Regional Sea Kayaking Series

Guide to Sea Kayaking on Lakes Superior & Michigan

The Best Day Trips and Tours

Bill Newman, Sarah Ohmann,
and Don Dimond

The Globe Pequot Press

Old Saybrook, Connecticut

Copyright © 1999 by William A. Newman and Sarah M. Ohmann

Cover design: Adam Schwartzmann
Text design: Casey Shain
Cover photograph: © Gary Nelkie/Nordic Sports, East Tawas, Michigan
Map design: Mary Ballachino
Interior photo on page 179 by Gary Nelkie. All others by Bill Newman, Sarah Ohmann, and Don Dimond.

Library of Congress Cataloging-in-Publication Data is available
Newman, William.
    Guide to sea kayaking on lakes Superior and Michigan: the best day trips and tours / by William Newman, Sarah Ohmann, and Don Dimond. —1st ed.
        p.   cm. — (Regional sea kayaking series)
    ISBN 0-7627-0416-0
        1. Sea kayaking—Superior, Lake—Guidebooks. 2. Sea kayaking—
—Michigan, Lake—Guidebooks. 3. Superior, Lake—Guidebooks.
4. Michigan, Lake—Guidebooks.   I. Ohmann, Sarah.   II. Dimond,
Don. 1964-   .   III. Title.   IV. Title: Best day trips and tours on
Lakes Superior and Michigan.   V. Series.
GV776.S86N49   1999
917.7404'43—DC21   99-12396
                                              CIP

Manufactured in the United States of America
First Edition/First Printing

Help Us Keep This Guide Up to Date

Every effort has been made by the authors and editors to make this guide as accurate and useful as possible. However, many things can happen after a guide is published—establishments close, phone numbers change, facilities come under new management, and so on. We would love to hear from you concerning your experiences with this guide and how you feel it could be improved and be kept up to date. While we may not be able to respond to all comments and suggestions, we'll take them to heart and we'll also make certain to share them with the author. Please send your comments and suggestions to the following address:

The Globe Pequot Press
Reader Response/Editorial Department
P.O. Box 833
Old Saybrook, CT 06475

Or you may e-mail us at:

editorial@globe-pequot.com

Thanks for your input, and happy travels!

Guide to Sea Kayaking
on Lakes Superior & Michigan

Contents

Lake Michigan

Lake Superior Routes

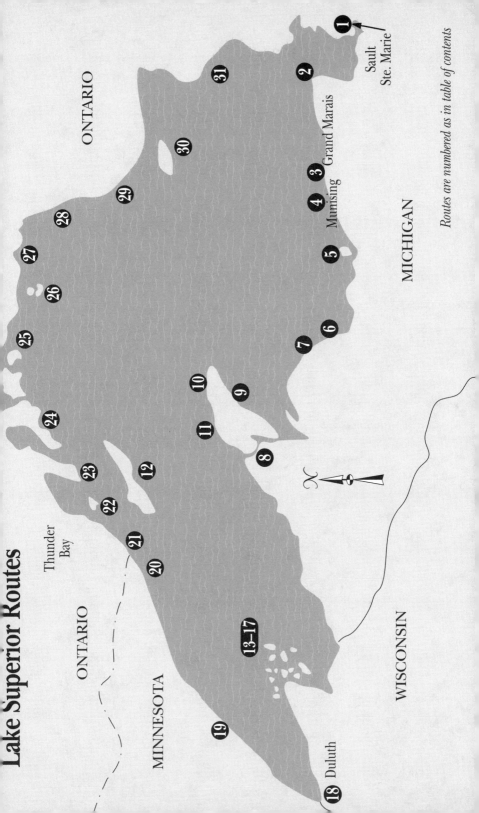

ONTARIO

Sault
Ste. Marie

Grand Marais

Munsing

MICHIGAN

Thunder
Bay

ONTARIO

MINNESOTA

WISCONSIN

Duluth

Routes are numbered as in table of contents

Lake Michigan Routes

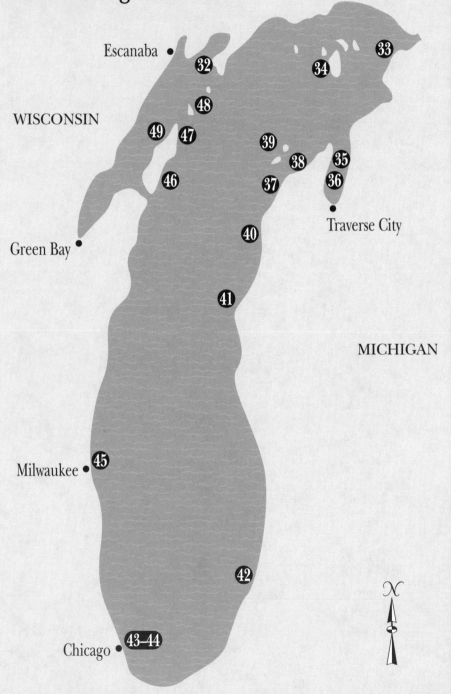

Escanaba •

32

48

WISCONSIN

49   47

46

Green Bay •

Milwaukee •   45

42

Chicago •   43–44

ILLINOIS

33

34

39

38

35

36

37

Traverse City

40

41

MICHIGAN

Routes are numbered as in table of contents

Acknowledgments

We are grateful to the many people who helped us in researching this book. In particular we would like to thank: Dave Brewster, Gerry Brindel, John Browning, Bill Day, Al Kasinskas, Peter Labor, Bruce Lash, Gary Mechanic, Ritchey and Nancy Newman, Nancy Parrish, Mike Petzold, Jim Prieur, Jeff Stasser, Kathi Talley, Bill Thompson, David Wells, and Anne Willis.

blank

Preface

When I first moved from Seattle to the Midwest in 1990, I felt very glum indeed about the prospect of being landlocked in such a flat and featureless place. I missed the mountains and the ocean badly and dreamed of going back west after finishing school. Even the Boundary Waters, I felt, didn't measure up to the landscape of the Pacific Northwest or the hills of New England where I grew up. One day, on my way back from a canoeing trip in the Arrowhead of Minnesota, I took the shoreline road instead of the inland route, and ended by standing, amazed, on the north shore of Lake Superior as the waves rolled in. I had no idea that such a wildly beautiful place existed in the middle of the continent, or that the Great Lakes were capable of such weather and waves. Within two months I had a kayak and was tentatively venturing out on the water. Within a few years I found that I no longer wanted to move west again, that the western landscape no longer measured up to the country I found here. I hope this book will help you find your way to some of the last, best places, anywhere.

—*Sarah Ohmann*

I bought my first sea kayak a little over ten years ago, while living on the shores of West Grand Traverse Bay on the Old Mission Peninsula. Having paddled white water for years, I was a bit worried that sea kayaking would be dull. Confident in my skills from white-water paddling, I was surprised to feel uncomfortable being as little as a mile offshore, but three years later, I found myself in the middle of Lake Michigan 40 miles from the nearest shore. Our group of four paddled almost 30 hours to cross 80 miles of open water. Paddling all day, all night, and on into the next day gives you a unique perspective on the size of these freshwater seas. Paddling in stormy November seas at the Gales of November Rendezvous in Agawa Bay removed all doubts about sea kayaking being dull and gave me an appreciation for the awesome power of the lakes. Kayaking the Great Lakes is not just for thrill junkies. Without a sea kayak, I would never have entered beautifully sculpted sea caves, played hide-and-seek with a family otters, shared a cobble beach with a timber wolf, or watched an incredible display of northern lights far from the glare of the city. I hope this book will help you explore the lakes and find your own adventures.

—*Bill Newman*

Introduction

Those who haven't explored the Great Lakes may be surprised to find that they have some of the best sea kayaking in the country: sand beaches; tall cliffs; long stretches of undeveloped shoreline with excellent wilderness camping, beautiful rock formations, and sand dunes hundreds of feet high; and some very fine sea caves. In particular, those from the United States may not be familiar with the rugged and rocky north shore of Lake Superior, so different from the sand and limestone shores of the southern Great Lakes.

The range of the landscape, geology, vegetation, and fauna in the region is well represented by Lakes Michigan and Superior, the two western-most lakes. The eastern hardwood forests and low sandy terrain of southern Lake Michigan change to the dolomite of the Niagara Escarpment seen in Door County, Wisconsin, and the Garden Peninsula near Manistique, Michigan. On the south shore of Lake Superior, the landscape becomes more hilly, and sandy shoreline is interspersed with the sandstone and other sedimentary rock formations seen in Pictured Rocks National Lakeshore and the Apostle Islands.

The igneous rock cliffs of the Keewenaw Peninsula in Michigan, along the Minnesota shore, and Thunder Bay were formed by enormous amounts of lava that poured through a midcontinental rift. The northeastern half of Superior is Canadian Shield country, characterized by worn and weathered gray bedrock. The country north of Superior is mainly boreal forest, inhabited by moose, wolves, bear, and even woodland caribou. The incredible variety of the lakes provides a diversity of kayaking opportunities, from urban day paddles to extended wilderness trips. Get ready to treat yourself to some great paddling.

Sea Kayak Safety

The power of the Great Lakes should not be taken lightly. While they are called lakes, don't mistake them for millponds. The day after finishing the last trip for these guidebooks, we heard that the first November gale of the season brought 80-knot winds and 20-foot waves to Lake Superior. The lakes have wrecked thousands of ships and claimed the lives of kayakers as well. Make sure you're prepared before paddling the routes described in this book.

Equipment

Don't leave shore without a seaworthy kayak with watertight bulkheads and/or flotation bags, a personal flotation device (PFD), bilge pump, compass, and paddle float. Just as important as having this safety equipment is knowing how to use it. Those who are getting started in the sport should take classes, join a club, or learn from more experienced paddlers. Regardless of their experience level, all kayakers should practice self- and assisted rescue techniques until they are automatic. Most important of all is your good judgment, which can save you from having to use rescue techniques and gadgets in the first place.

Trip Ratings

The trips in this book are rated by us as *beginner, intermediate,* or *advanced,* with the assumption that a beginning paddler (as opposed to a novice) will have a basic working knowledge of the common paddle strokes and braces, a paddle float self-rescue, and at least one of the assisted rescues (such as the T rescue). Intermediate paddlers should be comfortable paddling in higher winds (over 15 knots) in waves of 2–4 feet, and have the endurance to paddle 20 miles or more per day in good weather. They should be proficient in several group-rescue and self-rescue techniques, paddle bracing skills, and the Eskimo roll.

Advanced paddlers should be able to paddle in very rough conditions, have strong bracing skills, and a reliable Eskimo roll—preferably on both sides. They should be comfortable paddling in winds up to 30 knots and be able to paddle 30 miles per day or more in good weather. Advanced paddlers should have mastered several group-rescue and self-rescue skills and be able to complete most rescues in less than one minute. In some cases advanced trips can be done with intermediate level skills if extra time is allowed to wait out bad weather. Trip ratings are based on the assumption that you will be paddling in good weather during the summer months, but the stormy weather of fall and spring, or sudden squalls at any time, can easily turn a beginner trip into an advanced level one.

Weather

One of the recurring factors in deaths or near-deaths on the Great Lakes seems to be a failure to check or to heed marine forecasts before setting out. Sudden squalls or changes in weather can cause rapid changes in wind and wave conditions, turning calm sunny days into a kayaker's worst nightmare. Be especially wary of the weather when making an open-water crossing. We have written up a number of routes that include such crossings with mixed feelings. Although many kayakers have completed these trips safely, we would like to emphasize that the longer the crossing, the greater the risk and chance of encountering a change in the weather or other mishap. In many cases ferries or charter boats can be used to shuttle boats and gear to an island or start of a trip, and if you have limited experience with open-water paddling, please consider these options.

Another factor that must be considered is water temperature. Early in the season, particularly in the northern lakes, the surface water temperature may be only a few degrees above freezing. Paddling on water this cold introduces an extra level of risk. Even in late summer, Lake Superior is cold enough to quickly cause hypothermia in the event of a capsize. Dress for the water temperature, not the air temperature: We strongly encourage the use of a wet suit or dry suit for cold-water paddling.

Maps

The maps provided for each trip give a general idea of the location of the places mentioned in the route descriptions and are not to be used for navigation: Refer to the nautical charts or topographic maps recommended for routes. All distances are given in statute miles as this is the usual custom for inland waters on U.S. charts (apologies to Canadian paddlers who will have to convert to kilometers). Global positioning system (GPS) waypoints are given for some of the landmarks mentioned in the trip descriptions. Do *not* rely on these as your sole means of navigation, always carry a chart and compass. We generated most waypoints using handheld GPS units (without DGPS correction) and have made a reasonable effort to ensure that these are correct, but you should check them against a nautical chart before using them, especially when making an open-water crossing. Even if you carry a GPS, make sure you carry a chart and compass and know how to navigate using them.

It is not our intention to scare people away from the sport. In nearly all cases sea kayaking accidents have involved boaters who did not learn basic skills or did not follow the basic safety rules that we have listed. The authors and our many kayaking friends have paddled for thousands of miles without ever having a serious accident of any kind. We hope you will have the same experience, enjoying the beauty and the adventure that the Great Lakes offer without taking needless risks.

Lake Superior
Michigan

Route 1:

██ ██ ██ ██ ██ ██ ██ ██ ██ ██ ██ ██ ➤

Sault Ste. Marie: St. Mary's River

All of the Great Lakes shipping that is upbound for Lake Superior or downbound from the lake must pass through the Sault Locks. This makes Sault Ste. Marie a great place for boat watching as the huge ships pass down the relatively narrow St. Mary's River. The Canadian Sault is also a place of huge contrasts, from the industrial waterfront of Algoma Steel to the wildlife found in a maze of islands, bays, channels, and marshes just a stone's throw away. The following route provides a sample of both urban waterfront and wildlife, as well as the opportunity to lock through the historic locks on the Canadian side of the river.

TRIP HIGHLIGHTS: Great boat watching, bird watching, locking through a historic lock.

TRIP RATING:
Intermediate: 9-mile loop.

TRIP DURATION: Part or full day.

NAVIGATION AIDS: NOAA charts 14884 and 14883.

CAUTIONS: River currents up to 3 knots, Great Lakes shipping, small craft traffic near marinas, dams and rapids in some parts of the river.

TRIP PLANNING: This can be a complicated area in which to captain your kayak. Note that we refer to two route maps with different scales. With the complexity of shipping lanes, rapids, dams locks, and channels, having a chart of the upper river (NOAA chart 14884) is a must. If you intend to explore more than the short portion of the route downstream from Bellevue Park, consider getting NOAA chart 14883 for the lower St. Mary's. Follow the circular route in the direction described because it takes advantage of backwater areas to ease the upstream paddle, while using the full current for the return trip downstream.

LAUNCH SITE: Coming from the United States, cross the international bridge, and after clearing customs, take Business Highway 17 east until you are on Queen Street. Stay on Queen Street and follow it until you see the signs for Bellevue Park. Turn right into the park and follow the road to the river until you reach the Bellevue Park Marina. There is a low stone wall next to the boat ramp that makes a good kayak launch site, or you can use the boat ramp. Rest room facilities and ample parking are available at the park.

DIRECTIONS

START: Head downstream at roughly south-southeast to the east dock of the Sugar Island Ferry on **Island 1**. As you head downstream with the current, watch for any logs or debris. *Caution:* There is a small log boom just upstream from Island 1 that should be avoided, and watch for the ferry so you will not be in the way as it heads for the east dock.

MILE 1.0: At Mile 1.0 you reach the ferry dock for the **Sugar Island Ferry.** You are now in the United States so don't even think about smoking those Cuban cigars that you bought in the Canadian Sault. Head south along Island 1, hugging the bank to stay out of the shipping lanes.

MILE 1.75: About 0.75 mile south of the ferry dock, you come to a shore-mounted **navigation marker 96**. Check for shipping traffic and cross due west to the shore-mounted **navigation marker 95**. Paddlers who want to bird watch can continue downstream to explore the marshes, bays, and islands of the lower St. Mary's River.

MILE 2.5: From navigation marker 95 paddle south, hugging the right bank to stay out of the shipping channel. After about 0.75 mile (Mile 2.5), you round the south end of the island, and turn north.

MILES 2.5 TO 4.0: Heading north along the U.S. side, you stay in a backwater area with little current. You can either stay on along the mainland shore, which is a suburban neighborhood, or thread your way through the channel between **Islands 2** and **3** to enjoy a more natural setting. At Mile 4.0 you reach the ferry dock on the mainland side of the Sugar

Island Ferry. From here head upstream to the urban portion of the paddle and the Sault Locks.

MILES 4.0 TO 6.0: Heading west and hugging the American shore to stay out of the shipping lanes, you pass a boat ramp and small marina. Then you pass industrial docks and the **U.S. Steel Marine and Drydock Facility**. At about Mile 6.0 you come to the **United States Coast Guard base** at the foot of the **U.S. Locks**.

MILE 6.0 TO 7.0: The U.S. Locks are very busy with huge bulk freighters, so they don't want to bother with small craft. If you want to experience going up the locks, use the renovated historic locks on the Canadian side of the St. Mary's. Head north from the Coast Guard base, passing just east of the south and north shipping canals. These are shipping lanes, but the ships are moving quite slowly as they leave or approach the locks. You then paddle north along the base of the St. Mary's Falls (rapids).

MILE 7.0: On reaching the **Canadian Locks**, you can line up at the call box and wait for your turn to head upstream with the other small craft. In addition to the working small craft locks, this is a historic site, so it is worth landing on the shore of St. Mary's Island to explore the park on land. If you lock through stay near the bank on the Canadian side (Algoma Steel Plant); do not venture to the middle of the river above

Saute Ste. Marie: St. Mary's River

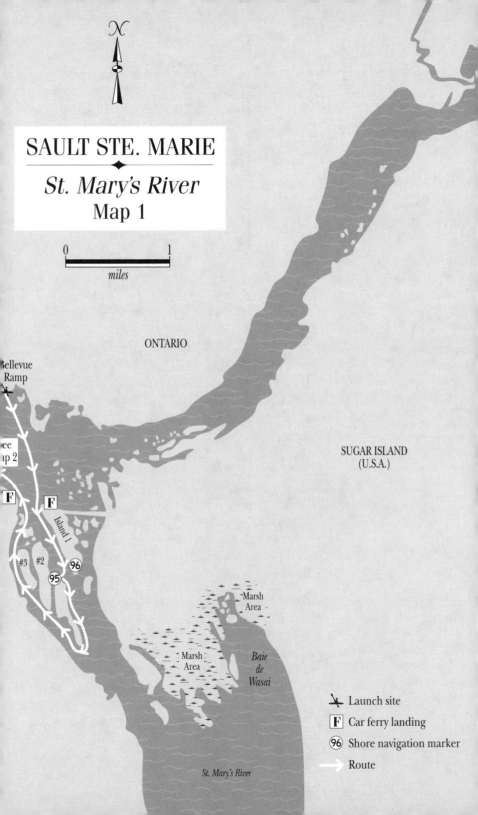

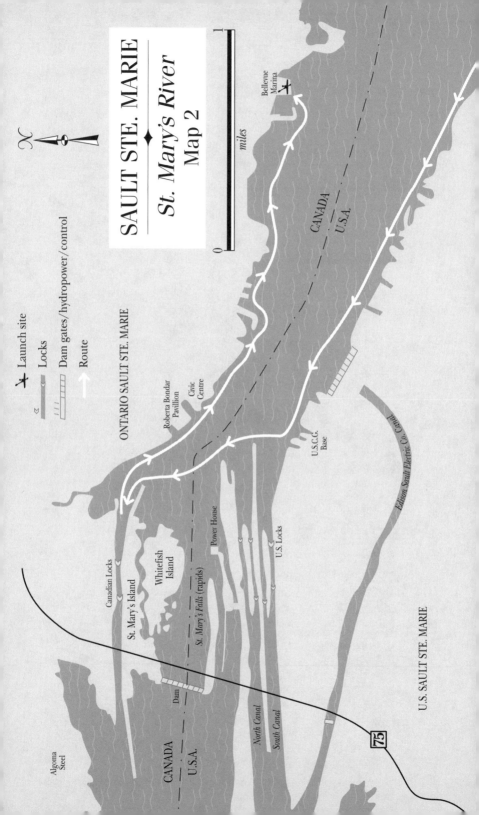

SAULT STE. MARIE
St. Mary's River
Map 2

Launch site
Locks
Dam gates/hydropower/control
Route

0   miles   1

ONTARIO SAULT STE. MARIE

Roberta Bondar
Pavillion

Civic
Centre

Bellevue
Marina

CANADA
U.S.A.

U.S.C.G.
Base

Edison Sault Electric Co. Canal

Canadian Locks

St. Mary's Island

Whitefish
Island

St. Mary's Falls (rapids)

Power House

U.S. Locks

Algoma
Steel

CANADA
U.S.A.

Dam

North Canal
South Canal

75

U.S. SAULT STE. MARIE

the locks or dams. *Caution:* Above the locks in center stream, the current can be swift, and a kayak could be swept downstream into the rapids, into a hydro power dam headrace, or over a flow control dam.

MILE 7.0 TO 8.0: Heading back down river from the locks on the Canadian side, stay near the bank, but watch for a sport fishing dock. *Caution:* The sport fishing dock sticks out from the bank into a fairly swift current, so swing wide enough to clear the fishing dock. You pass the city boardwalk and many waterfront attractions, including the **Roberta Bondar Pavillion**, with its large tentlike canopy, the **Norgoma Museum Ship**, the **Civic Centre**, the **Art Gallery of Algoma**, and the **Bush Plane Heritage Center**.

MILE 8.0 TO 9.0: You continue with the current along the Canadian shore until you return to the launch site.

Where to Eat & Where to Stay

RESTAURANTS The Canadian Sault is the larger of the sister cities, and so it offers more opportunities for dining. For tourist information for Ontario, including the Sault, stop by the Tourist Centre just after you cross the bridge, or call (800) ONTARIO. **LODGING & CAMPING** The Canadian Sault has many lodging options. For tourist information for Ontario, including the Sault, stop by the Tourist Centre just after you cross the bridge, or call (800) ONTARIO.

For More Information on Paddling the St. Mary's River

**Pick up a brochure on the St. Mary's Water Trail.
The pamphlet has maps and detailed route descriptions
for much of the river. Call Friends of the St. Mary's River
at (705) 759–6191.**

Route 2:

■ ■ ■ ■ ■ ■ ■ ■ ■ ■ ■ ■ ■ ■ ➤

Whitefish Point & the Great Lakes Shipwreck Museum

Paddlers interested in the history of the Great Lakes will enjoy a trip to the Great Lakes Shipwreck Museum, including the museum itself, the beautifully restored lightkeeper's house, and a movie about the raising of the ship's bell from the *Edmund Fitzgerald,* which is in the museum. The museum itself is a kick, with its murky underwater atmosphere, pieces and artifacts retrieved from many different wrecks (starting with the first ship lost on Superior, the *Invincible*), and the inevitable "The Wreck of the *Edmund Fitzgerald*" playing in the background. Other reasons to visit include the fine beach near the lighthouse and the Whitefish Point Bird Observatory. Whitefish Point is a great place to watch the spring raptor migration (as is Duluth for the fall migration) as they move northward and around Lake Superior. In addition it is one of the few remaining places on the Great Lakes where the piping plover returns each year to nest. Once down to a global population of twelve nesting pairs after being hunted to near extinction, the plover has made a partial comeback on the Atlantic Coast, where it is a threatened species, but remains endangered in the Great Lakes region with only twenty-six breeding pairs. Habitat destruction and the extreme vulnerability of chicks during nesting season to foot traffic, ATVs, and other animals, such as racoons, have made it hard for the plover to thrive here.

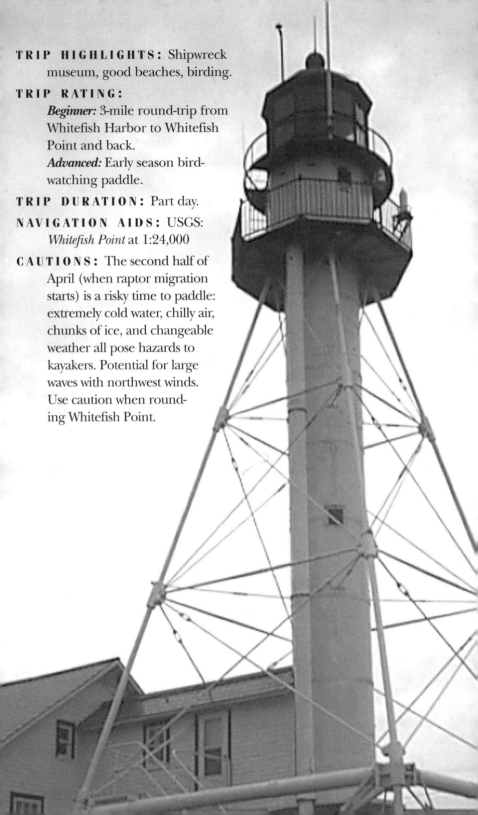

TRIP HIGHLIGHTS: Shipwreck museum, good beaches, birding.

TRIP RATING:

Beginner: 3-mile round-trip from Whitefish Harbor to Whitefish Point and back.

Advanced: Early season bird-watching paddle.

TRIP DURATION: Part day.

NAVIGATION AIDS: USGS: *Whitefish Point* at 1:24,000

CAUTIONS: The second half of April (when raptor migration starts) is a risky time to paddle: extremely cold water, chilly air, chunks of ice, and changeable weather all pose hazards to kayakers. Potential for large waves with northwest winds. Use caution when rounding Whitefish Point.

TRIP PLANNING: For calm weather, plan your trip before August, when winds and crowds pick up.Unfortunately for those who want to combine birding with paddling, raptor migration peaks in April and May. Paddling will be easier in May when the ice is more likely to be gone. The weather is extremely variable in May, but it is certainly possible to have some warm spring days. Be warned, however, that the surface water temperature is usually about 35° F after ice out, and for water that cold, a dry suit is strongly recommended. The launch site is protected from north and west winds, but conditions can be surprisingly different around a big point like Whitefish, so check the marine forecast before starting your paddle.

LAUNCH SITE: Drive north from Paradise on Whitefish Point Road for 11.2 miles to the turn off for the Whitefish Point Harbor Public Access Boat Launch (0.8 mile south of the museum parking lot). There is no charge to launch or park.

DIRECTIONS

START: Launch from the **beach (N 46° 45.715' W 84° 57.904')** next to the breakwater. North from the breakwater are a number of private cottages before the point itself.

MILE 0.5: Turn west after rounding the point. Use caution when rounding the point—north and west winds can create large waves over the sandbar extending from the point's tip.

MILE 1.0: There is one main boardwalk from the beach to the museum parking lot. *Caution:* Beyond the main path are submerged pilings.

MILES 1.5 TO 3.0: Return to the harbor beach.

Where to Eat & Where to Stay

RESTAURANTS & LODGING There are a fair number of motels in Paradise, and more in Newberry (about forty minutes away from Paradise). If you are planning to visit during July or August, advance reservations are recommended. Call the Paradise Tourism Council (906–492–5562) or Newberry Tourism Council (906–293–5562) for a list of motels and restaurants. **CAMPING** Both **Taquahemenon Falls State Park** (906–492–3415) and **Hiawatha National Forest** (906–786–4062) have campgrounds in the area.

Launch site
P Public parking
Lighthouse
→ Route

Whitefish Point Light

Great Lakes
Shipwreck Museum

P

Whitefish
Point

P

LAKE

SUPERIOR

TO
ADISE

N

WHITEFISH POINT

& the Great Lakes
Shipwreck Museum

0   .25   .50
miles

Route 3:

━ ━ ━ ━ ━ ━ ━ ━ ━ ━ ━ ━ ━ ━ ━ ━ ➤

Grand Marais Harbor to Hurricane River

Unlike the high sandstone cliffs of Miners Castle, the coast between Grand Marais and the Hurricane River consists of sand beaches and the huge dune bluffs of the Grand Sable Dunes. Other points of interest include a waterfall just a short hike from the lake and a historic lighthouse at Au Sable Point. The harbor of Grand Marais is also the site of the largest annual sea kayak symposium in the Midwest.

TRIP HIGHLIGHTS: Sand beaches, high sand dunes, a scenic waterfall, shipwrecks, and a historic lighthouse.

TRIP RATING:

Beginner: 5 to 6 miles out and back from Hurricane River to just past the lighthouse or from Grand Marais Harbor to just past the Sable River Falls.

Intermediate: About 10 miles one way from Grand Marais Harbor to Hurricane River.

TRIP DURATION: Part or full day.

NAVIGATION AIDS: NOAA chart 14963, USGS: *Alger County* at 1:100,000.

CAUTIONS: Clapotis waves off the breakwall, debris near shore from two shipwrecks, and cold water.

TRIP PLANNING: A north or a northwest wind can make for high seas. Rounding the Grand Marais Harbor breakwall with a north or westerly wind can be very rough because of clapotis waves off the breakwall. A calm day or a southerly wind is preferable, but most of the shoreline has sand beaches that will allow for an emergency landing if the weather deteriorates.

Pictured Rocks National Lakeshore

The Pictured Rocks National Lakeshore is named after the unique coloration of the sandstone cliffs along the coast. Mineral laden seeps have colored the cliffs with streaks of ochre, tan, brown, white, and green. The vertical cliffs rise 50 to 200 feet from Lake Superior along the coast from Sand Point to Spray Falls. Spray Creek shoots out from the high cliff wall to plunge directly into Lake Superior, forming the spectacular Spray Falls. Many of the sandstone cliffs have been carved by the elements to form arches and sea caves. In 1820 the explorer Henry Rowe Schoolcraft summed it up well when he said, "We had been told of the variety in the colour and form of these rocks, but were wholly unprepared to encounter the surprising groups of overhanging precipices, towering walls, caverns, and waterfalls mingled in the most wonderful disorder!"

The National Lakeshore includes 40 miles of the Lake Superior coast and 72,000 acres of park land. Wilderness camping along the coast is not allowed, but there are thirteen "hike-in" campgrounds and seven group sites spaced every 2 to 5 miles along the Lakeshore Hiking Trail that can be accessed by kayakers. Permits are required, and because this is an area heavily used by backpackers, it may be difficult to get the necessary permits to do a multiday trip along the coast. Kayakers can access the coast at Sand Point, Miners Beach, Twelvemile Beach Campground, Hurricane River Campground, and the Harbor at Grand Marais. For camping information, sea kayak policies, and permit reservations, call (906) 387–3700. (Much of the most interesting coastline can be accessed by day trips as described in Rtes. 3 and 4.)

LAUNCH SITES:

Grand Marais: Grand Marais Avenue runs along the edge of the harbor in downtown Grand Marais, Michigan. At the southwest corner of the harbor along Grand Marais Avenue just across from the town hall is a city swimming beach with rest rooms and road access leading down to the water. There is also a boat ramp at the west end of the harbor between the city beach and the Coast Guard station.

Hurricane River: Head west out of Grand Marais on County Road 772 until it feeds onto County Road H58. North of Grand Sable Lake, H58 becomes a gravel road. From where H58 becomes gravel to the turnoff to Hurricane River Campground and Picnic Area is about 4 miles. Outhouses and potable water are available.

DIRECTIONS

START TO MILE 1.0: From the Grand Marais City Beach, paddle northeast then north out of the harbor.

MILES 1.0 TO 3.0: Rounding the west breakwall at the **harbor light (N 46° 41.01' W 085° 58.31')**, turn west and follow the shore along low sand beach. *Caution:* The end of the west breakwall can be very rough from clapotis waves if there are winds from the north or west. Heading west down the coast at Mile 3.0 (about 2 miles west of the base of the breakwall), you come to the mouth of the **Sable River (N 46° 40.33' W 086° 00.84')**. The river mouth is often blocked by a sandbar so it may be difficult to see from far off shore. If you hike upstream a short distance, you will be treated to a cascading waterfall.

MILES 3.0 TO 8.0: From the mouth of the Sable River west, the low sand beaches are replaced with high sand dunes. These huge dune bluffs rise as much as 400 feet from the lake. At approximately Mile 7.0, you come to the **Log Slide Scenic Overlook**. Here there is road access to the top of the dune bluffs at the site where a large wooden log slide ramp was used to slide timber down to the lake during the lumber boom of the late 1800s. Nothing remains of the original structure, but those who drive up or those kayakers who foolishly decide to trudge up 400 feet of loose, steep sand are treated to a fantastic view.

Grand Marais Harbor to Hurricane River

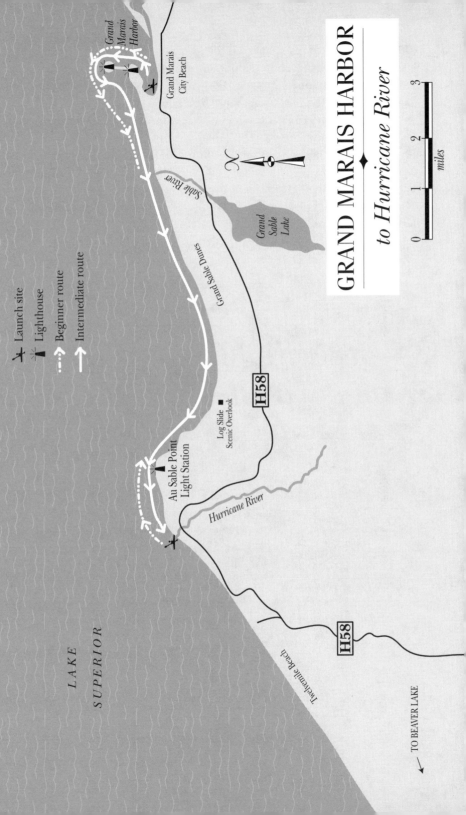

GRAND MARAIS HARBOR
to Hurricane River

Grand Marais Harbor

Grand Marais City Beach

Sable River

Grand Sable Lake

Grand Sable Dunes

Log Slide Scenic Overlook

H58

Au Sable Point Light Station

Hurricane River

Twelvemile Beach

H58

TO BEAVER LAKE

LAKE SUPERIOR

Launch site
Lighthouse
Beginner route
Intermediate route

0   1   2   3
miles

MILE 8.0 TO 10.5: After Mile 8.0 the sand dunes and sand beaches transition to a mixed shoreline of cobblestone beaches with some low sandstone shelves. At approximately Mile 9.0 you come to the **Au Sable Point Light Station** at the end of **Au Sable Point**. The Au Sable Point Light was put into service in 1874 and is still in operation. A short distance west of the lighthouse, you come to the remains of multiple shipwrecks that can be seen in the shallow water and from the shore. Continuing west about another mile, you come to another shipwreck as you near the mouth of the **Hurricane River**. Take out at the picnic area at the mouth of the Hurricane River. For a 5.0-mile round-trip the beginning paddler can launch at the mouth of the Hurricane River, paddle 2.5 miles to the light station, and return.

Great Lakes
Sea Kayak Symposium

This annual event is the largest sea kayak symposium in the Midwest. Well over 300 kayakers attend. Experts from all over the world come to give lectures and offer instruction on sea kayaking and kayaking skills. The city beach in Grand Marais is within the sheltered harbor and provides an ideal location for lessons and boat demos. Guided trips to Grand Island and Pictured Rocks National Lakeshore are included as part of the symposium activities. For information call Great River Outfitters at (248) 683–4770.

Where to Eat & Where to Stay

RESTAURANTS Grand Marais is a small town with only a few restaurants. A popular brew-pub and restaurant is the **Dunes Saloon** (906–484–2337). Another bar and restaurant in downtown Grand Marais is the **Sportsmans Restaurant** (906–494–2671). There is also a restaurant associated with the Welkers Inn Motel down by the Coast Guard station. For a more complete list of restaurants in the area, call the Alger County Chamber of Commerce at (906) 387–2138 or the Grand Marais Chamber of Commerce at (906) 494–2766. **LODGING Alversons** and the **Welkers Inn Motel** are two motels near the water in Grand Marais. For a more complete list of motels in the area, call the Alger County Chamber of Commerce at (906) 387–2138 or the Grand Marais Chamber of Commerce at (906) 494–2766. **CAMPING** At the west end of Grand Marais, there is the **Woodland Park Township campground** with modern campsites and showers. Within the National Lakeshore, there are several sites with outhouses and potable water, but they do not have shower facilities, these include Hurricane River and Twelvemile Beach. For information on camping in the National Lakeshore, call (906) 387–3700. The Grand Marais Chamber of Commerce has detailed area camping guide—call (906) 494–2766.

Grand Marais Harbor to Hurricane River

Route 4:

====================================➤

Miners Castle to Spray Falls

This route covers some of the most spectacular sandstone cliff shoreline in Pictured Rocks. Miners Castle is named after the castlelike sandstone tower that rises up from the lakeshore cliffs. At its base are some beautifully carved sea caves and delicate rock columns. The route also includes two huge sea arches and a waterfall that plunges off the cliffs into Lake Superior. Although most of this section of coast consists of vertical sandstone cliffs up to 200 feet high, it also includes beautiful sand beaches at Miners Beach and Chapel Beach.

TRIP HIGHLIGHTS: Spectacular sandstone cliffs, sea caves, sea arches, and beautiful sand beaches.

TRIP RATING:
Intermediate: 8 miles round-trip from Miners Beach to Miners Castle then to just east of the Mosquito River to a large sea arch and back.
Advanced: 15 miles round-trip from Miners Beach to Miners Castle then east to Spray Falls and back.

TRIP DURATION: Part or full day.

NAVIGATION AIDS: NOAA chart 14963, USGS: *Alger County* at 1:100,000.

CAUTIONS: Exposed cliff coast offers few places to land, clapotis waves from cliffs, falling rock, and cold water.

TRIP PLANNING: Grand Island offers some shelter to the coast for the first part of the trip, but a north or northwest wind can produce large seas. Even moderate seas can build into violent clapotis along the cliffs and sea caves. Rough weather landing beaches are few, with only Miners Beach and Chapel Beach being suitable for landing in large seas. Even in summer the water can be very cold—often less than 50° F—so a wet suit or dry suit is strongly recommended.

LAUNCH SITE: From Munising and the Highway 28/County Road H58 intersection, head east for about 5 miles, then go north on County Road H13 for about 5 miles until you see the sign for Miners Beach. After the turnoff it is about 2 miles to the parking lot. From the lot to the beach, there is a wooden-planked path that takes you to the beach, about 500 feet away.

DIRECTIONS

START: Try to launch your kayak well away from the swimmers using the beach. The Global Positioning System (GPS) coordinates for the **Miners Beach** are **N 46° 29.81' W 086° 32.61'**. Head west 0.5 mile to explore the interesting rock formations and sea caves before returning east to Miners Beach.

MILES 1.0 TO 3.0: Paddle along the beautiful sand beach heading east until you reach the start of the sandstone cliffs. For the next 2.0 miles the sandstone cliffs continue until you reach the low sandstone cliffs at the mouth of the **Mosquito River (N 46° 31.64' W 086° 29.61')** about 3.0 miles east of Miners Beach. The shoreline and the lake bottom at the river mouth consist of flat sandstone rock shelves. In calm weather you can land on the smooth rock shore. For those fortunate enough to get permits, you may camp here at a designated campsite.

MILE 3.5: About 0.5 mile east of the mouth of the Mosquito River is a huge **sea arch** with an opening that is about 50 feet high by 100 feet wide. After passing through the arch, you come to some of the beautiful mineral-streaked cliffs for which the Pictured Rocks are so aptly named.

MILE 4.5: 1.0 mile east of the arch and about 4.5 miles east of Miners Beach, you come to a place where huge slabs of sandstone have fallen off the cliffs into the lake. One unusual looking rock is flat and only about 6-feet thick, but measures about 30 feet by 40 feet in width and height. This upturned flat slab is known as **Sail Rock**. *Caution:* Although it is a very rare occurrence, falling rock from the cliffs can be a hazard.

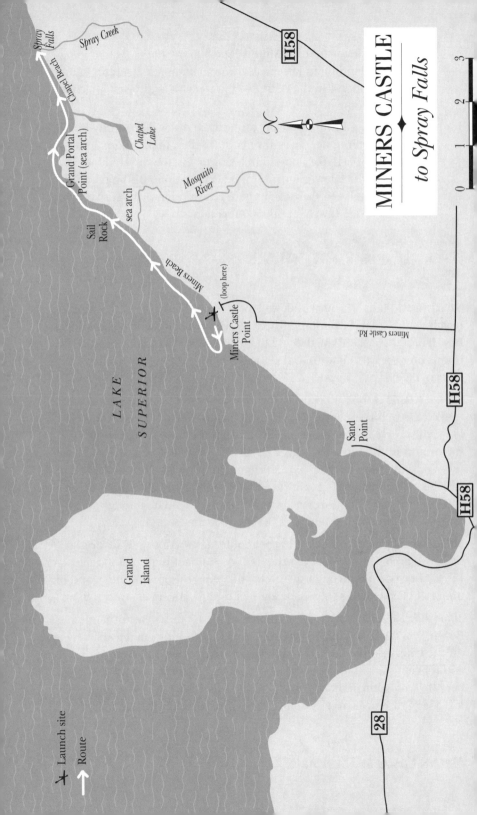

MINERS CASTLE
to Spray Falls

H58

0 1 2 3

Spray Falls
Spray Creek
Chapel Beach
Chapel Lake
Grand Portal Point (sea arch)
Sail Rock
sea arch
Mosquito River
Miners Beach
(loop here)
Miners Castle Point
Miners Castle Rd.
Sand Point
H58
H58
28

LAKE SUPERIOR

Grand Island

✈ Launch site
⬆ Route

On this very stretch of coast, a good friend of mine once watched a boulder the size of a school bus fall in the water 100 feet behind him exactly where he had just been in his kayak!

MILE 5.5: About 5.5 miles east of Miners Beach, you pass through the **Grand Portal (N 46° 33.19' W 086° 27.80')**. Here the elements have formed a sea arch that tunnels through a huge sandstone point with high cliff walls. The arch opening is similar to the large arch east of the Mosquito River, but tunneling through the high cliff point makes it all the more spectacular. Inside the arch is a second smaller arch.

MILE 6.0: About 6.0 miles east of Miners Beach, you come to **Chapel Beach (N 46° 32.86' W 086° 26.57')** at the mouth of the Chapel River. In addition to a lovely sand beach and low rock waterfall at the river mouth, there is a large rock on the shore called **Chapel Rock**. The large, sculpted house-sized boulder sits at the eastern edge of the beach. If you are lucky enough to get a permit, there is a campsite at Chapel Beach.

MILE 6.5: A short distance from Chapel Rock, you come to a **sea cave** about 30 feet wide by 30 feet high by 80 feet long.

MILE 7.5: About 7.5 miles east of Miners Beach, you come to **Spray Falls**. Here Spray Creek soars out from the high cliff wall to plunge directly into Lake Superior. This is the end of the advanced trip; retrace your steps to Miners Beach to complete a total of 5.0 miles.

Where to Eat & Where to Stay

See Route 5: Grand Island for information about restaurants, lodging, and camping.

Route 5:

Grand Island

G rand Island is located about a half mile from the mainland near Munising, Michigan. Originally owned by the
Cleveland Cliffs Mining Company, the island has now
been designated as a National Recreation Area. This large
island of 13,500 acres is covered in hardwood forests and
has a beautiful shoreline, ranging from sheltered bays with
sand beaches to towering sandstone coastal cliffs that rise
over 200 feet from the water. Many of the cliffs have been
carved by the elements, forming sea arches and sea caves.
For nonpaddlers a ferry run by the National Forest Service,
which makes four trips a day in summer months, is available
from Powell Point. The island has many dirt roads and trails
for hikers and mountain bikers.

TRIP HIGHLIGHTS: Spectacular sea cliffs, arches, and sea caves;
lovely sand beaches; hardwood forests, and many hiking trails.

TRIP RATING:
Intermediate/Advanced: A 27-mile circumnavigation of Grand Island.

TRIP DURATION: Overnight or multiday trip.

NAVIGATION AIDS: NOAA chart 14963, USGS: *Alger County* at
1:100,000.

CAUTIONS: Long stretches of sea cliffs, clapotis waves, and cold
water.

TRIP PLANNING: There are six designated campsites, two on
Murray Bay and four on Trout Bay. Wilderness camping is also
allowed along the coast with the exception of the north beach
study area and on the few private land holdings. At this time no

permits are necessary for camping, but pick up a brochure at the ferry dock to become familiar with island regulations. Lake Superior has very cold water, with temperatures of less than 50° F common even in summer. A wet suit or dry suit is strongly recommended. The north half of the island is primarily sea cliffs, here clapotis waves are likely, and landing may not be possible except on the sandy north beach. *Caution:* To round the north end of the island, start early in the day and only paddle north of Trout Bay in relatively calm conditions.

LAUNCH SITE: Heading west on Highway 28 out of Munising about 3 miles out from the County Road H58/Highway 28 junction, watch for the sign for the Grand Island Recreational Area, then turn right on Grand Island Landing Road. The road dead-ends at the ferry dock. There are porta-john bathrooms available, but no potable water at the ferry landing. There is a good sand beach for launching kayaks just to the left of the ferry dock.

DIRECTIONS

START: From the **ferry dock (N 46° 26.71' W 086° 39.83')**, head northwest to the nearest land on Grand Island if you intend to circumnavigate the island. *Caution:* The northern half of the island is exposed sandstone cliffs with few suitable landing sites. If there is any question about the weather conditions, or if it is too late in the day to circle most of the island, then head for the shelter of either Murray Bay or Trout Bay.

MILE 1.0: After making the 0.5-mile crossing to **Grand Island**, you paddle around the southwest corner of the island along a low sand beach shore and turn north.

MILES 1.0 TO 2.0: You paddle along a narrow sand beach that transitions to cobblestones and then to low red **sandstone cliffs** up to 30 feet high at Mile 2.0.

MILES 2.0 TO 4.5: The sandstone cliffs continue with 10-foot- to 50-foot-high sandstone cliffs right to the waters edge. At Mile 4.0 there is a **small bay** and a nice **sand beach**. There are some private cabins, but there is room to land and use the beach without trespassing. Take advantage of this rest stop, the next acceptable beach for landing in rough weather is more than 5 miles down the coast.

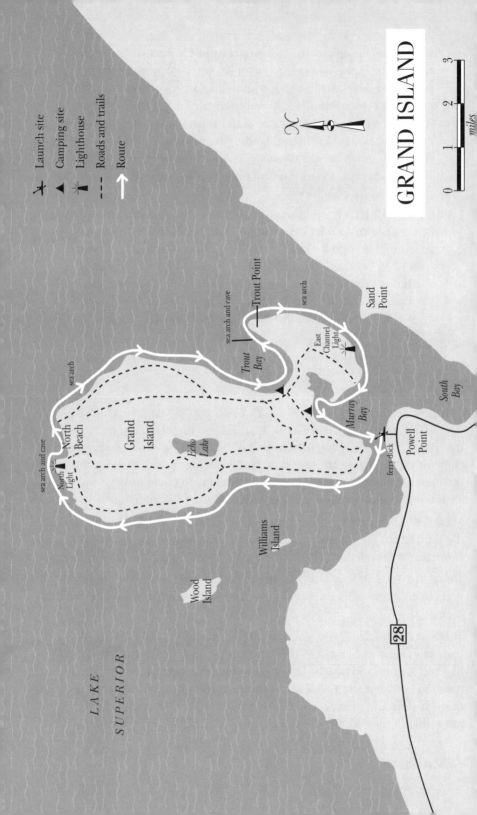

GRAND ISLAND

Launch site
Camping site
Lighthouse
Roads and trails
Route

miles
0 1 2 3

LAKE
SUPERIOR

Wood
Island

Williams
Island

Grand Island

Echo
Lake

North Light
sea arch and cave
North Beach
sea arch

Trout
Bay
sea arch and cave
Trout Point
sea arch

East
Channel
Light

Murray
Bay

South
Bay

Sand
Point

Powell
Point
ferry dock

28

MILES 4.5 TO 9.5: Head north along a **vertical cliff coast**. The colorful wave-carved sandstone cliffs rise 50 to 200 feet from the water. Much of the sandstone has eroded and been shaped by waves. If you are lucky, springs seeping from the rocks high above on the cliffs will provide you with a refreshing shower. *Caution:* This is a bad place to be with a strong northwest wind. Large violent clapotis waves form along the cliffs if there are significant seas coming from the north or west.

MILE 10.0: At the northern most point of the island, cliffs tower 150 feet overhead. Although it is difficult to see when close to shore, the **Grand Island North Light** is perched high on the cliff top overhead. The light-house tower, which was constructed in 1868, is still in use today. Just before the lighthouse there is a small bay with a sand beach that would allow a landing in most weather. Heading east of the lighthouse, you pass through a sea arch with a long, narrow crack on the shoreward side **(N 46° 33.28' W 086° 38.84')**. If the water levels are down and the sea is dead calm, you can squeeze your boat into the crack and follow it back to a domed sea cave about 20 feet in diameter.

MILE 10.5: Passing through the sea arch east, you come to a beautiful **sand beach (N 46° 33.40' W 086° 40.16')** almost 1 mile long on the north end of the island. Take advantage of this opportunity to rest because the next good landing beach is about 6 miles to the south on the east side of the island. But note that this north beach area is designated as a natural study area for day use only.

MILES 12.0 TO 16.0: Leaving the beach behind you, head east, then south, once again paddling along high cliff faces with small sea caves and reentrants. Less than 1 mile from the north beach, you pass through a **sea arch** with a window in the arch **(N 46° 33.70' W 086° 40.69')**. At about Mile 13.0 the cliffs are lower for about a mile, and then as you approach **Trout Bay,** they once again rise up to 50 feet or more.

MILES 17.0 TO 18.0: At the south end of Trout Bay is another lovely sand beach **(east side of the beach, N 46° 28.71' W 086° 37.61')** about 1 mile in length. There are four designated campsites in Trout Bay. There also appear to be private cabins in the center of the beach so please respect the rights of the landowners. This is a great spot to take a break or to camp and wait out bad weather.

MILE 19.0: Heading north along the east side of Trout Bay, you come to a **large arch and sea cave (N 46° 29.61' W 086° 36.81')**.

MILES 20.0 TO 21.0: Rounding **Trout Point** and heading south, you are once again paddling along a high cliff coast. At about Mile 21 there is a small sea arch and some small sea caves.

MILE 22.0: At about Mile 22 you reach the old abandoned **East Channel Lighthouse** on the south end of Grand Island. This old wooden lighthouse is on private land, so you will have to enjoy it from the water. The lighthouse was put in service in 1868 and operated until 1913, when it was replaced by more modern harbor range lights.

MILE 24.5: Rounding the south end of the island, the cliffs give way to cobble and sand beach as you turn north into the sheltered harbor of **Murray Bay**. There are two designated campsites on the north end of Murray Bay.

MILES 24.5 TO 26.5: Heading south down the west side of Murray Bay, you make the crossing back to the National Forest Service dock on the mainland.

Where to Eat & Where to Stay

RESTAURANTS The **Dogpatch Restaurant** (906–387–9948) is a popular bar and restaurant in Munising. For a complete list of restaurants, call the Alger Chamber of Commerce at (906) 387–2138. **LODGING** For a list of motels in the area, call the Alger Chamber of Commerce at (906) 387–2138. **CAMPING** There are several options on the mainland near Munising. To the west of the ferry landing, there is the **Munising Tourist Park** campground with modern campsites. Farther west **Bay Furnace** campground and **Five Mile Point** campground offer more primitive campsites. To the east there are four drive-in campgrounds within the **Pictured Rocks National Lakeshore**. For information on campsites in Pictured Rocks National Lakeshore, call (906) 387–4845; for National Forest campsites, call (906) 387–3700. For information on private campgrounds, call the Alger Chamber of Commerce at (906) 387–2138.

Route 6:

▬▬ ▬▬ ▬▬ ▬▬ ▬▬ ▬▬ ▬▬ ▬▬ ▬▬ ▬▬ ➤

Presque Isle to Little Presque Isle

T his is a beautiful stretch of coast with a rocky bedrock shoreline, high ridges, and rocky islands. There are also great sand beaches at Little Presque Isle, Wetmore Landing and at the launch site on Presque Isle. The shoreline between Little Presque Isle and Presque Isle is also relatively sheltered. Although some of the shoreline in the middle section of the trip is private land, most of the land around Presque Isle and between Little Presque Isle and Sugarloaf Mountain is public land.

TRIP HIGHLIGHTS: Volcanic bedrock cliffs, many small rocky islands, sheltered shoreline.

TRIP RATING:
Beginner: 5 miles out and back, exploring Presque Isle and rounding Partridge Island.
Intermediate: About 7 miles one way, exploring the coast between Presque Isle and Little Presque Isle.

TRIP DURATION: Part or full day.

NAVIGATION AIDS: NOAA chart 14963 (14970 for beginner trip, Presque Isle detailed), USGS: *Marquette County* at 1:100,000.

CAUTIONS: Exposed rocky shoreline, clapotis off cliffs.

TRIP PLANNING: The first half of the intermediate trip or all of the beginner trip is well sheltered unless there is a north wind. The second half of the intermediate trip is sheltered unless there is a wind from the north or northeast. Beginners should pick a calm day or a day with a gentle southerly breeze. Starting early in the day will improve your chances of having calm conditions. Lake Superior is very cold. Water temperatures of less than 50° F are common even in summer. A wet suit or dry suit is strongly recommended.

LAUNCH SITES:

Presque Isle: From Marquette head north along Lakeshore Drive to Presque Isle Park. Take the left branch of the road where the one-way loop around Presque Isle starts. The launch site is the sand beach on the west side of Presque Isle. At this time there are porta-johns on site, and a pavillion that will include public bathroom facilities is under construction.

Little Presque Isle: Head west out of Marquette on County Road 550 toward Big Bay. Watch for the sign for Sugarloaf Mountain on the right-hand side. The dirt road to Little Presque Isle—the second dirt road on the right after the parking lot for Sugarloaf Mountain—is not marked. The entrance to the road is between two metal guardrails just before a creek about 6.5 miles from Marquette. Follow the road to the end of the parking lot. From there it is about a 500-foot hike to the water. An outhouse is available, but there is no potable water supply. Use the sand beach on the west side of the peninsula, because it has fewer rocks and boulders.

DIRECTIONS

START: From the beach on the west side of **Presque Isle (N 46° 33.12' W 087° 23.12')**, head north along the west side of the peninsula.

MILE 1.0: Rounding the north end of Presque Isle, you turn south into a **small cove with black cliff walls** and a gravel beach at the south end. These are the "black rocks," and assuming the weather is warm and the water is above freezing, it's likely that you will see local kids or college students cliff diving here.

MILE 2.0: Heading west from the cove, you make the crossing to the north end of **Middle Island** at Mile 2.0. It's a small rocky island with rock walls that rise about 100 feet above the lake. For the beginner trip, head west for Partridge Island; for the intermediate trip, head west toward the mainland coast.

MILE 3.0: At Mile 3.0 you pass the south end of **Partridge Island**, a small but high-cliff island that rises over 200 feet above the lake. For the beginner loop, circle the island, then head back to the sand beach landing to the southeast for a loop of about 5.0 miles in length. For the intermediate trip, head toward the mainland shore and follow the coast west and north.

Presque Isle to Little Presque Isle

LAKE
SUPERIOR

PRESQUE ISLE
◆
to Little Presque Isle

0   1   2
miles

Launch site
Lighthouse
Route

Little
Presque
Isle

Wetmore
Landing

Larus
Island

Sugarloaf
Mountain
elev. 1,077 ft.

Partridge
Island
elev. 816 ft.

Black
Rocks
Cove

Middle Island

Middle
Island
Point

Presque
Isle

Yacht Harbor
Ore Dock
Breakwall

MILE 4.0 TO 5.0: After Mile 4.0 the shore consists mainly of huge boulders or a low, volcanic bedrock cliff wall. *Caution:* Avoid this stretch of coast if there are large seas from the north because clapotis can be quite bad. At about Mile 5.0 you pass the **Sugarloaf Mountain** scenic overlook, a high rock escarpment that towers about halfway up the mountain at 500 feet above the lake.

MILE 5.0 TO 6.0: Shortly after Sugarloaf the rock and low-cliff shoreline becomes a lovely sand beach at **Wetmore Landing**. This is public land so feel free to land and enjoy the beach. There is road access (first dirt road past Sugarloaf), but it is a rather long carry to the water, making Little Presque Isle the preferred trip landing.

MILE 6.0 TO 7.0: After Wetmore Landing the shore returns to low volcanic bedrock cliffs and huge boulders until you approach **Little Presque Isle (N 46° 38.12' W 087° 28.06')**; on the east side of the peninsula there is a sand beach. Avoid landing

on the beach on the east side: There are numerous large cobbles and rounded boulders hiding along the shore. Little Presque Isle is a small rock and cliff island connected to shore by a shallow rock shelf. On a calm day with higher lake levels, you can float a kayak between the island and the shore, otherwise paddle around the point. *Caution:* The cliff walls, shoals, and hidden boulders off the tip of Little Presque Isle can create confused seas in rough weather. To end the trip, land on the west side of Little Presque Isle where there is a good sand beach for a safe landing.

Where to Eat & Where to Stay

RESTAURANTS & LODGING   There are many restaurant and lodging choices in the Marquette area. For lists of both, call the Marquette Convention and Visitors Bureau at (800) 544–4321. **CAMPING**   There is a campground in Big Bay at **Perkins Park**, not far from the put in. In Marquette you can camp at **Tourist Park**. For a list of other camping options in the area, call the Marquette Convention and Visitors Bureau (800–544–4321).

Route 7:

Big Bay to Little Presque Isle

Although much of this stretch of coast consists of private land, almost all has been left in a wild, undeveloped state. Loma Farms is a private estate that has been left wild along the coast—with exception of a large log cabin mansion and private harbor! The coast is very rugged, and although there are a few sand beaches, most is either sandstone cliffs or volcanic bedrock coast. There are several rocky headlands that although beautiful can make for very rough conditions. This trip is a very long advanced one: 22 miles of rugged coast that must be paddled in one day, but in good weather it is a rewarding paddle well worth the effort.

TRIP HIGHLIGHTS: Sandstone and bedrock cliffs, rocky headlands, bird watching for eagles, a huge log mansion on the coast.

TRIP RATING:
Advanced: 22 miles of exposed coast and rocky shores.

TRIP DURATION: A very long day trip—no camping available at this time for overnight trips.

NAVIGATION AIDS: NOAA chart 14963, USGS: *Marquette County* at 1:100,000.

CAUTIONS: Exposed rocky shoreline, clapotis off cliffs and rocky headlands, limited rough water landing harbors or beaches, and cold water.

TRIP PLANNING: Pick a calm day or a day with winds from the southwest. Don't try to do this coast with significant wind or waves coming from the northeast because the cliffs and headlands will get very rough. Get an early start—you need to complete the entire 22 miles in one day. At this time camping is not allowed along the coast. A water trail from Big Bay to Grand Marais is proposed so this may change in the future. Lake Superior is very cold. Water temperatures of less than 50° F are common even in summer. A wet suit or dry suit is strongly recommended.

LAUNCH SITES:

Little Presque Isle: Head west out of Marquette on County Road 550 toward Big Bay. Watch for the sign for Sugarloaf Mountain on the right-hand side. The dirt road to Little Presque Isle is not marked. The road is the second dirt road on the right after the parking lot for Sugarloaf Mountain. The entrance to the road is between two metal guardrails just before a creek at about 6.5 miles from Marquette. Follow the road to the end of the parking lot. From there it is about a 500-foot hike to the water. An outhouse is available, but there isn't a potable water supply. Use the sand beach on the west side of the peninsula for launching because it has fewer rocks and boulders.

Big Bay Harbor: After shuttling a car to Little Presque Isle, continue northwest on County Road 550 to the town of Big Bay (about 26 miles from Marquette). In Big Bay, 550 becomes Bensiger Street, then curves and becomes Balke. Watch for a truly tiny sign that marks the turnoff for the harbor, at the intersection of Balke and Schenk Streets. Turn right on Schenk for about 0.3 miles, then left on KF/KCB and follow for about 0.2 miles to the harbor. There are no public bathrooms or water at the private yacht basin so take care of these needs in town.

DIRECTIONS

START: Heading out of the **Big Bay Harbor (N 46° 49.71' W 087° 43.52')** turn east and paddle down the coast toward Big Bay Point.

MILES 1.0 TO 2.0: You pass along the **sand beach of Big Bay**.

MILES 2.0 TO 3.0: At Mile 2.0 you turn north and head to the end of **Big Bay Point**. The sand beach transitions to cobbles and then red sandstone cliffs as you reach the end of the point at Mile 3.0. At the tip of the point is the **Big Bay Point Lighthouse**. The lighthouse was put into service in 1896. It is now privately owned, and the buildings are run as a bed-and-breakfast.

Big Bay to Little Presque Isle

LAKE

SUPERIOR

N

Big Bay Point

Big Bay

G BAY

Lake Independence

BIG BAY
to Little Presque Isle

0   1   2   3

miles

Launch site
Lighthouse
Route

Granite Point

550

Granite Island

Saux Head Point

Garlic Island

Thoney's Point

Little Garlic River

Little Presque Isle

MILES 3.0 TO 5.0: As you round the point, you pass **red sandstone cliffs** about 50 feet high and paddle in shallow water off the point. *Caution:* The combination of a rocky headland, cliffs, and shoals can make rounding the point very rough when breaking waves and/or clapotis are present. South down the east side of the point, the cliffs diminish and transition to a cobble beach.

MILES 5.0 TO 6.5: Once you get past the base of the point, the cobble beaches become sand beach, and there is about a mile-long sand beach at the mouth of the **Iron River**. The shore then returns to rocks and cobbles. The sand beach is private land, but it is still a possible bad weather bail-out point.

MILES 6.5 TO 10.5: The shoreline alternates between rock and steep cobble beaches. There are no suitable rough-water landing beaches. At Mile 10.5 you round a small rocky headland, **Granite Point**. *Caution:* The cliffs and rocky headland may create clapotis and confused seas. There are also shoals and partially covered boulders off the point.

MILES 10.5 TO 11.5: After rounding the point you pass **red sandstone cliffs** for about 1 mile with no landable shoreline.

MILES 11.5 TO 13.0: After about Mile 11.5, the sandstone cliffs are replaced by a **steep boulder and cobble shoreline**—still not a good beach to land on in rough weather.

MILES 13.0 TO 14.0: From Mile 13.0 to 14.0 you come to a good **sand beach** that is suitable for landing in rough weather. This land is private so only land in an emergency, or if you are invited to come ashore.

MILES 14.0 TO 16.0: After the sand beach ends, you paddle along either steep cobble beaches or a shoreline of huge boulders or low cliffs. Much of this coast is part of one huge land holding, the Loma Farms. At Mile 16.0 you come to a rocky point and a small island just off shore called **Garlic Island**. *Caution:* The cliffs and rocky headland may create clapotis and confused seas. There are also shoals and partially covered boulders off the point and near the island. On the point is a huge log mansion with a private harbor and large boathouse.

MILES 16.0 TO 21.0: Passing Garlic Island you continue down a low cliff and boulder coast that has few suitable beaches for rough wea-ther landing. You pass **Thoney's Point**, a rocky headland with a small rock island just off shore. *Caution:* The cliffs and rocky headland may create clapotis and confused seas. There are also shoals and partially covered boulders off the point and near the island. Rock and low cliffs predominate the shoreline until Mile 21.0; here you reach the sand beach on the northwest side of Little Presque Isle.

MILE 22.0: At Mile 22.0 you reach **Little Presque Isle (N 46° 38.12' W 087° 28.06')**, a small island connected to the mainland by a shallow rock shelf. At higher lake levels on a calm day, you can just float a kayak between shore and the island. The island has both sandstone and vol-

Big Bay to Little Presque Isle

canic bedrock cliffs with sand beaches on either side of the point. Land on the west side of the point because there are large cobbles and rounded boulders on the east side.

Where to Eat & Where to Stay

RESTAURANTS & LODGING There are many restaurant and lodging choices in the Marquette area. For a list of restaurants and hotels, call the Marquette Convention and Visitors Bureau at (800) 544–4321.

CAMPING There is a campground in Big Bay at **Perkins Park** not far from the put in. You can also camp in Marquette at Tourist Park. For a list of other camping options in the area, call the Marquette Convention and Visitors Bureau at (800) 544–4321.

Route 8:

Keewenaw Water Trail

T his short and easy paddle serves as a brief introduction to the Portage Waterway portion of the Keewenaw Water Trail. Unlike the other Keewenaw trips in this guide, this one is an urban paddle with views of old mine buildings, now falling to ruin. Although some of the copper mines on the Keewenaw Peninsula have been turned into museums or historical displays (such as the Quincy Mine Hoist visible on the ridgeline above Hancock), the buildings along this section are simply abandoned and have the eerie appearance of a ghost town. The setting is appealing; the waterway runs below the two cities of Houghton and Hancock, each on a ridge, facing the other across the waterway. The views are especially good when fall color is at its best.

TRIP HIGHLIGHTS: Old mine buildings, urban paddling.

TRIP RATING:
Beginner: 2-mile round-trip paddle east of Houghton.

TRIP DURATION: Part of a day.

NAVIGATION AIDS: USGS: *Chasell* at 1:24,000, Keewenaw Waterway navigational chart 14972.

CAUTIONS: Boat traffic.

TRIP PLANNING: An introductory brochure and a more detailed map of the water trail are available from the Keewenaw Tourism Council at (800) 338–7982. The entire trail includes about 50 miles on the Portage Waterway and Torch Lake, so an extended trip is certainly possible. There are several campgrounds in the area and even a few primitive water trail sites, which make an overnight paddle a possibility. Although this route is fairly protected, winds can funnel down the channel and create some steep, choppy waves; for calmest conditions paddle early in the day.

LAUNCH SITE: There are several possible launch sites, only one is listed here. Contact the Keewenaw Tourism Council (see above) for more options. Most of the Houghton waterfront is lined with public parking and docks, but the docks are so far above the water that they are unusable for kayaks. The Houghton waterfront park has a small beach east of the bridge that can be used to launch. From the M 26/US 41 bridge, go south on M 26 for 0.5 mile. Turn right on Canal Road and drive 0.25 mile to the parking lot on your left. There is no charge to park in the lot.

DIRECTIONS

START: Put in at the beach and paddle east toward the bridge. Most boats will pass through the center channel under the bridge, and it's best to stay to the side and out of the way.

MILE 0.5: The NPS headquarters for Isle Royale National Park are on the right. The *Ranger III* will be at the dock if it is not on its way to and from the park.

MILE 1.0: When the shipping channel is clear, cross to the north side of the waterway to view the old mine buildings. You may see old ore carts next to some structures.

MILE 1.5: Continue back west along the north side of the channel. Note the old fishing boats beached on the shore: The spread of the parasitic sea lamprey to Lake Superior in the 1950s decimated trout and other

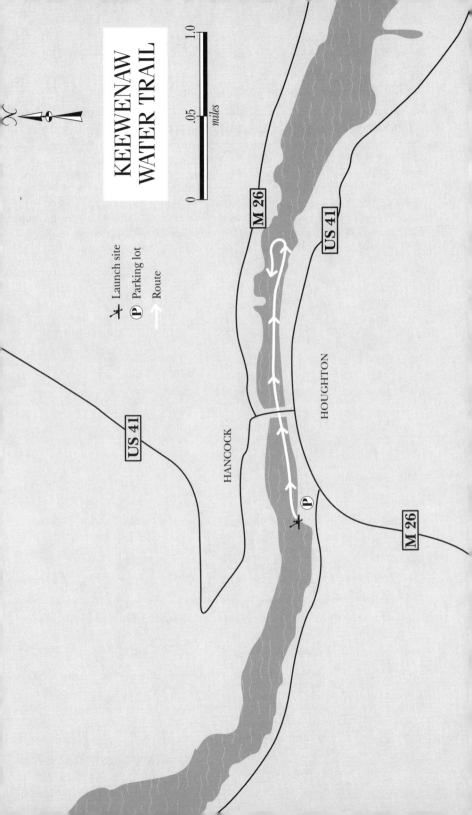

KEEWENAW
WATER TRAIL

1.0 .05 0
miles

↟ Launch site
Ⓟ Parking lot
↑ Route

M 26

US 41

US 41

M 26

HANCOCK

HOUGHTON

fish populations and caused a drastic decline in Great Lakes commercial fishing.

MILE 2.0: Cross back to the waterfront park or extend your paddle west.

Where to Eat & Where to Stay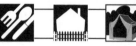

RESTAURANTS & LODGING Many choices here, contact the Keewenaw Tourist Council for a listing and map. **Marie's Deli** on Sheldon (906–482–8650) serves good Greek and Middle Eastern food. **CAMPING** **McLain State Park** is located at the western entrance to the Portage Waterway and is another possible access point to the water trail. Call (906) 482–0278 for more information. Both Houghton and Hancock have city campgrounds. Call (800) 338–7982 for more information.

Route 9:

━━ ━━ ━━ ━━ ━━ ━━ ━━ ━━ ━━ ━━ ━━ ➤

Bete Grise Bay

This day trip is a good introduction to the Keewenaw, along shoreline that is still undeveloped and reminiscent of the rocky north shore and Isle Royale in terms of appearance. Bete Grise Bay has a pretty beach where the water may even be warm enough for a comfortable swim.

TRIP HIGHLIGHTS: Good sand beach, lighthouse, waterfall, rocky shoreline.

TRIP RATING:
Intermediate: 12-mile trip to the waterfall and back.

TRIP DURATION: Day-long.

NAVIGATION AIDS: USGS: 47087-1 at 1:250,000, or *Lake Medora* at 1:24,000.

CAUTIONS: Shoreline open to southerly winds, few landing spots in rough
weather.

TRIP PLANNING: Calmer conditions are more usual early in the season.

LAUNCH SITE: From Highway 41 turn east onto Bete Grise Bay Road, drive 10.8 miles to Bete Grise Beach. Cars park along the side of the road on the shoulder at the north end of the beach, near the changing room and toilet. There is no charge to park here.

DIRECTIONS

START: Paddle east from the **beach (N 47° 23.148' W 087° 57.488')** **launch site.**

MILE 1.0: As you near the end of the houses, look at the rock shoals beneath to see colorful bands of sedimentary rock. From here to the waterfall, there are only cobble beaches. Furthermore, there is an underwater rock shelf along most of the shore, so landing may be very difficult in rough weather.

MILE 3.0: To the right are **two impressive peaks** close to the shore.

MILE 3.5: Look for a **sea stack** close to shore.

MILE 6.0: The **Montreal River falls** empty directly into the lake. To the left is a narrow sand beach that may be underwater in high-water years. There are trails along the side of the river.

MILES 6.0 TO 12.0: Return to Bete Grise Bay. For an extension, head to the south end of the bay where the lighthouse, which is now privately owned, stands at the entrance to the canal, which connects **Lac La Belle** with Lake Superior. A canal, built by the Conglomerate Mining Company, was intended for moving copper out to Lake Superior, but the mines in the Lac La Belle area were operational for only a few years. Before the arrival of the sea lamprey, fishing was the mainstay of the Lac La Belle community.

Where to Eat & Where to Stay

RESTAURANTS & LODGING The nearest restaurants and hotels will be in Eagle Harbor and Copper Harbor. Call the Keewenaw Tourism Council at (800) 338–7982 for information. **CAMPING** Try **Fort Wilkins State Park** in Copper Harbor (906–289–4215) or **McLain State Park** (906–482–0278) for campsites.

Bete Grise Bay

BETE GRISE BAY

COPPER HARBOR

US 41

Big Bay

Montreal River

falls

Fish Cove

LAKE SUPERIOR

Bete Grise Bay

dirt road

Mt. Houghton
elev. 1,466 ft.

P

ship canal

Lac La Belle

Mendota
Lighthouse

←TO US 41

Launch site
P Parking lot
Lighthouse
Route
Route extension

0   1   2
miles

Route 10:

▬ ▬ ▬ ▬ ▬ ▬ ▬ ▬ ▬ ▬ ▬ ▬ ▬ ▬ ➡

Copper Harbor Lighthouse

This is a short but scenic trip across sheltered Copper Harbor to visit the Copper Harbor Lighthouse, now a museum and part of Fort Wilkins State Park. The original lighthouse was built in 1849, a year after Whitefish Point Lighthouse. Near the lighthouse is the vein of chrysolite or greenstone (a copper containing ore) that led to the discovery of copper on the Keewenaw and the copper rush of the mid-nineteenth century. Thousands of prospectors de-scended on the Keewenaw, and cavalry troops were posted at Copper Harbor to keep the peace. They built Fort Wilkins, which has been reconstructed and is now a state park and historic complex, complete with reenactors in period costume.

TRIP HIGHLIGHTS: Good scenery, lighthouse museum.

TRIP RATING:

Beginner: 4-mile round-trip from marina to Copper Harbor Lighthouse and return.

TRIP DURATION: Part day.

NAVIGATION AIDS: USGS: *Fort Wilkins* at 1:24,000.

CAUTIONS: Boat traffic around the harbor, some exposure to north winds.

TRIP PLANNING: Copper Harbor is fairly sheltered, but the gap between Porter's Island shoals and Hayes Point is open to north winds. Check the marine forecast before going.

LAUNCH SITE: The Copper Harbor Marina is open to the public and does not charge for parking or launching. There is no beach, however, and kayakers must share a cement ramp with other

boaters. Take M 26 west from its intersection with US 41, go 0.25 mile and turn right into the marina parking lot. An alternate launch is the Lighthouse Overlook, 1.3 miles east of the 26/41 intersection. This is part of Fort Wilkins State Park, and a $4.00/day vehicle permit is required for parking in the lot. There is a sheltered gravel beach to launch from, and the lighthouse is less than a half mile away.

DIRECTIONS

START: From the marina paddle east. Be careful of the lighthouse tour boat, which leaves the marina dock hourly in the summer, as well as other boat traffic.

Copper Harbor Lighthouse

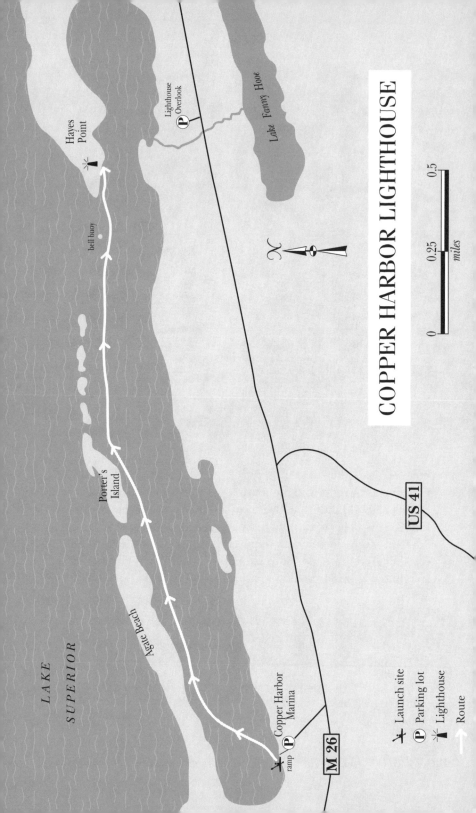

COPPER HARBOR LIGHTHOUSE

LAKE SUPERIOR

Hayes Point

bell buoy

Porter's Island

Agate Beach

Lighthouse Overlook

Lake Fanny Hooe

Copper Harbor Marina

ramp

M 26

US 41

N

0   0.25   0.5
miles

- Launch site
- Parking lot
- Lighthouse
- Route

MILE 1.0: On the left is **Porter's Island**. If the weather is calm, it is possible to pass through the gap between the island and the mainland, around the point and visit Agate Beach. Otherwise paddle east past the dock for the *Isle Royale Queen III*, which leaves at 8:00 A.M. daily for Rock Harbor.

MILE 2.0: Boats must pass between **Hayes Point** and **the bell buoy**, making for a narrow channel. As you cross the channel to the lighthouse, please use caution. At the lighthouse kayakers are asked not to use the tour boat dock. There is a rocky beach on the south side of Hayes Point that you can use. Tour the buildings and take the footpath to the green chrysolite vein, which runs out from shore and under the lake.

MILES 3.0 TO 4.0: Return along the same route.

Where to Eat & Where to Stay

R E S T A U R A N T S   There are several restaurants in Copper Harbor, call the information line for Copper Harbor at (800) 338–7982 for a list and map. The **Harbor Haus** (906–289–4277), located on the waterfront, has German-American cuisine, and their ethnically attired wait staff sometimes greets the returning *Isle Royale Queen III* by doing the can-can. **L O D G I N G**   Again, there are many choices. Call the information line for Copper Harbor at (800) 338–7982. Advance reservations are recommended. The **Norland Motel** (906–289–4285), while not on the waterfront, is on Lake Fanny Hooe and is quiet and has reasonable rates. **C A M P I N G**   **Fort Wilkins** is most convenient. Call the park for more information (906) 289–4215, or call (800) 44PARKS for state park reservations.

Route 11:

━━ ━━ ━━ ━━ ━━ ━━ ━━ ━━ ━━ ━━ ━━ ━━ ➤

Eagle Harbor to Agate Harbor

Like other Keewenaw towns, Eagle Harbor got its start from one of the nearby and short-lived mines, but it survived after the mine closed by serving as a harbor for ships carrying supplies for other inland mines. It has an old lighthouse that has also been coverted into a museum (actually three museums: maritime, copper mining, and local history), and a good swimming beach inside the harbor.

TRIP HIGHLIGHTS: Good swimming, lighthouse museum.

TRIP RATING:

Beginner: 6-mile trip to entrance of Agate Harbor and back.

TRIP DURATION: Part to full day.

NAVIGATION AIDS: USGS: *Eagle River* and *Delaware* at 1:24,000.

CAUTIONS: Exposed rocky shoreline, reflection waves, shoals.

TRIP PLANNING: There are not many places to land between Eagle and Agate Harbors should the weather turn ugly. So check the marine forecast and plan on doing this trip early in the season and early in the day.

LAUNCH SITE: There is an old Coast Guard station on the north arm of Eagle Harbor that is now used as a public boat launch. There is no fee for launching or parking. Drive north from the center of the town of Eagle Harbor on M 26. Take the first possible left turn, where M 26 leaves the shore and heads inland. Drive 0.7 mile to the parking area at the end of the road.

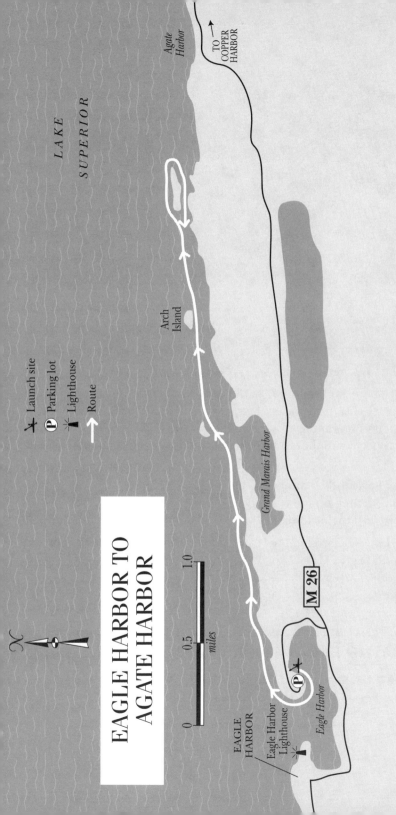

EAGLE HARBOR TO AGATE HARBOR

Launch site
P Parking lot
Lighthouse
→ Route

LAKE

SUPERIOR

Agate Harbor

TO
COPPER
HARBOR

Arch
Island

Grand Marais Harbor

M 26

EAGLE
HARBOR

Eagle Harbor
Lighthouse

Eagle Harbor

KEEWENAW PENINSULA

0   0.5   1.0

miles

DIRECTIONS

START: There is a former life-saving boat, which is being restored by the Keewenaw Historical Society, at the put in. Paddle south from the ramp and then west into the lake. From here to the larger islands is mostly private property, and the steep rocky beaches make for poor landing in any case.

MILE 2.0: Near the entrance to **Grand Marais Harbor**, look for an island with a rock arch on the west side. Continue paddling past a school of rocks toward the next islands.

MILE 3.0: Loop around the island at the entrance of **Agate Harbor** and return to **Eagle Harbor**. The best views of the lighthouse at the south end of the harbor entrance are from the water, but it may be easiest to visit the museums via the land route, since the beach at the lighthouse is small, steep, and rocky.

Where to Eat & Where to Stay

RESTAURANTS & LODGING The nearest restaurants and hotels will be in Eagle Harbor and Copper Harbor. Call the Keewenaw Tourism Council at (800) 338–7982. **CAMPING** Try **Fort Wilkins State Park** in Copper Harbor (906–289–4215) or **McLain State Park** (906–482–0278).

Route 12:

━ ━ ━ ━ ━ ━ ━ ━ ━ ━ ━ ━ ━ ━ ━ ━ ━ ━ ➤

Isle Royale National Park

Isle Royale is a wilderness park with no roads and few
amenities; and it is a popular destination for backpackers
and boaters. Isle Royale is great for kayaks, too. Paddlers
can choose protected, scenic areas, such as Rock Harbor
and the Five Fingers, or the challenge of more rugged and
exposed shoreline. Because the ferry, *Voyager II*, completely
circles the islands and makes stops at the major campsites, it
is possible to paddle a one-way section of the island and
arrange for the ferry to pick up you and your boat at the
end of a segment.

TRIP HIGHLIGHTS: Protected scenic areas, excellent trail system
for sidetrips and hikes, good fishing.

TRIP RATING:
Beginner: 10 miles and up one way from Rock Harbor to Daisy
Farm, Belle Isle area.
Intermediate: 20 miles—plus extra for sidetrips—Five Fingers:
McCargoe Cove, Amygdaloid Channel, Duncan Harbor, Tobin
Harbor, and Rock Harbor, one way.
Advanced: 110 miles: island circumnavigation.

TRIP DURATION: Part day to two weeks: Getting to the island is a
trip in itself; plan to stay awhile and make the most of your visit.

NAVIGATION AIDS: USGS and NPS topographic map of Isle
Royale at 1:62,500, which shows campsites and trails.

CAUTIONS: Exposed rocky shoreline, cold water (wet suit or dry suit
recommended), fog, remote area.

TRIP PLANNING: One of the first things you should do is contact
the park office at (906) 482–0984 and request an information pack-
et, which should include useful pamphlets on the ferries, their

schedules and fares, campsites and permits, and the canoe portages around the island.

The hardest part of paddling Isle Royale is getting there in the first place. Ferries leave from Grand Portage, Minnesota (the *Wenonah* and *Voyager II*), Copper Harbor, Michigan (*Isle Royale Queen III*), and Houghton, Michigan (*Ranger III*). Round-trip fares for one person and a canoe/kayak run about $120, but price and voyage times vary by boat. Once there, you must obtain a camping permit from either the Rock Harbor or Windigo ranger station, at $4.00/person/night. There may also be parking fees for your car while you're on the island; make sure to check with the company you travel with. Although taking the ferry is a bit of a hassle, we advise kayakers against attempting to paddle to the island, as the shortest crossing is 15 miles from Pigeon Point, Minnesota. Fog, rapid changes in weather and wind, extremely cold water and boat traffic make this an extremely risky crossing.

Most campsites have sleeping shelters with a screen wall on one side, but don't plan on finding a free one every night—they are available on a first come, first serve basis. There are portages that circumvent the exposed and rocky points of the Five Fingers area, but portaging a loaded kayak is difficult, and unless you have experience doing this, a better approach may be to allow for extra wind days in your trip plan.

Although paddling early in the year is often a good crowd and wind avoidance strategy, there are some drawbacks, such as more fog, bugs, and cool weather. Late-season paddling will definitely be rougher—July is probably the optimum month for kayaking.

LAUNCH SITE: Ferries leaving from the Keewenaw Peninsula go to Rock Harbor; the Grand Portage ferries stop either at Windigo (the *Wenonah*), or they make a complete circuit around the island (*Voyager II*), stopping at the major camping areas.

Isle Royale National Park

DIRECTIONS

These directions are for the entire shoreline, starting at Rock Harbor and going counterclockwise. Refer to the appropriate locations and mile points for the shorter trips.

START: Rock Harbor (N 48° 08.724' W 88° 29.021') is the busiest place on Isle Royale. There is a small beach near the lodge, but it's a little far to carry all your gear from there to the campground. Allow enough time after your arrival to paddle someplace more convenient for kayakers.

MILE 2.0: Heading northeast cross **Tobin Harbor** from **Scoville Point**. The islands at the mouth of Tobin Harbor have old vacation cottages in various states of decay, though some are still in use. *Sidetrip:* If you have time, take a sidetrip down to the end of the harbor and look for a trail-head in a small bay on the north side. The trail leads to Lookout Louise on the Greenstone Ridge, and the view is well worth the walk.

MILE 3.0: Hug the north shore of Tobin Harbor and follow it into **Merrit Lane**, a narrow and protected channel.

MILE 4.0: There is a nice but popular campsite with one shelter here. If the weather is a bit rough, wait it out here before attempting to round **Blake Point**.

MILE 4.5: *Caution:* Kayakers know **Blake Point** is trouble. It is extremely exposed to winds from most directions, and rough conditions and reflection waves are common, so wait for calm seas before going around. If you get stuck in bad weather, consider doing the Tobin Harbor portage instead.

MILE 6.0: After rounding Blake Point, turn southwest and paddle toward **Locke Point**. Your reward for passing the point is what many paddlers feel to be the best scenery on the island, so take your time and explore the coves and islands between here and McCargoe Cove. *Sidetrip:* Follow the shoreline into Duncan Narrows (where there is a campground on the south side) and beyond to Duncan Bay. Though part of Lake Superior, the bay is so protected it feels like an inland lake. At the end of the bay is another campground. Both campsites tend to be pretty busy. After leaving or passing Duncan Narrows, continue paddling southwest.

Isle Royale National Park

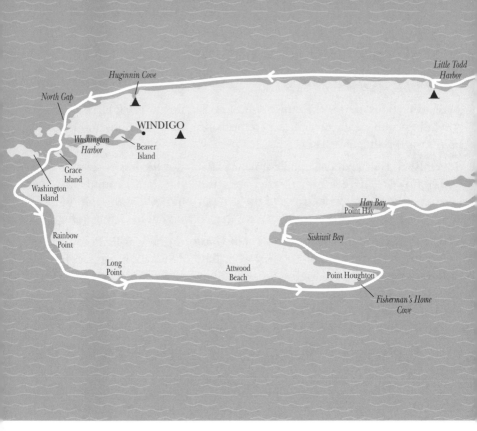

MILE 7.0: After **Locke Point** there is a series of small islands and shoals that will give some protection from waves on your way into **Five Finger Bay**.

MILE 10.0: Make a sidetrip into **Stockly Bay** or continue onto Hill Point.

MILE 11.0: After **Hill Point** there are numerous islands and shoals that provide protection from the open lake.

MILE 13.5: The campground at **Belle Isle** is in a great spot, but it is also popular. From Belle Isle you have the choice of going through the **Amygdaloid Channel** or down through **Pickerel Cove** and over the very short portage to Herring Bay; the distance is about the same either way. Do a little of both, if you have time. Pickerel Cove is the last of the long, thin harbors of the Five Fingers area. Near the end of the bay on the north side of the channel is the campsite and portage. The site is pleasant but not roomy; the portage is short but steep enough to make carrying a loaded boat a challenge. The other route, through the Amygdaloid

Isle Royale National Park

Channel, is more exposed but also worth a visit. Look for the trail to the lake on Amygdaloid Island, which leaves from the middle of the south side of the island.

MILE 18.0: Whichever route you take, you will end up at **Indian Point.** *Caution:* You are now leaving the shelter of Amygdaloid Island; use caution in approaching the entrance to McCargoe Cove.

MILE 19.0: The **Birch Island** campsite is located near the entrance to McCargoe Cove. Many paddlers begin their trip to Rock Harbor from here. *Sidetrip:* It is 2.0 miles down McCargoe Cove to the campground, but even if you are not staying there, it can be a pleasant paddle. *Caution:* After leaving McCargoe Cove or Brady Cove, there will be no good sheltered landing spots until Todd Harbor.

MILE 23.0: Pass the entrance to **Todd Harbor**, a broad bay. There are a few small islands at the south end that help shelter the bay.

Isle Royale National Park

MILE 25.0: Look for a narrow beach and dock, on the south side of the point in the middle of Todd Harbor. The group sites are near the dock while the individual sites are farther down the small cove. *Caution:* There are no good landing spots between Todd Harbor and Little Todd Harbor.

MILE 31.0: Little Todd Harbor has a cobble/gravel beach with tent sites at the south end. *Caution:* If you are continuing to Washington Harbor from Little Todd Harbor, be aware that you are beginning an extremely challenging and dangerous section of shoreline, prone to reflection waves and characterized by cliffs and narrow boulder or cobble beaches at the foot of a rock wall 4 to 6 feet high. Although these beaches are usable for break stops in calm weather (you will find one every 1–2 miles), they will either be underwater or unapproachable even in moderate seas. Do not attempt this 13.0-mile section unless you are confident of fair weather but are prepared to deal with bad weather if conditions deteriorate.

MILE 46.0: Huginnin Cove, though small, is fairly protected and has a small gravel beach. It has tent sites but seems to get very heavy use by backpackers because of its proximity to Washington Harbor.

MILE 50.0: At **North Gap (N 47° 53.684' W 89° 13.446')**, look for the wreck of the *America*, a passenger and freight steamer, which sank in 1928 after hitting one of the many reefs in the area (no lives were lost). The bow is only a few feet underwater and is marked by a diving buoy.

MILE 50.5: The entrance to **Washington Harbor** stretches to the north. *Sidetrip:* Washington Harbor has a small store, laundromat, showers, ferry dock, and a ranger station that issues permits. Otherwise there is not much reason to make the 7.0-mile trip down and back out. The campground at **Beaver Island** is small and busy, as is the whole harbor, and the scenery is not especially compelling.

MILE 51.0: Pass by **Grace Island** (which also has a campground) and into Grace Harbor.

MILE 53.0: *Caution:* After **Cumberland Point** there are no good harbors until Siskiwit Bay, 18.0 miles away. Unlike the north side of the island, this stretch of shoreline has good cobble or gravel beaches, but it is wide open to southerly winds that can bring big waves and swell. Paddle this leg in good weather only and be prepared to wait out rough weather.

MILE 55.0: After **Rainbow Point** follow the shore as it begins turning to the northeast. The beaches become less steep, the cobbles smaller, and good stopping places more frequent. There are no facilities or established campsites between Rainbow Cove and Siskiwit Bay, and you are on

Isle Royale National Park

your own. Because few people travel this section, and there is no hiking trail access, you may get a rare chance at solitude.

MILE 57.5: Look for a section of rock cliffs with sea caves.

MILE 59.5: Long Point is a pretty spot and has plenty of room for tents if you don't mind camping on gravel.

MILE 65.0: Attwood Beach is another great spot to camp, with a broad, flat gravel beach. This is probably the best spot until Siskiwit Bay.

MILE 70.5: Fisherman's Home Cove is a nice sheltered spot, but there are several private cottages here.

MILE 71.0: Point Houghton forms the southern arm of **Siskiwit Bay**. Unless you want to skip directly to Point Hay, round Point Houghton and paddle south around the perimeter of the bay.

MILE 76.0: Siskiwit Bay Campground is at the south end of the bay.

MILE 80.0: Around **Point Hay** there is a small campsite in the shelter of Hay Bay. *Caution:* The shoreline from Hay Bay to Malone Bay is fairly exposed.

MILE 84.0: Once behind Wright Island, you will be well protected in **Malone Bay**.

MILE 86.0: The campground is next to a small pebble beach and has a number of shelters. It is only a five-minute walk from the campground to **Siskiwit Lake**.

MILE 87.0: The Malone Bay Ranger Station and dock are on the opposite side of the point from the campground. Paddle north between **Hat Island** and the main island. *Caution:* When going from Hat Island to Chippewa Harbor, there are only marginal landings at Little Greenstone Beach, Vodrey Harbor, Greenstone Beach and Blueberry Cove. Proceed with caution, especially in southerly winds. Much of the shoreline in this section consists of flat, gray rock, sloping into the water at an angle of about 30°—very pretty to look at and very prone to clapotis.

The Wolves of Isle Royale

The moose and wolves living on Isle Royale are relatively recent introductions: The moose swam from Ontario in the early 1900s, while the wolves (possibly a single pair) crossed over an ice bridge in 1949. They have been studied since 1958 to understand predator-prey relationships. Initially changes in the two populations were in sync so that increases or decreases in the wolf population lagged behind but mirrored changes in the moose population. But in 1980, the wolves were decimated by parvovirus, a canine disease brought from the mainland, which left only fourteen wolves living. Meanwhile the moose population, freed from predation by the wolves, increased to more than 2,400 by 1994 (During '94 and '95 it was hard not to see a moose on an Isle Royale visit.) Overbrowsing of balsam fir, severe cold, and winter tick infestation during winter of 1996 caused a crash in the moose population, which currently stands at about 700 animals. Unfortunately the drastic reduction in moose hit the wolves hard, and their total is back down to fourteen animals from twenty-four in 1997. With such a small population, it is possible that the wolves will not survive. Though there are fewer moose, it is still possible to see one, particularly near Rock Harbor and Washington Harbor. Annual reports on the wolves and moose are available in the park offices at Washington Harbor and Rock Harbor, or from The Isle Royale Natural History Association, 800 East Lakeshore Drive, Houghton, MI 49931–1869.

MILE 95.5: **Chippewa Harbor (N 48° 01.726' W 88° 38.439')** is extremely protected. The campground is located on the north side of the first narrows; it has several shelters but few good tent sites. Continue paddling northeast along the coast. *Caution:* There are no good sheltered landing spots until Conglomerate Harbor or Rock Harbor. Proceed with care.

MILE 99.5: Round **Saginaw Point** and turn west toward the entrance to Rock Harbor.

MILE 100.5: **Conglomerate Bay** provides a nice sheltered break from any wind and waves.

MILE 101.5: The southern entrance to Rock Harbor is through the **Middle Passage**. *Caution:* The Middle Passage can be a little rough, and on busy weekends it sees quite a bit of boat traffic. On the left is the **Rock Harbor Lighthouse**, built in 1855 and now a museum with exhibits on shipwrecks and life on Isle Royale before it became a park. The spot is definitely worth seeing. It can be reached either by landing at the small beach in front of the lighthouse or by paddling through the Middle Passage and south to the Edison Fisheries dock. A short trail connects the lighthouse and the fishery. Opposite the lighthouse is **Caribou Island**, which only has two shelters, but plenty of room for tents under the pines. *Sidetrip:* If you have time, take a day trip down to Daisy Farm. A trail runs from the campground up to Mount Ojibway on the Greenstone Ridge.

MILE 103.2: North of Caribou is **Mott Island**, which houses the park's headquarters. Just north of Mott is a parallel line of small islands with a channel between them, providing a nice detour.

MILE 106.0: **Tookers Island** is a nice place to stay but like all island sites is popular with motorboaters.

MILE 108.0: From Tookers Island paddle northeast along **Smithwick Island** then paddle north to **Rock Harbor** campground and ferry dock.

Where to Eat & Where to Stay

R E S T A U R A N T S & L O D G I N G   The only lodging and dining facilities on the island are at **Rock Harbor Lodge,** and they're not cheap. Call (906) 337–4993 for reservations and information. For lodging in Copper Harbor, see information for Rte. 9; for information on Houghton, see Rte. 7; for information on Grand Portage, see Rte. 14. **C A M P I N G**   As of 1997, there is a $4.00/person/day permit fee. There are also some restrictions on camping away from designated campsites. Please ask when getting your permit.

Lake Superior
Wisconsin

Apostle Islands
National Lakeshore

The northern tip of Wisconsin juts out into Lake Superior and ends in an archipelago of the twenty-two Apostle Islands. A total of 2,500 acres of the mainland coast and twenty-one of the twenty-two islands are protected within the Apostle Islands National Lakeshore, managed by the National Park Service. The Apostle Islands are a kayakers dream, offering you many islands to explore with varied coastlines, ranging from sand beaches to red sandstone cliffs. Distances between the islands are normally only a few miles, allowing kayakers to make short crossings and find shelter in the lee of the many islands in bad weather. The islands are popular with other recreational boaters during the peak summer season,

but you can always find a quiet corner of wilderness within the park. Many of the islands have a fascinating historical sites, including lighthouses, commercial fishing camps, quarries, and farms. The many sandstone sea caves are popular destinations for kayakers. Paddling your kayak is the perfect way to explore the intricate tubes, tunnels, natural arches, cracks, and caverns of sculpted rock.

Camping Within the Apostle Islands National Lakeshore

Many of the islands have designated campsites for individuals and small groups. Class A individual sites hold a maximum of seven campers and three tents. Class B sites allow only two tents and a maximum of five campers. A limited number of group campsites are available for groups of eight or more on Basswood Island, Oak Island, Stockton Island, and Sand Island. Group sites are limited and in high demand; we strongly recommend that you reserve them well in advance. A camping permit that costs $15 is required. On some islands wilderness camping is allowed for groups of five or less, with no fires allowed and strict low-impact camping practices enforced. Check with the park for details. The number of sites that are available for camping can vary from year to year—some sites are occasionally closed to protect sensitive wildlife (bald eagles get first pick). For camping information call (715) 779–3397. The park can also mail you their detailed brochure on camping, which lists all available sites for any given year.

Route 13:

Squaw Bay Sea Caves

The Squaw Bay sea caves are a magic place. On our last visit we arrived at the caves just before sunset. The water was like glass, and with the setting sun, the sandstone cliffs glowed red in the most fantastic colors. With the lake level at a record low, there were more arches and caves to explore than usual, and we were able to slide our kayaks hand over hand along the ceiling of deep passages that we had not entered in years. As a game we started to paddle through every sea arch, but we lost interest in the game and lost count somewhere after twenty-five arches. The previous month had been wet and rainy, and curtains of water cascaded from cracks in the cliffs, sparkling in the setting sun, and providing a cooling shower on a warm summer evening.

TRIP HIGHLIGHTS: Beautiful sandstone cliffs, sea caves, and sand beaches.

TRIP RATING:

Beginner/Intermediate: A 3.5-mile stretch of coast; 7.0 miles as an out-and-back day trip.

TRIP DURATION: Day or half-day trip.

NAVIGATION AIDS: NOAA chart 14966, USGS: *Squaw Bay* (7.5 minute).

CAUTIONS: The cliffs and sea caves form clapotis and confused seas when winds and waves come from the north or west. A wet suit or dry suit is recommended because water temperatures are often less than 50° F.

TRIP PLANNING: Always check the marine forecast: Winds from the north or west can make the sea caves too rough to explore. Glass calm conditions are needed to explore the caves, even a 1-foot chop will make exploring the caves difficult.

LAUNCH SITE: Four miles east of the Cornucopia Public Harbor and 17 miles west of Bayfield on Highway 13 is a dirt road that leads to Meyers Beach. Camping is not allowed, long-term parking is allowed for paddlers departing for multiday trips. There is an outhouse, but no potable water supply.

DIRECTIONS

START: You start your trip by carrying the kayaks down a wooden stairway to **Meyers Beach (N 46° 53.15' W 91° 02.91').** Heading east along the beach, you can see the red sandstone cliffs, which start about 1 mile from the beach.

MILES 1.25 TO 3.0: After 1.0 mile of sand beach the red sandstone cliffs begin. Within about 100 yards, you see the first small caves, arches, and pillars begin. There are too many caves and arches to describe in detail, but here are two of my favorites. The names I have used are my own, so feel free to name them yourself.

Crack-in-the-earth: A huge crack cuts into a cliff wall 50 to 100 feet high. The crack continues deep into the cliff and narrows to about 20 feet wide, where a natural stone bridge crosses this little canyon. Paddling into the shadows, you soon find that the crack goes deeper, continuing for another 30 to 50 feet and narrowing to a boat width or less. A small stream of water trickles into this cold, dark cave. The ceiling of the narrow crack arches up in a gentle curve and towers high overhead. At the end of the narrow crack is a jumble of driftwood, and I have often found ice deep in the crack as late in the year as July.

Low-wet-crawl: Look for an amphitheater-shaped chamber with a tiny arched hole that is about 3 by 3 feet when lake levels are low. By laying your paddle under a deckline and walking your hands along the ceiling, you can pass 100 feet under the cliff wall and exit on the other side through a series of arches and columns. With high lake levels, it may not be possible to enter the cave.

Squaw Bay Sea Caves

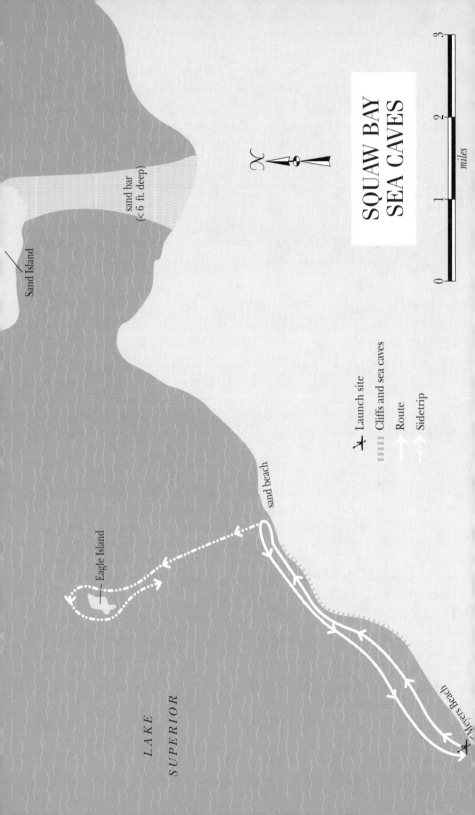

LAKE
SUPERIOR

Sand Island

sand bar
(<6 ft. deep)

Eagle Island

sand beach

Meyers Beach

SQUAW BAY
SEA CAVES

✈ Launch site
Cliffs and sea caves
Route
Sidetrip

0   1   2   3
miles

Sea Caves

The story of the Apostle Islands sea caves begins over one billion years ago. Rivers and streams carried sandy sediments from what is now southern Minnesota and deposited them in the basin where the Apostle Islands are now located. These sediments formed the Devil's Island sandstone formation, the thinly bedded, fine-grained sandstone that has been sculpted by Lake Superior into so many fantastic shapes. The erosion of the pounding waves and the seasonal freeze and thaw action on the fractured rock forms undercut stone formations called reentrants, which when combined together over the centuries can form caves, arches, and pillars.

Sea caves can be found on many of the islands, wherever sandstone cliff faces are exposed to the full force of spring and fall storms. The most spectacular sea caves and sculpted sandstone are found along the mainland coast at Squaw Bay, on Sand Island's Swallow Point, and at the north end of Devil's Island. On glassy calm days an adventurous kayaker can squeeze a kayak into every crack and crevice and thread through every arch. The caves and cliffs form confused seas and violent clapotis with very little swell, so that even with a small wave pattern of 1 to 2 feet, it is too rough to explore the inner caves.

MILE 3.5: From miles 1.25 to 3.0, the **sandstone cliffs** dominate the shoreline. From Mile 3.0 the cliffs diminish; at Mile 3.5 there is a narrow sand beach that makes an excellent lunch stop. This is one out-and-back trip for which there is no need to dread retracing your steps. It is hard to resist the urge to explore all of the caves again on the return trip. Try to leave enough time to arrive at the Meyers Beach landing site well before dark because it is very hard to see the stairs from the water. *Sidetrip:* Advanced paddlers can head offshore to explore Eagle Island, a small island about 2 miles northwest of the coast. Landing on the island is not permitted between May and September because this site is a sensitive heron and cormorant rookery. With care you can view the heron and cormorant rookery on the northeast corner of the island without disturbing the birds.

Where to Eat & Where to Stay

For information on restaurants, lodging, and camping, see Route 17: Outer Island Loop.

Squaw Bay Sea Caves

Route 14:

━━ ━━ ━━ ━━ ━━ ━━ ━━ ━━ ━━ ━━ ━━ ━━ ━━ ━━ ➤

Sand Island Circumnavigation

Located about 2 miles from Little Sand Bay, Sand Island is easily accessible as either a day trip or an overnighter. The island has many interesting areas to explore by kayak, including excellent sea caves at Swallow Point, sand beaches, and a sandstone lighthouse on the northern tip. Sand Island is the only island within the park that once had a year-round community. To learn more about the history of the island, pick up the Park Service brochure on Sand Island.

TRIP HIGHLIGHTS: Excellent sea caves, good sand beaches, abandoned farms and a historic lighthouse.

TRIP RATING:
Beginner/Intermediate: 15-mile round-trip

TRIP DURATION: A long day trip or an overnight trip (a 2.25 mile crossing, plus a 10-mile circumnavigation of the island).

NAVIGATION AIDS: NOAA charts 14966 or 14973, USGS: *Bayfield County* at 1:100,000.

CAUTIONS: Clapotis from cliffs and sea caves. A sandbar, which can produce shoaling seas far from shore, extends from the mainland to the island.

TRIP PLANNING: Kayakers who plan to camp on the island will need to reserve a campsite at the ranger station in either Bayfield or Little Sand Bay and pay a $15 fee for a camping permit. Beginning paddlers should only cross to the island with a good weather window, bringing camping gear and extra food to allow for an extended stay should they become windbound. Winds from the north or northeast will often bring rough conditions. Always check the marine forecast (Duluth 162.55 MHz); daily forecasts are also posted at the ranger station in Little Sand Bay. Fog can be a problem any time of the year on Superior, with May, June, and July being the most common months for fog. Every paddler must have a chart and compass to make the crossing safely. A wet suit or dry suit is recommended because water temperatures are cold, often less than 50° F.

LAUNCH SITE: From Highway 13, 7 miles east of Cornucopia or 5 miles west of Bayfield, you will see the sign for County Road K and the turnoff for Little Sand Bay. Follow the signs to the Little Sand Bay ranger station and the Russell Township campground and public boat ramp. The ranger station has potable water and toilet facilities. Fees are $1.00 per kayak to launch, $20.00 for a season's pass, and $100.00 for a season's pass for commercial outfitters.

DIRECTIONS

START: The kayak launching beach is located by the **boat ramp (N 46° 56.81' W 90° 53.35')**. Long-term parking is available about 100 yards inland from the ramp, and additional parking can be found along Shaft Road.

MILE 2.25: By crossing from **Little Sand Bay** to the nearest land, you come to the southeast corner of the island. There is a private residence located here so please respect private property and do not land on the beach except in an emergency.

MILE 3.25: Continuing north along the east side of the island, you pass the group campsites and come to the **Sand Island dock (N 46° 58.92' W 090° 56.06')** and individual campsites. There is a nice sand beach, potable water, and outhouses near the dock. The island is low,

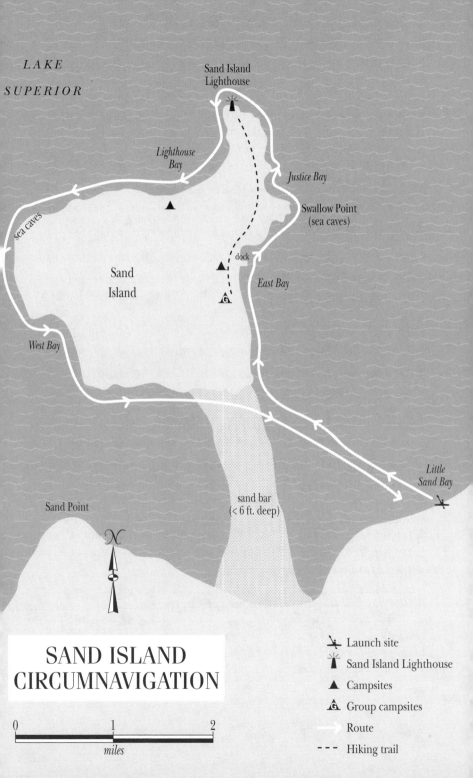

LAKE
SUPERIOR

Sand Island
Lighthouse

Lighthouse
Bay

Justice Bay

Swallow Point
(sea caves)

sea caves

Sand
Island

dock

East Bay

West Bay

Little
Sand Bay

Sand Point

sand bar
(< 6 ft. deep)

N

SAND ISLAND
CIRCUMNAVIGATION

0   1   2
miles

Launch site

Sand Island Lighthouse

Campsites

Group campsites

Route

Hiking trail

and some of the soil is clay so it can be muddy in wet weather. This is also prime mosquito habitat so bring your insect repellent.

MILE 4.0: Northeast from the dock the sand beaches change to red clay banks and then sandstone cliffs. At Mile 4.0 you reach the sandstone cliffs and sea caves of **Swallow Point**. On a calm day you can explore numerous caves, arches, and columns. Just past the point in Justice Bay is a lovely sand beach that makes a great lunch stop. *Caution:* Confused seas and clapotis can develop in this area from a north or northeast wind—only enter the sea caves in waves of 1 foot or less.

MILE 5.5: Heading north from **Justice Bay**, the shore transitions from sand back to sandstone blocks and low cliffs. At Mile 5.5 you reach the **Sand Island Lighthouse** on the northern tip **(N 47° 00.2' W 090° 56.2')**. Established in 1881 the lighthouse is staffed by park volunteers in summer months, and tours are available. On very calm days you can land on the flat rocks in front of the lighthouse; there is a hiking trail from the bay to the lighthouse. In rougher weather you can continue down the coast and land at Lighthouse Bay.

MILE 6.0: Following the coast south and west about 0.5 miles from the lighthouse, you come to **Lighthouse Bay**, which has a lovely sand beach.

MILE 9.0: Heading west along the north side of the island, there are some private land holdings along the sandy shore, and after about 1 mile, the beach transitions back to sandstone and sandstone cliffs. At the northwest corner of the island there are sea caves. Although not as spectacular as the Swallow Point caves, they are well worth exploring.

MILES 9.0 TO 13.0: Continuing south down the west side of the island, the sandstone cliffs give way to red clay bluffs. South of **West Bay** the shore reverts back to sand or cobble beaches with some private land holdings along the southwest and south end of the island. At Mile 13.0 you have reached the southeast tip of the island and can either return to Little Sand Bay via the 2.25-mile crossing or continue around the island another 1 mile to the campsites.

Where to Eat & Where to Stay

For information on restaurants, lodging, and camping, see Route 17: Outer Island Loop.

Route 15:

▬ ▬ ▬ ▬ ▬ ▬ ▬ ▬ ▬ ▬ ▬ ▬ ▬ ▬ ➡

Basswood Island

A day trip to Basswood Island is an excellent option when rough weather makes other trips difficult. Located about 1.5 miles from shore near the Red Cliff Buffalo Bay Tribal Marina, the island is well sheltered by the outer Apostle Islands from most wind directions. Basswood Island has a fascinating history, being the site of several farms, lumbering activity, and a sandstone quarry. For more detailed information on the island's history, pick up the Park Service's brochure on the island.

TRIP HIGHLIGHTS: Visiting the quarry, abandoned farms, sandstone cliffs, and a sea-stack named Honeymoon Rock.

TRIP RATING:
Beginner/Intermediate: An 8.5-mile loop. (A long beginner trip in good weather; rougher weather makes it an intermediate trip.)

TRIP DURATION: Day trip or overnight trip.

NAVIGATION AIDS: NOAA chart 14973, USGS: *Bayfield County* at 1:100,000.

TRIP PLANNING: For kayakers planning to camp on the island, a camping permit, which is available at the Bayfield or Little Sand Bay ranger stations, is required. Although the island is well sheltered from waves, always check the marine forecast from Duluth at 162.55 MHz. Wearing a wet suit or dry suit is recommended because water temperatures are often 50° F or less. Fog can occur on Superior even in summer months, so each paddler should have a chart and compass.

LAUNCH SITE: Three miles west of Bayfield on Highway 13, you will see the turnoff for the Red Cliff (Buffalo Bay) Tribal Marina. A kayak launching fee of $2.00 and a $2.00 parking fee are required.

Potable water and rest room facilities are available at the marina's campground.

DIRECTIONS

START: Leaving the marina **Red Cliff breakwater light (N 46° 51.2' W 090° 47.3')**, head east to make the 1.5-mile crossing to the island.

MILE 1.5: Adjust your course on the crossing to take you to the **National Park Service Basswood Island dock (N 46° 51.06' W 090° 45.42')**. Campsites are available just south of the dock, and you can access hiking trails that lead to three former farm sites and a brownstone quarry.

MILES 1.5 TO 3.5: Heading north and east, you follow a steep, wooded shoreline with little or no beach to the north end of the island, where sandstone cliffs begin. At Mile 3.5 you reach a sandstone column sitting just off shore. This sea-stack is called **Lone Rock** or **Honeymoon Rock**.

MILES 3.5 TO 6.5: Heading south the shore returns to steep, wooded hillsides with narrow cobble or gravel beaches until you approach the south end of the island. Watch for the remains of an old dock near a narrow gravel beach. Just north of the gravel beach is the abandoned **Breckenridge Quarry**.

MILE 7.0: At the southern end of the island is a flat, low shelf of sandstone along the shore. Near the sandstone shelf, there are some campsites. In calm weather you can land, and follow the trail northeast to the abandoned **Basswood Island Brownstone Quarry**.

MILE 8.5: Paddling round the corner and heading north along the shore, you complete the circumnavigation of the island and return to the dock. From here it is a short 1.5-mile crossing west back to the marina.

Where to Eat & Where to Stay

For information on restaurants, lodging, and camping, see Route 17: Outer Island Loop.

Basswood Island

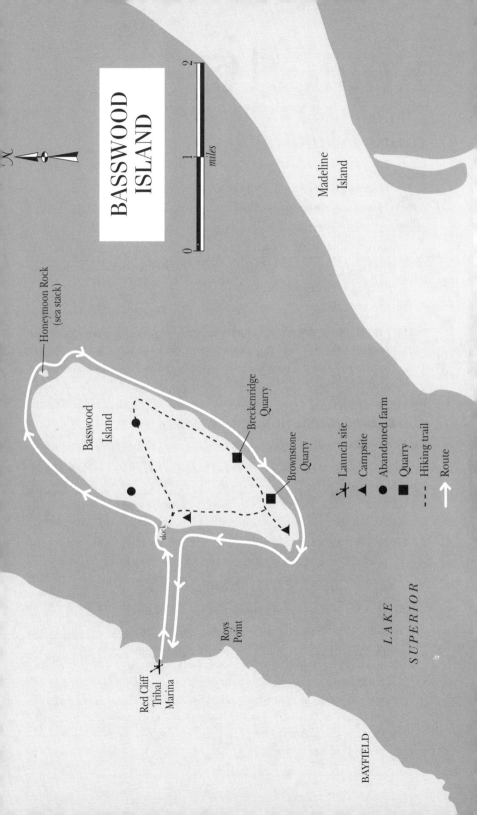

BASSWOOD ISLAND

0   1   2
miles

Honeymoon Rock
(sea stack)

Basswood
Island

Breckenridge
Quarry

Brownstone
Quarry

dock

Madeline
Island

Red Cliff
Tribal
Marina

Roys
Point

BAYFIELD

LAKE
SUPERIOR

Launch site
Campsite
Abandoned farm
Quarry
Hiking trail
Route

Route 16:

■ ■ ■ ■ ■ ■ ■ ■ ■ ■ ■ ■ ➤

Inner Island Loop

The Inner Island loop is a great way for paddlers to explore four beautiful islands as a weekend trip. The route is protected from northeast winds by the outer islands, allowing less-experienced paddlers to get a taste of the beauty of the Apostle Islands without the risks of paddling the exposed outer islands.

TRIP HIGHLIGHTS: Excellent sea caves (Sand Island), good sand beaches (Sand, York, Raspberrry, and Oak Islands), hiking trails (Sand and Oak Islands), and historic lighthouses (Raspberry and Sand Islands).

TRIP RATING:
Beginner/Intermediate: Total distance about 25 miles.

TRIP DURATION: Two or three day trip.

NAVIGATION AIDS: NOAA charts 14966 or 14973, USGS: *Bayfield County* at 1:100,000.

CAUTIONS: See Route 14 "Cautions." Clapotis and confused seas can develop along the sandstone cliffs of York Island and Oak Island.

TRIP PLANNING: Camping is available on Sand, York, and Oak Islands. No camping is allowed on Raspberry Island. Kayakers who plan to camp on any of the islands will need to reserve a campsite at the ranger station in either Bayfield or Little Sand Bay and pay a $15 fee for a camping permit. For groups of eight people or more, group sites are available on Sand and Oak Islands. Crossings from and to the various islands are about 2 miles or less in length, but beginning paddlers should only cross with a good weather window, and all kayakers should bring extra food and allow for an extended stay if they become windbound. Always check the marine forecast (Duluth 162.55 MHz). Daily forecasts are also posted at the ranger station in Little Sand Bay. A wet suit or dry suit is recommended;

water temperatures are often less than 50° F. Fog can be a problem any time of the year on Superior; every paddler must have a chart and compass to make the crossings safely.

LAUNCH SITES:

Little Sand Bay (Start): See Route 14: Sand Island for launch site information.

Red Cliff Buffalo Bay Tribal Marina (Finish): See Route 15: Basswood Island for launch site information.

DIRECTIONS

START TO MILE 4.0: See Route 14 for description.

MILES 4.0 TO 6.0: From **Swallow Point** you can make the 2.0-mile crossing east to the northwest tip of **York Island**. Kayakers who want to explore Sand Island further before crossing may want to continue north to the lighthouse (see Rte. 14). At Mile 6.0 you reach the shore of York Island, a rocky coast of low cliffs and large boulders.

MILE 6.5: Heading east along the north end of York Island, you reach a crescent-shaped sand beach.

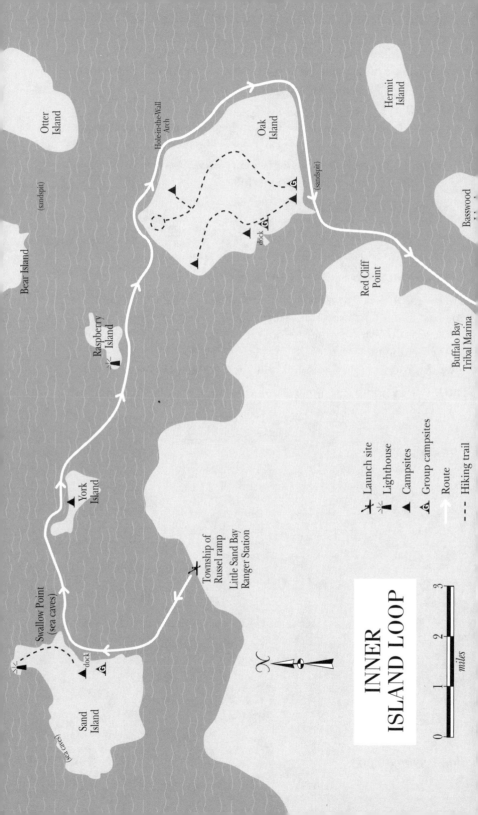

INNER
ISLAND LOOP

Otter
Island

Bear Island

(sandspit)

Hole-in-the-Wall
Arch

Oak
Island

Hermit
Island

Basswood

(sandspit)

Red Cliff
Point

Buffalo Bay
Tribal Marina

Raspberry
Island

York
Island

Swallow Point
(sea caves)

dock

Sand
Island

(sea caves)

Township of
Russel ramp
Little Sand Bay
Ranger Station

dock

Launch site
Lighthouse
Campsites
Group campsites
Route
Hiking trail

miles

0   1   2   3

MILES 6.5 TO 8.0: Continuing east along the north shore of the island, the sand beach gives way to low **sandstone cliffs** and **boulders**. Continue eastward to the southwest tip of **Raspberry Island**.

MILE 10.0: After a crossing of a little over 2 miles, you come to the **Raspberry Island lighthouse** (N 46° 58.3' W 090° 48.3') on the southwest tip of the island. There is a high dock that you can land at in calm weather, although stepping up out of your kayak may be tricky.

MILE 11.0: The easiest place to land on Raspberry Island is at the sand-spit on the southeast corner. This nice sand beach is a very popular mooring and day-use area for sailboats and power boaters. From here you can hike a 1.0-mile trail to the lighthouse.

MILE 13.0: After a southwest crossing of about 2 miles, you reach **Oak Island**. There is a campsite on this northwest side of the island. If you continue northeast along the shore, you will be heading around the point to North Bay. *Caution:* With north or northeast winds, the sandstone cliffs can create clapotis and confused seas. In rough weather you may want to paddle around the southern—more protected—side of Oak Island.

MILE 14.0: On the north end of Oak Island, you find a small bay with a sand beach called **North Bay**. There is a campsite here and a hiking trail

Inland Sea Symposium

The Island Sea Symposium, which has been held every June for more than a decade, is attended by hundreds of kayakers, including many internationally famous guest lecturers and instructors. For information write to the Inland Sea Society, P.O. Box 145, Washburn, WI 54891, or call (715) 373–0674.

that leads to a scenic overlook on the northwest tip of the bay. At the east end of the bay there is a natural arch on shore called **Hole-in-the Wall**.

MILES 14.0 TO 18.0: The landscape on the eastern side of Oak Island varies from sandstone cliffs to cobble and boulder beaches. At about Mile 18.0 you round the corner and head west along an increasingly low and sandy shoreline.

MILE 19.0: Heading west along the south shore of Oak Island, you come to a **sandspit** on the southwest corner of the island. The sandspit has a nice beach, group and individual campsites, and an artesian well with potable water.

MILE 20.5: Heading southwest from the sandspit, you go 1.5-miles to the sandstone cliffs of **Red Cliff Point**. The end of the point is at a shoal off shore marked by a bell buoy.

MILES 20.5 TO 24.5: Heading south and west down the coast, you pass **Red Cliff Bay** and follow the sandstone and red clay bluffs to the Buffalo Bay Tribal Marina.

Where to Eat & Where to Stay

For information on restaurants, lodging, and camping, see Route 17: Outer Island Loop.

Route 17:

---------------------------->

Outer Island Loop

The Outer Island loop includes eleven of the Apostle Islands and some of their best beaches, sea caves, and historic lighthouses. The larger islands also have extensive hiking trails. Rounding the north end of Devil's, Rocky, and Outer Islands can be very difficult in strong northerly winds. Plan for extra time to explore the islands on foot when it is too rough to paddle.

TRIP HIGHLIGHTS: Excellent sea caves (Sand Island/Devil's Island), good sand beaches (Sand, York, Raspberry, Rocky, Outer, Stockton, and Oak Islands), hiking trails (Sand, Stockton, Outer, and Oak Islands), and historic lighthouses (Raspberry, Sand, Devil's, and Outer Islands).

TRIP RATING:
Advanced: About 70 to 75 miles.

TRIP DURATION: Plan on a full week to explore the islands. Planning for extra food and windbound days is especially important in the outer exposed islands such as Outer Island and Devil's Island. By doing out and back trips to Devil's or Outer Island from the Red Cliff or Little Sand Bay launch sites, shorter trips of 25 to 50 miles can be done as an alternative to the full outer-islands loop.

NAVIGATION AIDS: NOAA charts 14966 or 14973; USGS: *Bayfield* at 1:100,000.

CAUTIONS: Confused seas and clapotis develop off the sandstone cliffs and sea caves. The north ends of Devil's Island and Outer Island are exposed to the full fetch of Superior in all directions. Wave heights of 8 to 10 feet are not uncommon with a strong northeast wind even in summer months.

TRIP PLANNING: Campsites are available on Sand, York, Devil's, Rocky, Ironwood, Cat, Outer, Stockton, and Oak Islands. No camping is allowed on Raspberry Island, and there are no campsites on Bear Island, although wilderness camping is allowed. Kayakers who plan to camp on any of the islands will need to reserve a campsite at the ranger station in either Bayfield or Little Sand Bay and pay a $15 fee for a camping permit. For groups of eight people or more group sites are available on Sand, Stockton, and Oak Islands.

Crossings to and from the various islands are about 2 to 5 miles. Bring extra food and plan extra days in case you become windbound. The exposed islands, such as Devil's and Outer, are notorious for rough conditions with a north or northeast wind. Always check the marine forecast (Duluth 162.55 MHz). Daily forecasts are also posted at the ranger station in Little Sand Bay. A wet suit or dry suit is recommended because water temperatures are often less than 50° F. Fog can be a problem any time of the year on Superior; every kayaker must have a chart and compass to make the crossings safely.

LAUNCH SITES:

Little Sand Bay (start): See Route 14: Sand Island for details.
Red Cliff Buffalo Bay Tribal Marina (finish): See Route 15: Basswood Island trip for details.

DIRECTIONS

START TO MILE 11.0: **Little Sand Bay–Sand Island–York Island–Raspberry Island Sandspit:** See Route 16: Inner Island Loop.

MILE 14.0: From the **Raspberry Island sandspit**, head northeast to the **Bear Island Sandspit (N 47° 00.01' W 090° 44.90')**, located on the southeastern tip of the island. There are several private land holdings along the beach so if you do land make it a brief stop and respect the no trespassing signs.

MILE 17.0: Weather permitting, the east side of Bear Island makes for a more scenic paddle. The west side is mostly eroded clay bluffs, while the east side is red sandstone cliffs and jumbles of huge boulders. At Mile 17.0 you reach a crescent-shaped **beach (N 47° 01.54' W 090° 45.00')** on the northeast side of Bear that makes a great lunch stop. This beach

Outer Island Loop

develops dumping surf next to the shore, which can make landing difficult, when there are big waves from the north or northeast. On either side of the beach, the north end of the island is sandstone cliffs with reentrants and small sea caves. *Caution:* When winds are from the north the confused seas and clapotis on the north shore can create difficult paddling conditions.

MILE 20.0: From the beach to Devil's Island, you make a 3.0-mile crossing, heading roughly NNE to the southern tip of the island. At the south end there is a **small harbor (N 47° 03.73' W 090° 43.66')** with rock breakwalls and a large boathouse. In rough weather this the only safe place to land on Devil's Island. Just up from the hill are the designated campsites for Devil's—wilderness camping is not allowed on the island. There is a two-track road that heads north for about 1 mile to the lighthouse and sea caves at the north end of the island.

MILE 21.0: Heading north up the west side of the island, the rock and gravel beaches give way to boulders and then sandstone cliffs. The sea caves start on the northwest corner of the island and continue around the north end. Devil's Island columns and arches are the most intricate of any of the Apostle Island sea caves. The columns are so numerous that at some points you feel like you are paddling in a forest, with sandstone trunks rising all around you.

I call one of my favorite caves. "The Hanger" because it is big enough to house an airplane. The entrance is only about 15 feet high by 30 feet wide, but it soon flares out to about 50 feet wide and is perhaps 100 feet long. *Caution:* Never attempt to explore the sea caves when there are any significant seas coming from the north. Confused seas and violent clapotis form even with small waves. On very calm days there is a flat rock shelf east of the caves where you can land kayaks for a lunch break and a quick trip to **Devil's Island Light (N 47° 04.8' W 090° 43.7')**. During the summer months a park volunteer is usually available to give tours of the lighthouse, which is equipped with a huge brass-and-glass Frensel lens.

MILE 25.0: Paddling down the east side of Devil's Island, you pass low sandstone cliffs and jumbles of huge boulders. From the south end of the island, paddle southeast to make the 2.5-mile crossing to Rocky Island. Heading east along the north end of the island, you pass a large crescent-shaped beach that is a good place to land and take a break.

MILE 27.0: Rounding the northeast tip of **Rocky Island** and heading southwest along the coast, you enter the sheltered harbor formed by

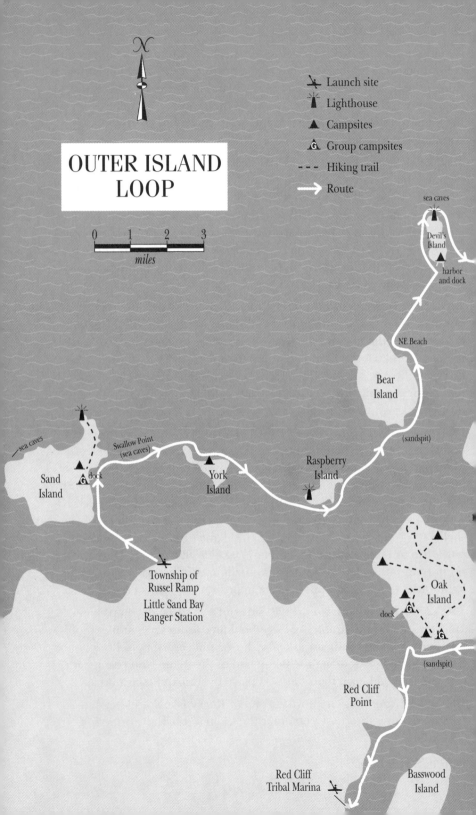

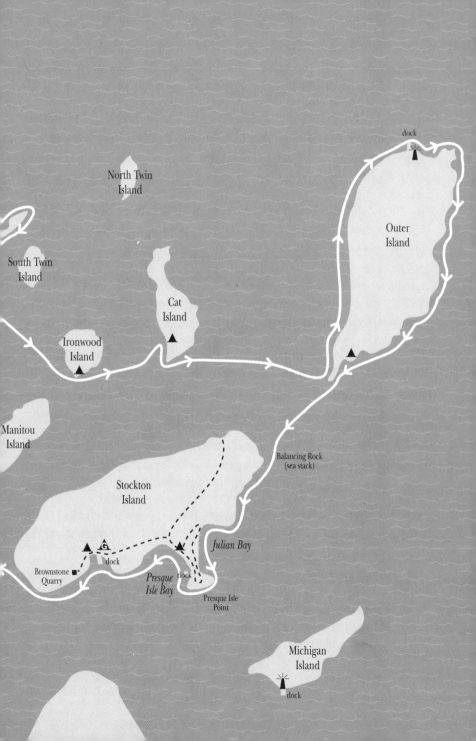

North Twin
Island

South Twin
Island

Ironwood
Island

Cat
Island

Outer
Island

dock

Manitou
Island

Stockton
Island

Balancing Rock
(sea stack)

Julian Bay

Brownstone
Quarry

dock

Presque
Isle Bay

dock

Presque Isle
Point

Michigan
Island

dock

Rocky Island and South Twin Island. *Caution:* The rocky shore and shallow water off the point at the northeast tip of Rocky Island produces very rough conditions with large seas from the north. Avoid the point in rough weather and stay well offshore while rounding the point. Watch out also for the sandbar/shore connecting Rocky Island and South Twin. It is very dangerous in northerly winds. There are some private land holdings and a park dock with several campsites available on the east side of the island. The sheltered harbor is very popular with powerboats and sailboats, so it is not a place to seek solitude. Some of the campsites are less than optimally accessible by kayak. **Campsite 1 (N 47° 01.27' W 090° 40.75')** provides the best landing and access to the water for kayakers.

MILE 31.0: Heading southeast from Rocky Island, you pass **South Twin Island** and continue on to the south end of **Ironwood Island**. There is small sandspit and beach at the southern tip that has a **campsite (N 46° 59.39' W 090° 37.09')** on it. The campsite does not have an outhouse or potable water.

MILE 33.0: From Ironwood Island head east to the southern tip of **Cat Island**. There is a lovely **sandspit** with a campsite **(N 46° 59.94' W 090° 33.77')**, located just north of the spit on the west side of the island. The campsite does not have a outhouse or potable water. There is also a cabin on the south end of the island that is stocked with provisions for fishermen who are windbound and need to stay there in an emergency. Please only use this cabin in an emergency.

MILE 38.0: From the Cat Island sandspit, head east to make the 4.5-mile crossing to the **Outer Island** sandspit. *Caution:* This very exposed crossing should not be attempted if strong winds are forecast from the north or northeast, making large seas likely. The **sandspit at Outer Island (N 46° 56.68' W 090° 28.03')** is a large curved spit on the south end of the island. At the base of the sandspit, there is a campsite nestled in a shallow depression in a wooded area. This is a lovely spot and a great place to stay sheltered from the wind when bad weather comes roaring out the north. Just west of the camp along the shore are the remains of old fishing boat.

MILES 38.0 TO 45.0: If you journey all the way out to Outer Island, it is well worth taking the time to circumnavigate the island. It is about 15 miles around the island, so plan on taking most of a day. From the sandspit head north along the west side of the island. The west side consists mostly of eroded red clay bluffs with some cobbles and small rounded boulders. The

Outer Island Loop

water is often stained red from the clay, and it is often shallow so be careful of rocks, or you may get to do a little boat repair on your trip.

MILES 45.0 TO 47.0: Rounding the corner and heading east along the north end of the island, the red clay bluffs give way to a rocky sandstone coast. At Mile 47.0 you reach the **Outer Island lighthouse (N 47° 04.6' W 090° 25.0')** . This lighthouse, located high on the clay bluffs, can be seen for a long distance on a clear night. This spot does not get may visitors, but if you are lucky, you may be able to find a ranger or volunteer to give you a tour of the lighthouse.

The first time I saw the lighthouse, I arrived the hard way after making a 46.0 mile crossing from Grand Marais, Minnesota, with Don Dimond and Brian Day. The crossing was a training trip for an expedition that the three of us had planned, across Lake Superior from the Keeweenaw to Agawa Bay. As luck would have it the weather was perfect and we were amazed to see the lighthouse light from more than 30 miles offshore.

MILES 47.0 TO 51.0: Rounding the north end of island and heading south, you pass some of the most beautiful sandstone cliff coast in the Apostle Islands. There are interesting cracks, crevices, reentrants, and small sea caves. Although not as intricately carved as the Squaw Bay, Sand Island, or Devil's Island caves, this is still one of my favorite sections of coast. *Caution:* There are miles of cliffs with few places to land. This is not a good place to be when large seas are coming from the northeast, confused seas and clapotis develop here.

MILES 51.0 TO 55.0: The sandstone cliffs continue, becoming a sandy shoreline as you approach the sandspit. After the cliffs end there is a small bay with a nice beach on the southeast side of the island. At approximately Mile 55, you have completed the circumnavigation of the island and returned to the sandspit.

MILE 58.0: Heading southwest from the sandspit, you can make the 3.5-mile crossing to the north end of **Stockton Island**. The northeast side of Stockton is a sandstone cliff coast with reentrants, small sea caves, and sea-stacks. *Caution:* This crossing offers no shelter from a north wind, and large seas are likely. The cliffs at the northeast end of Stockton create clapotis and very confused seas when seas hit the island from the north or east.

MILES 58.0 TO 62.0: As you paddle southwest along the south side of Stockton, the cliffs give way to the sandy shores of **Julian Bay**. There is a

marsh and lagoon near the shore so watch for sandhill cranes and great blue herons. Near the marsh outlet in 15–20 feet of water is a shipwreck that is visible on calm days. Heading south you then paddle to the tip of **Presque Isle Point**. Presque Isle is a *tombolo*—a peninsula formed when sand filled in the gap between a small island and the Stockton Island shore. On the west side of Presque Isle Point, there is **small harbor (N 46° 54.9' W 090° 33.1')** and dock. Campsites and a ranger station are also located on the point. If you want to stretch your legs, you can access an extensive series of hiking trails from the point. In all the park service maintains 14 miles of trails on Stockton Island.

MILES 62.0 TO 64.0: Rounding the point and paddling northwest down the coast, you come to **Presque Isle Bay**. This sheltered area near the point is very popular in the summer months with powerboats and sailboats for mooring and day use. It is not the place to find solitude in August. Heading west from Presque Isle Bay, you come to **Quarry Bay (N 46° 55.3' W 090° 36.45')**. Here a second campsite and ranger station are located. The Quarry Bay Trail and Quarry Trails lead east and west from this point. The Quarry Trail leads west to the abandoned Brownstone Quarry.

MILE 65.5: Paddling 1.5 miles west from Quarry Bay, you come to the abandoned **sandstone quarry** that was operated by the Anderson Brownstone Company from 1889 to 1897.

MILE 66.5: Continuing down the coast another 1 mile, you come to the western tip of Stockton Island. From here it is an easy crossing of less than 2 miles to Oak Island. Because it is sheltered from north by numerous islands, rough conditions are rarely a problem.

MILE 70.0: After reaching **Oak Island** paddle west along the south shore until you reach the sandspit on the island's southwest tip. Here you'll find campsites, outhouses, and an artesian well for potable water. Not only is there a great sand beach, but you can access the Oak Island hiking trails. The park maintains 11.5 miles of trails on the island.

MILE 72.0: Crossing to the mainland to the southwest, you reach **Red Cliff Point**. You will pass a bell buoy that marks a shoal a short distance offshore.

MILES 72.0 TO 75.0: Heading down the mainland coast to the southwest, you pass red clay bluffs and sandstone cliffs on your way back to the Red Cliff Tribal Marina in Buffalo Bay.

Where to Eat & Where to Stay

RESTAURANTS   Bayfield is a tourist town of only about 700 people, with no shortage of choices in dining. **Greunkes** (715–779–5480) serves a good breakfast, and for dinners has an all-you-can-eat fish boil. **Maggies** (715–779–5641) is a popular tavern and restaurant with a rather strange obsession with pink flamingo decor (ask at the bar—they will explain it), but good meals for lunch and dinner. For more information contact the Bayfield Chamber of Commerce at (800) 447–4094 or their Web page: www.bayfield.org.   **LODGING**   Bayfield has many motels and bed-and-breakfast inns to choose from. For more information call the Bayfield Chamber of Commerce at (800) 447–4094 or try their Web page: www.bayfield.org. During the peak of the tourist season, you may need to explore options to the south in Washburn or Ashland.   **CAMPING**   Private campgrounds are conveniently located at both of the major launch sites. At Little Sand Bay, the **Township of Russell Campground** has outhouses and a pump for potable water—campsites are available on a first come first serve basis. At the **Red Cliff Tribal Marina**, there is a campground with potable water, bathrooms, and showers (715–779–3743). There is also a state park campground on **Madeline Island**, and several other private campgrounds in the area. For more information contact the Bayfield Chamber of Commerce (800) 447–4094 or their Web page: www.bayfield.org.

Lake Superior
Minnesota

Route 18:

━━ ━━ ━ ━━ ━━ ━ ━━ ━━ ━ ━━ ━━ ━ ━━ ━━ ━━ ➤

The Twin Ports: Duluth-Superior Harbor

Duluth and Superior together called the "Twin Ports," are the leading bulk cargo ports on the Great Lakes, with forty to forty-five million tons of cargo shipped each season, and total tonnage as high as seventy-five million tons in some years. Located at the westernmost edge of the Great Lakes—St. Lawrence Seaway System, the Twin Ports are the farthest inland seaport in the world, 2,342 miles from the Atlantic Ocean. The Duluth-Superior Harbor has approximately 17 miles of channels, 45 miles of frontage, and dozens of commercial docks, serving well over a 1,000 lake and ocean vessels every year, including some 200 vessels under foreign flags. The harbor provides great boat watching at a major international port. Just outside the harbor is a good surfing beach.

TRIP HIGHLIGHTS: Great boat watching at a busy international port, sand beaches, and good surfing outside the harbor at Park Point.

TRIP RATING:

Beginner/Intermediate: A 10-mile loop starting at Park Point and circling the harbor in a counterclockwise direction.

Intermediate/ Advanced: The 10-mile loop plus a side trip through the ship canal out to Lake Superior. Paddlers who want a longer trip can add miles by exploring the ore and coal docks of St. Louis Bay.

TRIP DURATION: Part or full day.

NAVIGATION AIDS: NOAA chart 14975. Additional harbor and shipping information: The Army Corps of Engineers Visitor Center and Historical Museum has shipping schedules for daily ship traffic and many informational pamphlets on the harbor and Great Lakes shipping.

CAUTIONS: Boat traffic—both commercial shipping and small craft. Shipping lanes along the commercial docks extend all the way to the shore, and there are obvious hazards associated with large vessels at dockside. A hazard that is not marked on the chart is a seaplane landing area located between Park Point and the airport.

TRIP PLANNING: Although the harbor is well sheltered from any reasonable weather always check the marine weather forecast on weather channel 1,162.55 MHz (Duluth). A harbor chart is a must for planning because of the many shipping lanes and hazards associated with the harbor. Paddlers who plan to paddle out the ship canal to Lake Superior should wear wet suits or dry suits because water temperatures are often less than 50° F.

LAUNCH SITES: The boat ramp at Park Point provides a good launching site and has parking and bathroom facilities. Please take the time to note where the seaplane landing area is marked along the shore between the airport and Park Point—stay out of this area for obvious reasons. Park Point can be very crowded at the peak of the summer tourist season so parking may not always be available. The University of Minnesota–Duluth Kayak and Canoe Institute (KCI) has generously agreed to be listed as an alternate launch site.

Both KCI and Park Point are located on Minnesota Point in Duluth near the lift bridge on the ship canal harbor entrance. Exit from Highway 35 and follow the signs for Park Point to the lift bridge. Cross the bridge to Minnesota Park. The KCI facility is located approximately 0.7 mile past the lift bridge. Watch for the sign for the Army Reserve Center (15th Street) and turn right. The preferred launch site, the Park Point boat ramp, is located another 3.2 miles past the turnoff for KCI (about 3.9 miles from the lift bridge).

DIRECTIONS

START: *Caution:* Before starting from the Park Point ramp, familiarize yourself with the boundaries of the seaplane landing area, marked by signs along the shore in the small bay between the boat ramp and the airport to the southeast.

MILE 1.0: Follow the shore to the right in a northwesterly direction—you pass relatively undeveloped shoreline—to the **Duluth Boat Club** building.

MILE 2.0: Hearding Island is a small island marked on the south end as a Wildlife Management Area and Colonial Bird Habitat.

MILE 3.5: Past Hearding Island, you paddle along a residential area, pass the **Army Reserve Center**, and come to the KCI aquatic center.

Canal Park Visitor Center: Marine Museum / Army Corps of Engineers Visitor Center

To get the most out of your harbor tour, we strongly recommend visiting the Marine Museum/Army Corps Visitors Center. The museum provides an excellent overview of the history of Great Lakes shipping and the Twin Ports harbor. The visitors center also lists all scheduled shipping for the day, so you can determine in advance which ships you'll see at dock or entering and leaving the harbor during your trip. The museum and visitors center are located on the northwest side of the aerial lift bridge. The visitors center also has general tourist information on the Duluth-Superior area.

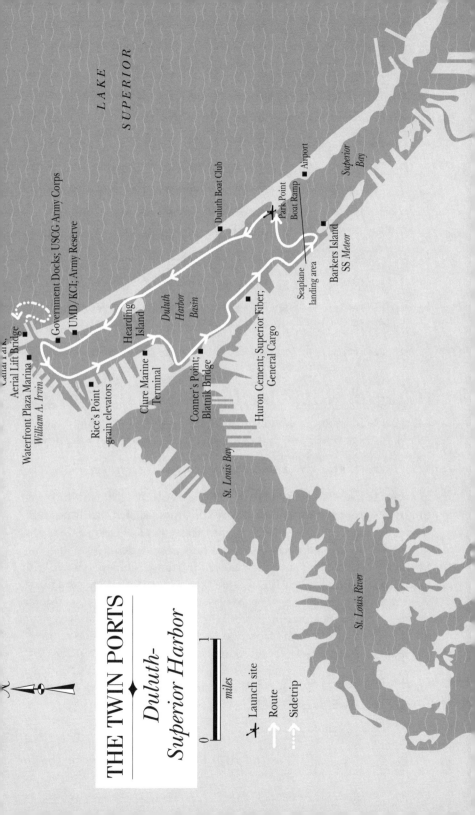

THE TWIN PORTS
Duluth-Superior Harbor

0   1
miles

✈ Launch site
⬆ Route
⬆ Sidetrip (dashed)

LAKE SUPERIOR

Canal Park;
Aerial Lift Bridge ■
Waterfront Plaza Marina ■
William A. Irvin
Government Docks; USCG; Army Corps ■
UMD/KCI; Army Reserve ■
Rice's Point
grain elevators ■
Clure Marine
Terminal ■
*Duluth
Harbor
Basin*
Hearding
Island
Conner's Point;
Blatnik Bridge ■
Huron Cement; Superior Fiber;
General Cargo ■
St. Louis Bay
St. Louis River
Duluth Boat Club ■
Seaplane
landing area
Park Point
Boat Ramp
Airport ■
Barkers Island
SS Meteor ■
*Superior
Bay*

University of Minnesota, Duluth (UMD) Kayak and Canoe Institute

The UMD/KCI program provides guided trips, and both student and instructor training courses for white-water and coastal kayaking. The center for coastal kayaking is located 0.7 miles past the aerial lift bridge on Minnesota Point (the turnoff is on 15th Street at the sign for the Army Reserve Center). The Aquatic Center is next to the Army Reserve Center and consists of a large sheet metal building next to a sand beach. For information on the many programs that KCI offers, call Randy Carlson at (218) 726–6177.

MILE 3.75: Just past KCI there is a marina and **Coast Guard center and government docks** for the Army Corps of Engineers. Just past the docks you reach the ship canal and the aerial lift bridge. *Caution:* Carefully check for boat traffic and make sure that the lift bridge is in the down position before crossing the shipping lane to the other side of the bridge.

Sidetrip: Advanced or intermediate paddlers: Assuming the lift bridge is down and the coast is clear for boat traffic, more skilled paddlers may want to paddle out through the ship canal into Lake Superior. Exiting the harbor to the right brings you to a long sand beach that follows the shore for several miles southeast along the Minnesota Point shore. With a northeast wind this beach can offer excellent surfing. *Caution:* The ship canal is only 300 feet wide. Never enter the canal when you think a large vessel may be entering it. Both the canal and breakwalls have sheet piling sides that can form clapotis, especially on the south side of the breakwall near shore, where a square corner of vertical walls makes for very strong reflex-wave patterns with an easterly wind. On calm days paddlers who make a left turn out of the harbor can land on a cobblestone and gravel beach in canal park.

MILE 4.0: Paddling past the lift bridge to the northeast corner of the harbor, you can enter the **Waterfront Plaza Marina**. On entering the marina you will see a large Army Corps of Engineers tug, and the *William A. Irvin,* a large iron ore bulk freighter built in 1938. The ship is permanently docked as a Great Lakes shipping museum. *Caution:* The Vista harbor tour boats use this area for their tour boat docking so keep an eye out for these large excursion boats heading out from the marina.

MILE 5.5: Heading southwest along the shore, you pass the convention center, then turn to the southeast and begin paddling along the grain elevators and docks of **Rice's Point**. Duluth has been the center of international grain exports since the late 1800s, and these docks serve hundreds of grain ships every season. *Caution:* Because of the docks the shipping lanes extend to the shore, so keep an eye out for incoming ship traffic. Continuing along the shore at Rice's Point, you reach the **Clure Public Marine Terminal**, a multimillion dollar center that is at the core of the port's general cargo activity.

MILE 8.0: Continue southeast along Rice's Point until the shore turns westward toward the highway bridge at the mouth to St. Louis Bay. Crossing under the bridge allows kayakers to cross the shipping lane at a narrow point. *Caution:* There is a marina nearby so there is a great deal of motorboat traffic under the bridge. Paddling southeast along Conner's Point, you will pass another general cargo facility, the Huron Cement loading terminal, Superior Fiber Products pulp and paper mill, and another grain elevator.

MILE 9.0: Continuing down the shore to **Barkers Island**, you come to a marina, and a ship/museum that displays the now landlocked whale-back freighter, *Meteor.* Whaleback freighters were among the first steel freighters on the lakes. Their unusual rounded deck and hull gave them an almost submarine-like appearance.

MILE 10.0: In order to safely cross the shipping lane and return to Park Point, we strongly recommend that you first backtrack about 0.25 miles to Barkers Island to the buoy marked GC9 on the chart, and then cross in a straight line to the buoy marked R10 on the chart. By staying on this range and following the line of position between buoys, you will return directly to the boat ramp at Park Point. *Caution:* If you cross too far to the northeast of this path, you could end up in the seaplane landing area located between the Park Point boat ramp and the airport.

Where to Eat & Where to Stay

RESTAURANTS   The Duluth-Superior area offers many options for dining. In Canal Park **Grandmas Saloon and Grill** (218–722–4724), located at the northwest side of the aerial lift bridge next to the Army Corps Visitor Center, is a popular destination. **Amazing Grace Delicatessen/Bakery** (218–723–0075) and **Taste of Saigon Vietnamese Restaurant** (218–727–1598) have many excellent vegetarian selections. The Amazing Grace Deli also has live folk music with no cover charge on many nights. Best of all they seem happy to serve people wearing dry suits or wet suits. **LODGING**   Duluth and Superior have many hotel and motel options. For information call the Duluth Convention and Visitors Bureau at (800) 4–DULUTH. **CAMPING**   Camping options include **Indian Point Campground** (218–624–5637); **Carlton KOA** (218–879–1819); and **Big Lake Campground**, Cloquet (218–879–1819). For scenic beauty it is hard to beat camping at the **Jay Cooke State Park** on the St. Louis River Gorge (800–246–2267).

Route 19:

▬▬▬▬▬▬▬▬▬▬▬▬▬➡

Lake Superior Water Trail

There are plans in the works for a water trail around the whole of Lake Superior, and currently two sections are in existence: the Minnesota trail and the Keewenaw waterway in Michigan's Upper Peninsula. Over the last fifteen years, the Minnesota shoreline has seen a huge increase in tourism and associated development, making it difficult for paddlers to tour there. Fortunately the water trail provides access and camping spots so that kayakers can continue to enjoy the great scenery. Although the water trail campsites are not numerous, they are still lightly used compared with other campgrounds along the shore, and they offer a rare opportunity to enjoy the view in relative solitude. Currently about 20 miles of the trail have campsites and rest areas for kayakers. This route runs from Gooseberry to Tettegouche State Park and includes excellent views of Split Rock Lighthouse, Shovel Point, and Palisade Head, where there are several sea caves and rock arches. Short hikes on the shoreline's numerous trails lead to waterfalls on the Gooseberry, Split Rock, and Baptism Rivers.

TRIP HIGHLIGHTS: Camping, Split Rock Lighthouse, Palisade Head, sea caves, and rock arches.

TRIP RATING:

Beginner: 1.5-mile round-trip from Little Two Harbors to Split Rock lighthouse, 2.0-mile round-trip from Little Two Harbors to Corundum Point.

Intermediate: 20-mile weekend round-trip from Gooseberry to

Tettegouche State Parks, or 5-mile part-day trip from Baptism River to Palisade Head and back.

TRIP DURATION: Half-day beginner trip and two-day intermediate paddle.

NAVIGATIONAL AIDS: USGS topographic map *Two Harbors* (47087-A1). The Minnesota DNR puts out a pamphlet with a map showing launches, rest areas, and campsites and giving general information. Call (800) 657–3929 for a copy.

CAUTIONS: Exposed shoreline, steep rock beaches or cliffs, reflection waves, cold water (< 50° F), difficult landing in rough weather.

TRIP PLANNING: This is a difficult shoreline to paddle in rough weather, as there are many stretches of cliffs, few good harbors, and no sand beaches for soft landings in surf. Make sure to check the marine forecast before setting out. Most of the launch spots are in Minnesota state parks, which require a $4.00/day vehicle permit. In addition kayak/backpack campsites within state parks require a $7.00/night fee (but water trail sites are currently free). You will also need to check in with the park rangers if you plan to be out overnight. Ask for a park map to help navigate the park roads when you pick up your permit. Note that the kayak/backpack campsites in Split Rock Park will likely be occupied in peak season (July–September), so unless you have a reservation, head for the water trail site instead. In general, pretty much everything on the North Shore will be booked solid during the summer, so if you are planning to stay at a campground, hotel, or resort, make reservations ahead of time! June is less busy, but expect more bugs and cooler weather. For those doing the whole trail, there is an alternative to there-and-back paddling. A shuttle runs along the length of the Superior Hiking Trail on Highway 61 on Friday, Saturday, and Sunday from late May through early October, making stops at all three state parks on the water trail. Call (218) 834–5511 for more information. *Note:* Most of the shoreline is private property. Please don't land or camp without permission. The DNR map of the water trail shows rest areas and campsites along the way.

LAUNCH SITES: Take Highway 61 north from Duluth past Two Harbors. All state park entrances are well marked and are accessible directly from 61.

Gooseberry State Park: Launch from the gravel bar at the mouth of the Gooseberry River. There is a short carry down some stairs to the river bank.

Split Rock State Park: Launch from the picnic area at Little Two Harbors. The harbor is fairly protected, but if the winds are from the northeast, consider some alternate activities (check the marine forecast before launching). Strong southerlies can also cause problems.

Tettegouche State Park: Park at the lot next to the Baptism River Bridge. There is a fairly hellish carry down a long set of stairs to the river below. The steep gravel bar at the river mouth has two rock cliffs on either side, making this a difficult launch when winds are offshore due to clapotis.

DIRECTIONS

START: Begin at the mouth of the **Gooseberry River (N 47° 08.521' W 091° 27.399')** and paddle north. *Caution:* If the river level is high, there may be standing waves at the river mouth.

MILE 1.5: Thompson Beach is your first rest area and water trail campsite.

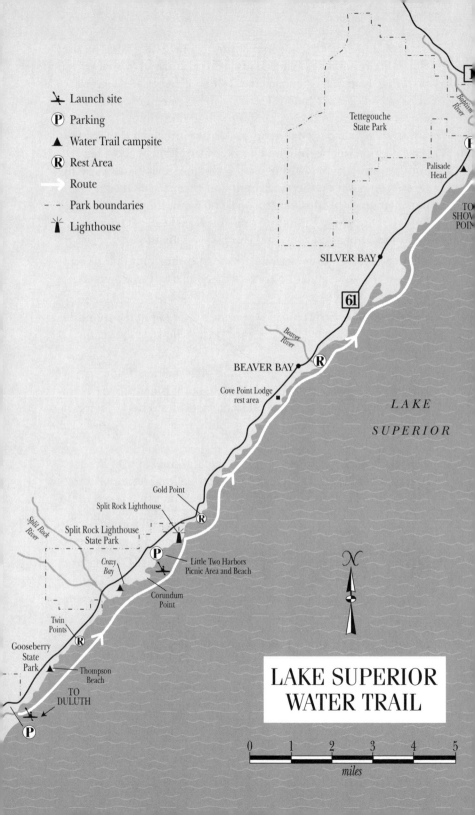

Legend

- ✈ Launch site
- Ⓟ Parking
- ▲ Water Trail campsite
- Ⓡ Rest Area
- → Route
- —·— Park boundaries
- ☀ Lighthouse

Tightum River

Tettegouche
State Park

Palisade
Head

TO
SHOV
POIN

SILVER BAY

61

Beaver
River

BEAVER BAY Ⓡ

Cove Point Lodge
rest area

LAKE

SUPERIOR

Gold Point

Split Rock Lighthouse Ⓡ

Split Rock Lighthouse
State Park

Split Rock
River

Ⓟ

Crazy
Bay

Little Two Harbors
Picnic Area and Beach

Corundum
Point

Twin
Points Ⓡ

Gooseberry
State
Park

▲ Thompson
Beach

TO
DULUTH

Ⓟ

N

LAKE SUPERIOR
WATER TRAIL

0   1   2   3   4   5
miles

Superior Hiking Trail

If the weather isn't cooperating or you feel like stretching your legs for a change, why not try a day hike on the Superior Hiking Trail (SHT)? Minnesota is not known for its tall mountains, but the SHT has surprisingly varied terrain and vegetation, waterfalls, and great views and has been voted one of the ten best trails in the country by *Backpacker* magazine. When finished, the trail will run from Duluth up to the U.S.-Canadian border; currently over 200 miles are completed. All the state parks have trails that connect with the SHT, and it's easy to do small segments. One of the most popular and prettiest stretches runs from the Split Rock River (from the parking lot/trailhead) up past a series of falls and cliffs to a ridge with a great view. Check park maps to find where park trails intersect the SHT. Maps are available for a small fee at all three of the state parks on the water trail, or contact the Superior Hiking Trail Association at (218) 834–2700 or visit www.shta.org for more information.

MILE 2.0: The beach on the south side of **Twin Points** is a water trail rest area.

MILE 3.5: There is a large gravel bar at the mouth of the **Split Rock River** that can be used for landing. The trailhead for the Superior Hiking Trail is just across the road, but it is probably not a good idea to leave your boat unattended because this area can get a lot of foot traffic. Paddle around the cliffs at **Split Rock Point**.

MILE 4.0: On the north side of the very impressive **Corundum Point** cliffs is the **Crazy Bay** water trail tent site, a small tent pad at the southwest end of the beach. *Caution:* There are potential reflection waves at Corundum Point.

MILE 5.0: **Little Two Harbors (N 47° 11.866' W 91° 22.601')** picnic area, toilets, and parking lot. If launching from here, try the south end of the beach for smaller rocks.

MILE 5.5: The best view of **Split Rock Lighthouse** and the cliff is from the water. Around the base are giant boulders far below the surface.

MILE 6.0: On the south side of **Gold Point** is a rest area. The remains of the *Madiera*, some of which may be seen in shallower water, are just off shore.

MILE 9.5: **Cove Point Lodge** allows kayakers to use the small bay and beach as a rest area.

MILE 12.0: Bayside Park picnic area and boat launch.

MILE 12.5: North of the long breakwater is **Silver Bay Harbor**, used by ore boats shipping taconite or iron pellets. *Caution:* Beware of the ships entering and leaving the harbor.

MILE 13.0: The shoreline here is composed of black mine tailings

MILE 16.0: The cliffs at **Palisade Head** are very impressive, and to top it off there are some excellent sea caves at the base. You may see climbers on the rock face high above the water. *Caution:* This is not a good place to be in rough weather.

MILE 17.0: Another water trail campsite and rest area, with room for several tents.

MILE 18.0: Take out at the **Baptism River (N 47° 20.185' W 91° 11.822')** in Tettegouche Park, or continue on for another 1.0 mile to Shovel Point (definitely worth it) before finishing your trip.

Where to Eat & Where to Stay

RESTAURANTS & LODGING Most of the restaurants and motels are in Two Harbors, but there are a few in Beaver Bay as well. Contact the Two Harbors Visitor Information Center for more information at (800) 554–2116. **CAMPING** There are campgrounds at each of the state parks on the water trail, but if you visit during peak season, make reservations in advance at (800) 246–2267. For more information on the specific parks, call (218) 834–3855 (Gooseberry), (218) 226–4372 (Split Rock), or (218) 226–3539 (Tettegouche).

Route 20:

--- --- --- --- --- --- --- --- --- --- --- --- ➤

Grand Portage Bay &
the Susie Islands

Like Isle Royale, the Susie Islands give paddlers a taste of the Canadian North Shore, with cobble beaches, rocky basalt and granite points covered with boreal forest, and a few arctic plants left behind after the retreat of the glaciers at the end of the last ice age. Access is a problem, however. There are no close public launch points, and camping is not allowed on the Susie Islands. Susie Island itself is owned by the Nature Conservancy, and the remaining islands belong to the Grand Portage Band of Chippewa. Both ask that boaters do not land on the islands without permission. Contact the Minnesota chapter of the Nature Conservancy at (612) 331–0750 or the Grand Portage Tribal Council at either (218) 475–2239 or (218) 475–2279 for information or permission to land on the islands. The lack of close launch points and restrictions on landing and overnight camping make this a long and therefore advanced day trip.

TRIP HIGHLIGHTS: Historical site, good scenery.

TRIP RATING:

Beginning: 4.5-mile day trip to Hat Point and back.

Advanced: 13-mile trip from Grand Portage around Susie Island and back.

TRIP DURATION: Full day.

NAVIGATION AIDS: USGS: *Pigeon Point* and *Grand Portage* 7.5-minute maps.

CAUTIONS: Exposed shoreline, potential for reflection waves along Hat Point, fog, and magnetic disturbances and unreliable compass readings near Pigeon Point and the Susie Islands.

TRIP PLANNING: Plan to paddle this route early in the season (before August when the weather turns rough).

LAUNCH SITE: The beach behind the National Monument stockade, next to the *Wenonah* dock has free daily parking, but the beach is rocky (the Voyageur Marina can also be used as a start point, but charges a $3.00/day parking fee). From Highway 61 take the southernmost exit to Grand Portage (Cook County Road 17). Turn east onto 17 and go 1.1 miles to the Grand Portage National Monument parking lot on the left. Follow a trail along the outside of the stockade (next to Grand Portage Creek) to the beach.

DIRECTIONS

START: The *Wenonah* ferry to Isle Royale moors at the **dock** behind the stockade **(N 47° 57.677' W 089° 41.034')** and gives a blast at 9:00 A.M. before departing. On some days the ferry will pass through the Susie Islands on its way out. Paddle toward Hat Point.

MILE 1.0: Pass by the sandspit on the north side of **Grand Portage Island**.

MILE 2.0: Pass by **Hat Point** at the northern entrance to Grand Portage Bay. Begin the 3.0-mile crossing to the Susie Islands, aiming for the channel between the **Susie** and **Lucille Islands**. The crossing has good views across Wauswaugoning Bay toward Mt. Josephine. *Caution:* Potential for reflection waves at Hat Point in southerly winds.

MILE 5.0: Paddle by the south side of Susie Island. Those who enjoy

Grand Portage Bay

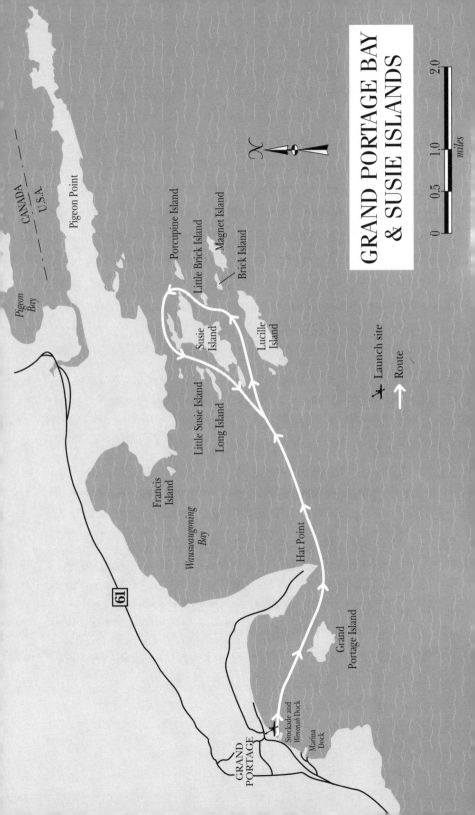

GRAND PORTAGE BAY & SUSIE ISLANDS

CANADA
U.S.A.

Pigeon Point

Pigeon Bay

Porcupine Island

Little Brick Island

Magnet Island

Brick Island

Susie Island

Lucille Island

Little Susie Island

Long Island

Francis Island

Wauswaugoning Bay

Hat Point

Grand Portage Island

61

GRAND PORTAGE

Stockade and Wenonah Dock

Marina Dock

⨉ Launch site

→ Route

0   0.5   1.0   2.0
miles

Grand Portage & the Fur Trade

The Grand Portage or Kitchi-Onigaming ("great carrying place" in French and Ojibway, respectively) was important to the Ojibway and Cree long before becoming a focal point for the fur trade in the 1700s. The 9-mile portage trail bypasses 20 miles of unrunnable rapids and falls on the Pigeon River before it empties into Lake Superior. This connection allowed canoes and trade goods to pass between the open waters of the Great Lakes and the maze of inland waterways leading as far north and west as Great Slave Lake.

The natives living inland traded beaver pelts and other furs to representatives of the Northwest Company. These pelts were then transported by "hivernants," or Northmen through the inland waterways to the Grand Portage. Meanwhile voyageurs set out from Montreal in 36-foot *canots de maitre*, carrying trade goods such as cloth, clothing, beads, and muskets. At the Grand Portage trading post, these goods were exchanged for the pelts, and the Montrealers and Northmen enjoyed the annual "Rendezvous," (a notoriously wild party), before returning home.

After the American Revolution, the U.S.-Canadian border was set along the Pigeon River, and eventually the Northwest Company was forced to move north to Fort William (near Thunder Bay) to avoid tariffs. The Ojibway continued to live at Grand Portage, however, and today the land belongs to the Grand Portage Chippewa. The site of the old trading post is now a national monument administered by the Park Service, with re-created buildings of the old post and interpreters dressed in period clothing.

botany can keep on the lookout for such "arctic disjunct" plant species as Norwegian witlow grass and Arctic lupine, remnants of the last ice age that have continued to survive near the lake due to the cool climate. More signs of the last glaciation are the parallel tracks left by glaciers as they dragged debris across the bedrock.

MILE 6.0: During late June and early July, herring gulls nest on small islands, such as **Little Brick Island**. Give them a wide berth during nesting season. Round the northeastern tip of Susie Island. The large bay at the north end is especially pretty.

MILE 8.0: Leave the southwestern tip of Susie Island and begin the trip back to Hat Point.

MILE 13.0: Finish at the *Wenonah* dock.

Where to Eat & Where to Stay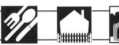

RESTAURANTS Try the **Grand Portage Lodge and Casino**, (800–543–1384). **LODGING** In Grand Portage itself, there is only the Lodge and Casino. There are many places in Grand Marais, an hour south of Grand Portage: Contact the Grand Marais Chamber of Commerce at (888) 922-2221. A real standout is the beautifully restored **Naniboujou Lodge**, built in the 1920s and decorated with a Cree theme (the dining hall is worth a look see even if you don't stay there). The lodge is located 15 miles northeast of Grand Marais on Highway 61, opposite the entrance to Judge Magney State Park. Call (218) 387-2688 for information and reservations. **CAMPING** A limited number of sites are available at the **Grand Portage Marina** (218–475–2476). Otherwise the closest campground is at **Judge Magney State Park**, about 25 miles south of Grand Portage. For more information, call the Minnesota Department of Natural Resources at (800) 766–6000. To make reservations for Minnesota's state parks, call (800) 246–2267.

Lake Superior
Ontario

Route 21:

━━ ━━ ━━ ━━ ━━ ━━ ━━ ━━ ━━ ━━ ━━ ━━ ━━ ➤

Little Trout Bay to Thompson Island

This trip is similar to the Susie Islands route in terms of scenery, but because the islands are Crown land, camping is permitted. The islands are popular with the Thunder Bay cruising crowd, who have put in a few trails and even a cabin and sauna on the north end of Thompson Island. It's not quite wilderness paddling, but the Pie Island vistas and the numerous rock cliffs of these islands make this a worthwhile paddle, and there are quiet beaches for camping if you prefer solitude. The linear shape of the chain of islands and the many sections of cliffs suggest that, like Pigeon Point, the islands are one long diabase (similar to basalt) dike. The flat tops of the mesas around Thunder Bay and on Pie Island also consist of a layer of diabase that is more resistant to erosion than the sedimentary rock beneath.

TRIP HIGHLIGHTS: Camping, cliffs, views of Pie Island.

TRIP RATING:
> *Intermediate:* 34-mile trip to Thompson Island and back.
> *Advanced:* Add a trip to Pie Island from Thompson (see Route 22: Thunder Bay to Pie Island).

TRIP DURATION: Three days.

NAVIGATION AIDS: Canadian topographic map *Jarvis River* (52 A/3) at 1:50,000.

CAUTIONS: Exposed shoreline and crossings, cold water (wet suit or dry suit recommended).

TRIP PLANNING: For calmer weather plan to go early in the year before the winds pick up in August. There is a $10/night camping fee for non-Canadian residents using Crown land. Permits can be picked up at any Ministry of Natural Resources office. Call the Thunder Bay MNR office at (807) 475–1471 for more information.

LAUNCH SITE: Little Trout Bay has a picnic area and boat launch. From Highway 61 turn east on Little Trout Bay Road. Follow the green and blue "C" signs to the conservation area. There is a $2.00 launch fee but no parking fee.

DIRECTIONS

START: The cement ramp may be preferable to the sharp rocks along the beach at **Little Trout Bay (N 48° 04.368' W 89° 26.869')** Paddle east towards the open lake.

MILE 2.0: After you pass **McKellar Point (N 48° 04.368' W 89° 26.869')** you will be exposed to southerly winds for the next 2.0 miles, so use caution before proceeding. Cross to the southern end of **Victoria Island**.

MILE 4.0: **Tiger Island (N 48° 04.435' W 89° 21.757')** is the closest landfall from McKellar Point.

MILE 4.5: Look for a black sand beach at the north end of **Cosgrove Bay** on Victoria Island—a good place to take a break or camp. This is one of the few sand or gravel beaches on the islands, and there are a few spots in the trees just off the beach that make good tent sites.

MILE 5.0: Paddle toward the southern point of Cosgrove Bay, then turn east into the channel between **Victoria** and **Albert Islands**. There are small sea caves in the cliffs. *Caution:* The route up the southeast side of the islands is very exposed to southerly winds, and there are few sheltered harbors. If winds are southerly, you may want to paddle the northwest side of the islands instead.

MILE 6.0: **Victoria Cove** is lined with cobble beaches.

MILE 7.5: Cross the short gaps between **Victoria, Devil's and Jarvis Islands**. There is a small beach on the southwest end of Jarvis Island.

MILE 8.5: Cross from Jarvis to **Spar Island**. The next 2.5 miles on the southwest side of Spar has only a few marginal landing spots.

MILE 11.5: You take a break on the beach at the north end of Spar Island; then begin your crossing to Thompson Island.

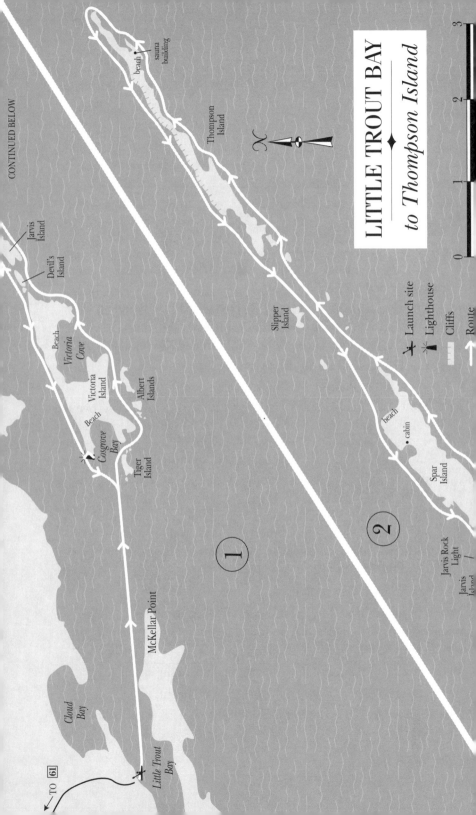

LITTLE TROUT BAY
to Thompson Island

CONTINUED BELOW

Jarvis Island

Devil's Island

Beach
Victoria Cove

Victoria Island

Albert Islands

Beach
Cosgrove Bay

Tiger Island

beach
sauna building

Thompson Island

Slipper Island

beach
• cabin

Spar Island

Jarvis Rock Light

Jarvis Island

McKellar Point

Cloud Bay

Little Trout Bay

TO 61

① ②

Launch site
Lighthouse
Cliffs
Route

0   1   2   3

MILE 12.5: **Slipper Island** has a nice tombolo and gravel beach on the south side, but it is likely to be covered with herring gulls, especially during nesting season.

MILE 13.5: The southwest tip of **Thompson Island (N 48° 08.906' W 89° 12.205')** is one of the places developed by local boaters and includes some ramshackle docks, a picnic table, an outhouse, and a string of electric lights, giving the whole thing a shantytown kind of feel. Although there is a small sand beach, there are not many great places to put tents.

MILE 15.0: There is a small bay with a cobble beach at the end.

MILE 16.5: The T-shaped point toward the northeast end of Thompson Island has a large cobble beach on its south side where camping is possible. Look for patches of gravel that have been used as tent pads. At the north end of the beach, there is a trail to the other side of the point, where you'll find a pretty spiffy building with a sauna inside. It is open to everyone, the only stipulation being that you replace the wood you use (this may be tough as the sauna is popular). It is also possible to paddle to the sauna by entering the harbor on the other side of the point. If you are interested in the trails on the islands, this is a good place to gather information from local boaters.

MILE 17.5: Round the tip of Thompson Island and begin your trip back along the northwest side of the island chain. This section of the island consists of cliffs that drop straight into the water. The cliffs are home to a variety of different colored lichens. *Caution:* There are no landing places at all for the next 3.0 miles.

MILE 21.0: There is a narrow cobble beach in a small bay, all right for a break but finding a tent site in the dense alder brush will be difficult.

MILE 21.5: Cross from **Thompson** to **Spar Island**.

MILE 24.0: The north end of **Spar (N 48° 07.303' W 89° 12.205')** is a pretty area, with cliffs towering over a cobble beach. Paddle down the northwest side of Spar Island.

MILE 24.5: There is a bay with a cottage at the end. According to one Thunder Bay boater, although this is on Crown land, it has been built for private use. The Ontario MNR lets it stand because it could be used as an emergency shelter by boaters. There is a sand beach a little way from the cottage, and there may be tent sites there.

MILE 25.5: Here you find a small bay, which has also been used by boaters. There is a small decaying dock and a narrow sand beach, obstructed by large boom logs chained together. Nonetheless it is possible to land and camp here. On the other side of this point is a cobble beach.

MILE 26.5: Cross from Spar to **Jarvis** to **Devil's** and then to **Victoria Island**. Paddle down the northwest side of Victoria Island. There are narrow cobble beaches lined with dense brush. There is one marginal beach about halfway down the island, but otherwise the first good landing spot will be back in Cosgrove Bay.

MILES 30.0 TO 34.0: Cross to McKellar Point and return to boat launch at Little Trout Bay.

Where to Eat & Where to Stay

RESTAURANTS & LODGING The nearest restaurants and motels are across the border in Grand Portage (see Rte. 3 for information) or in Thunder Bay. Call (800) 667–8386 for more information on Thunder Bay. **CAMPING** The closest campground is **Pigeon River Provincial Park** (formerly Middle Falls Provincial Park), near the U.S.-Canadian border. Call (807) 964–2097 for more information.

Route 22:

▬ ▬ ▬ ▬ ▬ ▬ ▬ ▬ ▬ ▬ ▬ ▬ ▬ ▬ ▬ ▬ ▬ ➤

Thunder Bay to Pie Island

Themal Thunder Bay area scenery evokes awe in visitors. It is easy to see why the Ojibwa believed that Mount McKay was the home of the Thunderbirds. When clouds enshroud the thousand-foot-high peak and thunder is heard, it is said that the Thunderbirds of Ojibwa legend have returned home. The entrance to Thunder Bay is marked by two huge cliff walls, those of Cape Thunder on the mainland and Pie Island. From the middle of entrance to the bay, the high cliff walls of Pie Island rise more than 800 feet above the lake to the summit of Mount Le Paté (elevation 1,461 feet).

TRIP HIGHLIGHTS: Spectacular cliffs, beautiful scenery, hiking trails, a wilderness island to explore.

TRIP RATING:
  Intermediate to Advanced: 38 to 44 miles round-trip.

TRIP DURATION: Over night to multiday.

NAVIGATION AIDS: Canadian chart 2314 for Chippewa Park and NOAA chart 14968, *Thunder Bay* and *Pie Island.*

CAUTIONS: Large waves can build quickly in this bay. Winds can shift suddenly and dramatically around the high cliffs. Shoals along islands can cause waves to break, and isolated boulders may lie hidden just under the water on calm days.

TRIP PLANNING: Check the marine forecast before setting out. Camping on Pie Island requires Crown land camping permits, which may be purchased at Canadian Border Information Centers. Lake Superior is very cold. Temperatures of less than 50° F are common even in summer. Wet suits or dry suits are strongly recommended. All paddlers must have a chart and reliable compass because fog is common on Lake Superior even during the summer months. Crown land camping permits are required for non-Canadian residents. They are $10/night and may be purchased at the Thunder Bay Ministry of Natural Resources (MNR) office (807–475–1471) or at any store selling fishing licenses.

LAUNCH SITE: South of Thunder Bay on Crown Highway 61, turn east onto Highway 61B just south of the Kaministiquia River. Travel east on 61B. After 3.2 miles you turn right on Mission Road. After 1.5 miles the road will fork, take the left road and drive 5.0 miles to find the dock in Squaw Bay. Park your car out of the way on the frontage road by the dock; leave a note about how long you plan on being gone and a description of your group. There are no parking or launching fees.

DIRECTIONS

START: Heading southwest, crossing the 1.5-mile mouth of **Squaw Bay (N 48° 18' 14.7" W 89° 13' 16.9")**, you will see a small island. Towering cliffs line the west side of this bay.

MILES 1.5 TO 3.5: Just before a sandy beach, you will find the entrance to the **Lomond River**.

MILES 3.5 TO 5.0: From Mile 3.0 to 5.0, you paddle along large cliffs along the shore.

MILES 5 TO 6.5: To save time you can cross a bay to reach **Russell Point**, or if you need to take a break, you can land on the shore midway across the bay.

MILES 6.5 TO 7.0: From Russell Point you will see Birch Island, a small island between the mainland and Flatland Island. Head for Birch Island. It is a 0.5-mile crossing to the west end of the island.

MILES 7.0 TO 7.5: Weather permitting you can choose to paddle along either side of **Birch Island**. A cabin is located on the south side, there is also a nice landing spot on the middle of the island's north side.

MILES 8.25 TO 9.5: To go from Birch Island to Flatland Island, you make a crossing of about 0.75 miles. Paddle along **Flatland Island** toward Pie Island. The island has a protected bay on the west side and the east side. *Caution:* The north side of the island has many shoals, and at the

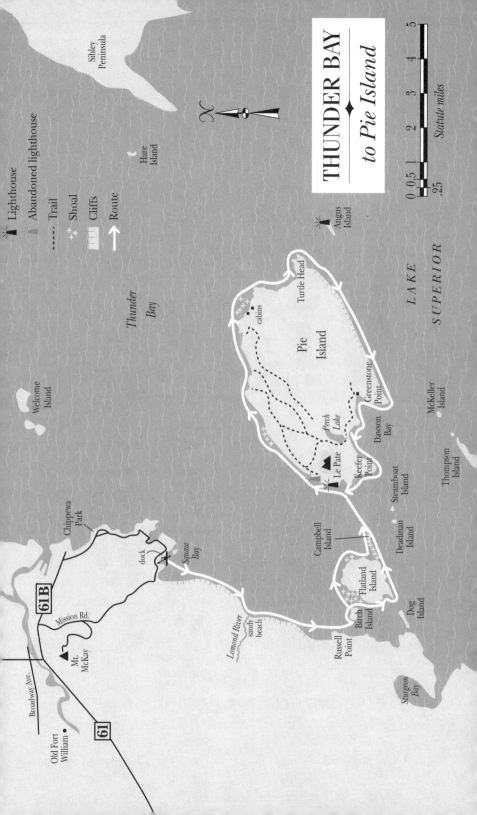

THUNDER BAY
to Pie Island

Statute miles

.25   0 0.5 1   2   3   4   5

Legend

☀ Lighthouse
🏛 Abandoned lighthouse
····· Trail
⁺⁺ Shoal
▥ Cliffs
→ Route

Sibley Peninsula

Hare Island

Angus Island

Thunder Bay

Welcome Island

Pie Island

Turtle Head

cabins

Perch Lake

Greenstone Point

▲ Le Pate

Keefer Point

Dawson Bay

McKeller Island

LAKE
SUPERIOR

Thompson Island

Steamboat Island

Deadman Island

Chippewa Park

dock

Squaw Bay

Campbell Island

Flatland Island

Dog Island

61B

Mission Rd.

▲ Mt. McKay

Lomond River

sandy beach

Russell Point

Birch Island

Broadway Ave.

Old Fort William •

61

Sturgeon Bay

south side of the island, there is a long barrier shoal, which extends out to **Campbell Island**.

MILES 9.5 TO 11.5: The 2.0-mile crossing between Flatland Island and Pie Island is the longest crossing on the route. There is a light at **N 48° 13' 45" W 89° 10' 30"** that can be used as a reference point during the crossing. Arriving on **Pie Island** near the light will put you at the base of the towering peak of **Mount Le Pate** (elevation 1461 feet).

MILE 12.0: Heading north along the coast, you pass an old wooden lighthouse building that is partially hidden by trees.

MILES 12.0 TO 19.5: The north side of the island gently gains elevation as it rises toward the south. A series of rugged hiking trails can be reached from the north end of the island.

MILES 20.0: At Mile 20.0 abandoned cabins are visible from shore.

MILES 21.0: After rounding the northeast tip of the island, you return to dramatic views of high cliffs. At Mile 21.0, close to the shoreline, the cliffs of **Turtle Head** rise hundreds of feet.

MILES 21.0 TO 25.0: The rocky coast continues with an interesting, steep seawall–like shore.

MILES 25.0 TO 26.5: Here you will see **Greenstone Point** extending inland, bare except for standing dead trees.

MILES 26.5 TO 27.5: Enter the east arm of **Dawson Bay** for the best camping area of the island with incredible cliff views.

MILES 27.5 TO 29.0: Paddle to the beach on the west arm of the bay and take a short hike to **Perch Lake**.

MILES 29.0 TO 32.0: Finish the circumnavigation of the island by paddling past **Keefer Point**. Sand beaches line the island's west side near the light. To return to Squaw Bay, simply retrace the route to the mainland via Flatland Island. Advanced paddlers could cross 6.0 miles directly back to Squaw Bay.

Where to Eat & Where to Stay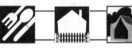

RESTAURANTS & LODGING There are many dining and lodging options in Thunder Bay. For information call Tourism Thunder Bay (800) 667–8386 or North of Superior Tourism (800) 265–3951. **CAMPING** Camping is available in **Chippewa Park** (807-623-3912) just north of the launch site and at Trowbridge Falls (807-683-6661). About 17 miles west of Thunder Bay, there is camping at the **Kakabeka Falls Provincial Park** by the 128-foot-high Kakabeka Falls. For more information call Tourism Thunder Bay (800–667–8386) or North of Superior Tourism (800–265–3951).

Route 23:

━━ ━━ ━━ ━━ ━━ ━━ ━━ ━━ ━━ ━━ ━━ ━━ ━━ ➤

Sleeping Giant Provincial Park: Silver Islet to Tee Harbor

Sleeping Giant Provincial Park is located on the Sibley Peninsula; it separates Thunder Bay from Black Bay. Like most of the north shore of Lake Superior, it is home to moose and other wildlife commonly found in the northern forests, but geologically it is not part of Canadian Shield Country. The striking flat-topped mesas of the Thunder Bay area are mainly sedimentary rock, covered with a flat layer of erosion-resistant diabase, a volcanic rock similar to basalt. The four mesas that make up the tip of the Sibley Peninsula resemble a "sleeping giant." For those who haven't been to this area, the change in topography is dramatic as you approach Thunder Bay, quite different from anything south of the border. The park has a wonderful set of hiking trails that leave from Tee Harbor and Sawyer Bay and climb steeply to the top of the sleeping giant, providing access to some of the most spectacular views of the Great Lakes region.

TRIP HIGHLIGHTS: Dramatic changing scenery, good day hikes with excellent views.

TRIP RATING:
Beginner: 2–4 miles: round-trip to Silver Islet and/or the Sea Lion sea arch; round-trip, overnight trip to Tee Harbor, 12 miles.
Intermediate: 12–50 miles: round trip, overnight.

TRIP DURATION: Half day to three days.

NAVIGATION AIDS: Canadian topographic map: *Thunder Cape* (52 A/7) at 1:50,000.

CAUTIONS: Exposed shoreline, stretches of shore with few and/or very poor landing sites, cold water (wet suit or dry suit strongly recommended).

TRIP PLANNING: To avoid windy conditions, plan your trip early in the year and paddle in the early morning. The park is open in the winter for skiers, but closes for a few months in the spring and may not reopen until mid-May. You will need a backcountry camping permit for Tee Harbor or Sawyer Bay, and if the park is not open, you will have to get your permit over the phone (call 807–977–2526 for more information). Spring comes late to the Canadian North Shore, so if you paddle in May or June, be prepared for cold weather, fog, and extremely cold water: Frost is not uncommon, and the lake surface temperatures are around 35° F early in the year.

LAUNCH SITE: From Highway 17, go south on the 587/Pass Lake exit. Follow this road to its end in the small town of Silver Islet. *Caution:* Beware of moose on the road at night. The general store at the main intersection offers parking for boaters and charges a few dollars a day. Make sure you check in with the owners, get permission, and pay the fee. The launch behind the store is rocky and not great, but the park has no lakeside road access.

DIRECTIONS

START: Paddle west from the Silver Islet general store. After you pass the western end of **Burnt Island**, paddle toward the island of **Silver Islet**, about 0.75 mile off shore. *Caution:* This crossing is short but exposed; don't try it unless the weather is fair.

MILE 1.0: At one time the island was entirely covered with buildings, but the lake has scrubbed it down pretty well, and there's not much left of the old mining complex now. Look for an old mine shaft visible near the southwest tip of the island in about 6 feet of water. The island is privately owned, so please look but don't land. Set your course back toward the shelter of Burnt Island and continue paddling west along the shore from there.

MILE 2.0: The **Sea Lion** rock arch is on the next point north of the town. It used to have a profile resembling a lion's head, but the wind

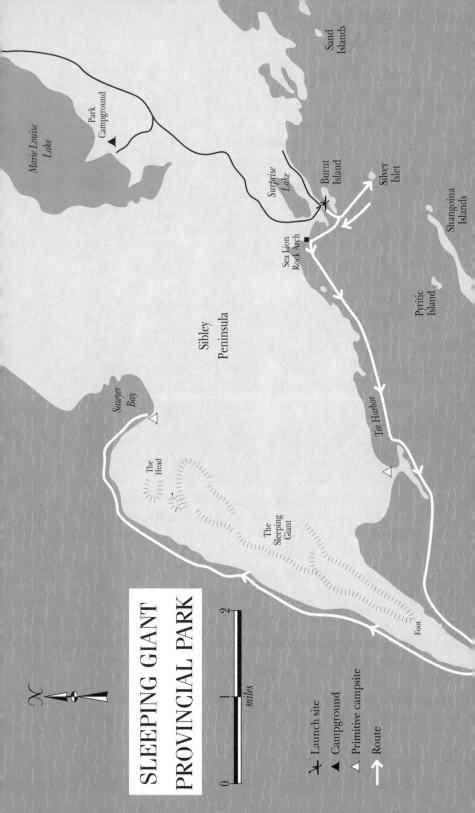

The Sleeping Giant &
the Silver Islet Mine

According to Ojibwa legends, the sleeping giant is really
Nanabiziew, trickster and teacher of the Ojibwa. Nanabiziew knew
that there was silver on the Sibley Peninsula, but told the Ojibwa
never to tell this to anyone because white settlers would come and
steal the land. Nanabiziew hid all the silver on one island, but one
person saw where it was hidden and used it to make weapons.
Eventually whites heard about this and came looking for the silver,
but Nanabiziew raised a storm and killed the men trying to reach
the island, breaking the manitou's rule. Nanabiziew's father turned
his sleeping son to stone as punishment.

Silver was discovered off the tip of the Sibley Peninsula in 1868,
and the tiny island of Silver Islet was quickly developed, soon
becoming one of the richest silver mines in the world. But the mining operations fought a constant battle against the lake and weather,
which constantly threatened to swamp the buildings and mine
shafts. Eventually the mine flooded when a shipment of coal did
not arrive in time to keep the steam-driven pumps working, and the
mine was abandoned. The lake has completely erased all traces of
the mine except for a sunken shaft just off shore.

and waves have changed it over the years. Paddle west past cobble beaches and small rock cliffs.

MILE 5.0: You can land on either side of the T-shaped point of **Tee
Harbor**, but the west side has a narrow cobble beach, while the east side
has a good sand beach. You will probably have company here, because this
spot is popular with sailboaters who anchor here, as well as with backpackers. Look for the trail going up to the "foot" of the sleeping giant. The
view is worth it, but be prepared to sweat a little on the climb up. To finish
the beginning trip, return to Silver Islet from Tee Harbor (5 miles back).
The intermediate trip continues west toward Thunder Cape.

MILE 6.0: Follow the shoreline into a big bay and follow it around to Thunder Cape.

MILE 8.5: The very tip of **Thunder Cape** is not in the park, and it is home to a bird observatory and the Thunder Cape Light. If the weather is clear, you should have a good view of Pie Island to the southwest. Big ships may be passing between Thunder Cape and Pie Island. Turn north after rounding Thunder Cape. *Caution:* Thunder Cape is extremely exposed, and there are no more sheltered landing spots until Sawyer Bay. There are narrow cobble beaches along the western shore, but nothing that would make a reasonable landing place in waves.

MILE 9.0: As you pass the foot of the giant, the mesas tower over you. At 800 feet, these are the highest cliffs in Ontario.

MILES 12.5 TO 25.0: Turn in to **Sawyer Bay** and paddle down the south side. *Caution:* The bay is quite open to the west and can get pretty choppy. There is a small picnic area/campsite with a small cobble beach where the shore turns north again. The trail to the "chest" leaves from here and it is short but steep. You can certainly paddle north from here, but the shoreline is not as scenic. Paddle back to Silver Islet via Thunder Cape and Tee Harbor.

Where to Eat & Where to Stay

RESTAURANTS & LODGING Although Silver Islet is a vacation town now, there are no motels. There are several motels on Highway 17 not too far from the 587 exit. **CAMPING** There is camping at the main campground in **Sleeping Giant Provincial Park**, just off 587. Call (807) 977–2526 for information and reservations.

Route 24:

▬▬ ▬ ▬ ▬ ▬ ▬ ▬ ▬ ▬ ▬ ▬ ▬ ▬ ➤

Silver Islet to Rossport

In our opinion this is one of the two best extended wilderness trips on Lake Superior (the other being Pukaskwa National Park). The outer islands of the Black Bay Peninsula and St. Ignace Island group are difficult to reach, with road and water access available only at Silver Islet, Red Rock, Nipigon, and Rossport. The remoteness has kept this area largely undeveloped, though this may change as the area becomes a more popular spot for vacation cottages. For now there's plenty of room, with wonderfully rugged scenery and hundreds of islands to explore (these will not be visible until you look at a detailed map of the area).

TRIP HIGHLIGHTS: Remote islands, wilderness camping.

TRIP RATING:
Beginner: See Route 25: Rossport Islands.
Intermediate-advanced: Silver Islet to Rossport is a minimum of 75 miles one way (150 miles round-trip); Silver Islet to Edward Island and back is 15 miles.

TRIP DURATION: 4 to 10 days.

NAVIGATION AIDS: Canadian topographic maps 52 A/7, 52 A/8, 52 A/9, 42 D/12, 42 D/13 at 1:50,000.

CAUTIONS: Remote wilderness with no facilities, rocky shoreline exposed to southerly winds, very cold water (wet suit/dry suit recommended), fog, exposed open-water crossings.

TRIP PLANNING: This is a very remote section of shoreline: Later in the season this route gets some sailboat and cruising traffic, but if you go early in the year (May–June), it is possible that you will not see another human being while you are out. Wilderness paddling has its rewards but also extra risks. This area is not a park and is not patrolled, so you must come prepared to be completely self-sufficient. A VHF radio is recommended in case you get into trouble, and so that you can check the marine forecast from Thunder Bay: Southerly winds can create very large waves in little time, and it's nice to have some warning, especially because the shoreline is extremely rocky with very few sand beaches. Steep, terraced cobble beaches are the rule, and they are extremely difficult to launch from or land on in surf. If you are lucky, you may find a gravel bar on some islands (check on the north end of the outer islands), but otherwise you should be prepared to camp on rock or cobble. The land here is a patchwork of private and Crown land, making this difficult for nonresidents of Canada, who must get a permit to camp on Crown land and pay a $10/night per person fee. Probably the most reasonable thing to do is to stay well away from any land with private cottages (this won't be hard) and assume that the rest is Crown land requiring a permit. Crown land permits can be obtained at any MNR Office. Call the Thunder Bay MNR office for more information at (807) 475–1471. If you are planning to set up a shuttle for a one-way trip, parking is available at either Silver Islet (see Rte. 23) or Rossport (see Rte. 25 for parking and launch information).

LAUNCH SITE: Follow directions to Silver Islet (Rte. 23) or Rossport (Rte. 25).

DIRECTIONS

START: Paddle east from **Silver Islet** past several small islands to the southeast tip of the **Sibley Peninsula**. If you have good weather, cross **Black Bay** to **Edward Island** (5 miles). *Caution:* Black Bay is more than 30 miles long, and you will be exposed to both north and south winds that can funnel through the channel between the Black Bay and Sibley Peninsulas.

MILE 5.0: Paddle past **Hardscrabble Island** and toward the southwest tip of Edward Island. **Horseshoe Bay (N 48°21.434' W 88° 38.992')** on Edward Island is sheltered but has only marginal, brushy camping possibilities. Head across to the bay on the northwest side of **Porphyry Island**. This island is used by boaters and has places to camp as well as a trail leading to the lighthouse at the south end of the island. Paddle northwest along the shore of Edward Island through one of the sheltered channels, and then out and along the shore as it curves north. Those touring only Edward and Porphyry Island may want to add a trip around Edward Island before returning to Silver Islet.

MILE 10.0: *Caution:* Once you leave the shelter of the islands, you will be very exposed to the open lake.

MILE 12.0: Leave Edward Island and cross to **Magnet Point (N 48° 24.584' W 88° 33.631')** on the **Black Bay Peninsula**. *Caution:* Magnet Point and **Magnet Island** are named for the magnetic disturbances found in the area. It is probably not a good idea to try this crossing in fog (these disturbances can be as high as 20 degrees in places along the north shore). There are a few cabins on the small island east of Magnet Point, but this area is otherwise empty.

MILE 17.0: Continue paddling northeast. Once you reach **Longfin Island**, you will have plenty of protection from the island group just beyond. It is hard to find a tent spot in the densely wooded islands, but this is a peaceful spot, reminiscent of the more sheltered places on Isle Royale. *Sidetrip:* If the weather cooperates, paddle out to the Shaganash Island Light, actually on Island 10 just off the northwest side of Shaganash. It is also possible to find tent sites there.

MILE 20.0: Once you leave the shelter of Shaganash Island, you will have to decide whether to follow the mainland around to the north or cut across the gap to **Gordeau** or **Swede Island**.

MILE 27.0: The Loon Harbor area is popular with the boating crowd. **Loon Harbor (N 48°31.77' W 88°21.557')** is formed by **Lasher**, **Borden**, and **Spain Islands**. It is a very pretty spot, with tiny islets and gray rock sloping down to the water. Tenting possibilities are marginal because of the lack of clear, level ground, but it's worth a visit even if you don't stay there. Paddle out through the east entrance and north toward Shesheeb Point.

MILE 30.0: Begin your crossing from **Shesheeb Point** to **Otter Island**. Alternatively you can make the long detour (about 5.5 miles each way) to the north end of Shesheeb Bay, where there is a real sand beach. *Caution:* This is another exposed, island-free gap, without really good shelter (except for the far recesses of Otter Cove). *Sidetrip:* Follow Otter Cove to its northern end, then into the small arm that turns south and zigs north again. If you follow this inlet to its end, you will find a waterfall with a few paths around it for exploring.

Silver Islet to Rossport

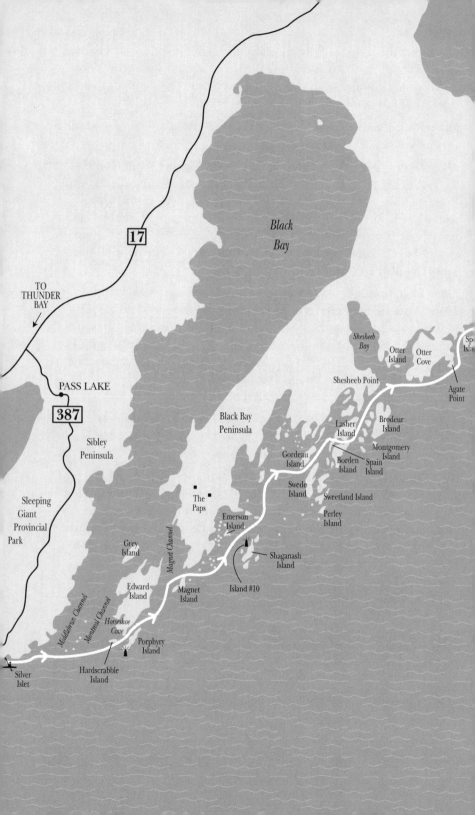

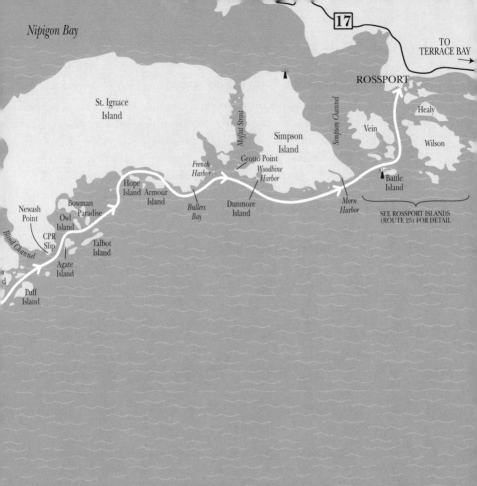

Nipigon Bay

17

TO
TERRACE BAY

ROSSPORT

St. Ignace
Island

Healy

Vein

Wilson

Moffat Strait

Simpson
Island

Simpson Channel

Grotto Point

*French
Harbor*

*Woodbine
Harbor*

Battle
Island

*Bullers
Bay*

Hope
Island Armour
Island

Dunmore
Island

*Morn
Harbor*

SEE ROSSPORT ISLANDS
(ROUTE 25) FOR DETAIL

Newash
Point

Bowman
Paradise

Owl
Island

CPR
Slip

Talbot
Island

Blind Channel

Agate
Island

*Puff
Island*

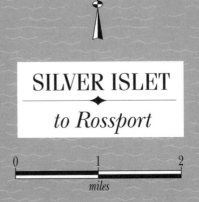

N

🛶 Launch site

☀ Lighthouse

➡ Route

SILVER ISLET
◆
to Rossport

0   1   2
miles

MILE 35.0: *Caution:* Use care when rounding **Agate Point**, which is exposed and is a likely place for reflection waves. There is a beach on the west side of the Agate Point Peninsula.

MILE 38.0: There is an enormous terraced, cobble beach east of Agate Point, stretching far back into the woods. Just ahead is **Spar Island**, with a decent gravel bar on the north end that makes a good stopping place. Paddle east toward **Fluor Island**. *Caution:* There is little shelter for the next 2.0 miles until you reach the chain of islands near Fluor Island. *Sidetrip:* If weather permits you can visit the lighthouse on Lamb Island just southeast of Spar Island.

MILE 40.0: Fluor Island is one of the scenic highlights of the trip. The rounded hills at the south end lead up into the **Nipigon Channel** and give the area a fjordlike feel. Follow the shore of Fluor Island to the northeast, putting the outer islands between you and the lake. The Nipigon Channel runs between the Black Bay Peninsula and **St. Ignace Island**. Those who encounter a prolonged stretch of bad weather off the lake may choose to follow the channel north into Nipigon Bay and follow the north shore of St. Ignace Island into the Rossport area. *Caution:* The Nipigon Strait may have current flowing in or out of Nipigon Bay, caused by wind or changes in atmospheric pressure over the lake. Monitor your progress to check for current.

MILE 45.0: The 0.5-mile-wide **Blind Channel** separate Fluor and St. Ignace Islands.

MILE 46.0: Use caution when approaching **Newash Point**. This shoreline is rife with shoals, so you may want to stand well off shore in rough weather.

MILE 47.0: Follow the shore as it turns north. Watch for a **small bay** to the east (**N 48° 41.871' W 88° 00.504'**). Follow it in and around to an incredibly sheltered little bay. You will see several buildings and some docks, and very likely some boaters. This is **CPR Slip**, privately owned but open to the public. The buildings include a bunkhouse (new, clean, and bug proof) as well as a sauna. You are welcome to stay and enjoy a sauna, but please keep it cleaner than you found it and replace any wood you use.

MILE 50.0: Paddle east to **Owl** and **Agate Islands**. There are a few cabins on these islands and the bay east of here is the most heavily populated, with small cabins scattered along the shore all the way to Armor Island. South of Agate Island is **Talbot Island**, site of the infamous "Lighthouse of Doom," so called because all three of the keepers died. One of the keepers, Thomas Lamphier died soon after the lake became impassable, leaving behind his wife who was unable to bury him in the frozen ground. She was forced to leave his body in a rock crack and wait for help to arrive in the spring. She survived, and her husband was eventually buried on **Bowman Island**. Paddle east to Paradise Island, known for its brilliant white rock beaches.

MILE 55.0: Continue paddling east along the shore of St. Ignace island to **Armor Island**. The shore is characterized by a rock shelf that extends out and underwater. In rough weather waves will break on the rock shelf, making landing difficult. Armor Island now has a few cabins on it, but there is a very narrow beach at the back of **Armor Harbor (N 48° 45.099' W87° 52.004')** just opposite the island. This is not a great camping spot; the beach is too small, and the woods are brushy and buggy, but it is doable.

MILES 55.0 TO 58.0: *Caution:* The next few miles consist of rocky headlands with small, unfriendly cobble beaches. Although these can be used in calm weather, in rough conditions it is better to stay well away from shore because of reflection waves. The next good shelter from southerly winds can be found at **Bullers Bay** or **French Harbor**, though neither is particularly comfortable for camping. Paddle from the **St. Joe Islands** across the **Moffat Straight** to **Grotto Point** on **Simpson Island**. *Caution:* This is another exposed channel open to north and south winds.

MILE 60.0: Follow the shore toward **Dunmore Island**, which has some impressive cliffs. Paddle southeast toward Grebe Point. *Caution:* The next few miles have few "outs" or good sheltered landing places if the weather turns nasty. Proceed with caution.

MILE 66.0: As you paddle by Simpson Island, look for brown or black, octagonal columns of basalt, a volcanic rock. Look for the entrance to **Morn Harbor** behind Raymond Island, which offers the best shelter in the area. At the north end you may find a small shelter, and behind that a path leading up to O'Brien Lake.

MILE 67.0: *Caution:* Wait for good weather before attempting to cross from Morn Point to **Battle Island**.

MILES 70.0 TO 76.0: See Rte. 25 for a description of Battle Island and the Rossport Island group.

Terraced Beaches

The steplike beaches seen on this trip and all around the north shore were formed by wave action long ago when the lake level was higher (actually it was glacial Lake Minong, which existed about 10,000 years ago). In addition the land itself has been rising. This area was covered by a mile-thick sheet of ice, whose weight was so great it actually pushed the earth down underneath it, during the last ice age. Ever since the ice melted, the land has been slowly rebounding.

Where to Eat & Where to Stay

RESTAURANTS & LODGING Call North of Superior Tourism for information on dining and motels in Pass Lake, Nipigon, Red Rock and Rossport at (800) 265–3951. **CAMPING** Camping is available at **Sleeping Giant Provincial Park** (807–977–2526) or **Rainbow Falls Provincial Park** (807–824–2298).

Route 25:

■ ■ ■ ■ ■ ■ ■ ■ ■ ■ ■ ■ ■ ■ ■ ➜

Rossport Islands

The islands south of the town of Rossport provide enough shelter for canoes to visit the innermost islands, or paddlers can leave the protection of the Rossport harbor and head for the outermost islands and the open lake. The varied topography and sand and cobble beaches make this an increasingly popular place for kayakers, but there is plenty of peace and quiet to be had. The Rossport Islands have the same look and feel as the Black Bay Peninsula and St. Ignace Islands (see Rte. 24) but are much easier to reach. Battle Island is a good destination if the weather holds, and if the retired keeper is there, you may get to climb to the top for a great view of the Rossport area.

TRIP HIGHLIGHTS: Protected harbor, camping, and fishing.

TRIP RATING:

Beginner: 4–6-mile trip around the inner islands.

Intermediate: 12–30 miles from Rossport to Battle Island and back.

Advanced: Add as many miles as you like by extending your trip to Simpson and St. Ignace Islands (see Rte. 24).

TRIP DURATION: Full day to multiday.

NAVIGATION AIDS: Canadian topographic map: *Rossport* 42 D/13 at 1:50,000.

CAUTIONS: Sections of rocky, exposed shoreline with no landing in some areas, exposure to southern winds on the outer islands, and very cold water out on the open lake (wet suit or dry suit recommended).

TRIP PLANNING: Large swells are more common here than on the south and west shores because strong south or southwest winds are not unusual. If you would like to see the southern side of the island group without seeing a 3-meter wave, plan to paddle early in the season before the autumn gales start in mid- to late August. Build some wind days into your schedule if you are camping out in the islands. June is the calmest summer month, but the trade-off is cooler nights, colder water, more bugs, and fog. The local boating community has established campsites on many of the islands, but please note, however, that most of the islands are privately owned, and permission is required to camp on these islands. Minnie, Harry, Salter, and Battle Islands are Crown land and available for camping. Non-Canadian residents must pay a $10 per night camping fee. Crown land camping permits can be picked up at any Ministry of Natural Resources office; call the MNR office in Terrace Bay at (807) 825–3205 for more information.

LAUNCH SITE: The road to Rossport leaves Highway 17, passes through town, and then connects with 17 again. If you are doing a day trip, the city park has the easiest launch site. From the east intersection of the Rossport Road with Highway 17, drive no more than 0.1 mile west and look for the picnic area (with a gazebo shelter) on the south side of the road. There is a strip of sand along the grassy shore. If you plan to be out in the islands for a few days, drive to the center of town. There is a dock at the intersection of the main road and Dock Street that can be used for kayak launching. There is a fee to use the dock or ramp. The alternative is to ask the kayak outfitter, also located at the main intersection, whether it's all right to launch from his land about 15 feet west of the dock, for which there is no charge. Either way, after unloading your boat and gear, move your car to the parking lot by driving west on the main road 0.1 mile to the lot right next to the railway tracks. There is no charge for parking there.

DIRECTIONS

START: Launch from the **town park** and paddle under the **Nicol Island** Bridge. In low-water years you may have to get out and walk your kayak over the shallow bottom or paddle around the south side of Nicol Island. In recent years Nicol Island has become a popular place for vacation homes.

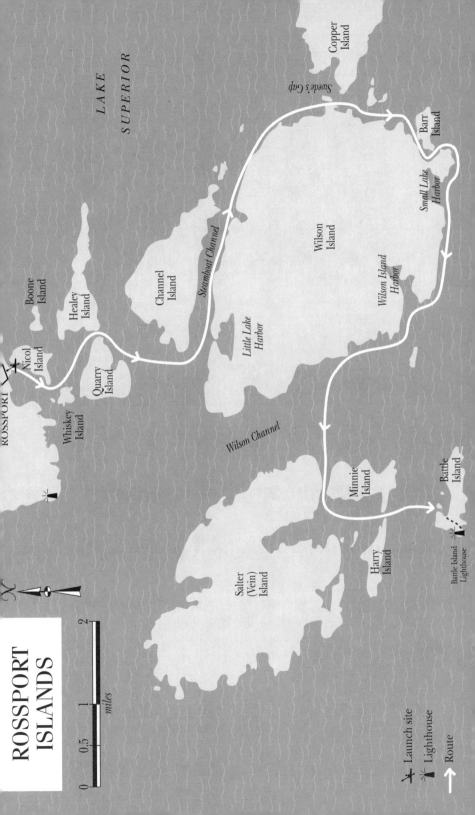

ROSSPORT ISLANDS

0   0.5   1   2
miles

Launch site
Lighthouse
Route

LAKE SUPERIOR

Copper Island

Swede's Gap

Barr Island

Small Lake Harbor

Wilson Island

Wilson Island Harbor

Boone Island

Healey Island

Channel Island

Steamboat Channel

Little Lake Harbor

Nicol Island

ROSSPORT

Quarry Island

Whiskey Island

Wilson Channel

Salter (Vein) Island

Minnie Island

Harry Island

Battle Island

Battle Island Lighthouse

MILE 1.0: Pass between **Nicol** and **Whiskey Islands** (the latter named for the bootleg whiskey stored there at one time) into a protected area surrounded by five islands. Paddle toward the narrow gap between **Quarry** and **Healey Islands**. *Caution:* You are now entering a less-sheltered area, use caution and be prepared to deal with small chop. *Sidetrip:* Paddle into the bay on the southeast side of Quarry Island, once the site of a sandstone quarry. At the north end of the bay is a small picnic area (it

may be obscured by weeds in late summer) with a fairly rugged trail that leads to the top of the cliffs; you may see abandoned machinery from the quarry operation. The trail is maintained by occasional volunteer labor, and hiking to the top may involve a bit of bushwacking.

MILE 3.0: Paddle toward the western tip of **Channel Island** then east into the **Steamboat Channel**. Immediately after entering the channel, look for a narrow gap in the shore of Wilson Island that leads into the sheltered waters of Little Lake Harbor. Continue east along the shore of **Wilson Island**.

MILE 5.0: Leave Steamboat Channel and follow the shore of Wilson as it curves southward. Look for black sand beaches along the east shore. *Sidetrip:* The northeast side of Channel Island has cliffs made of red, black, and gold sedimentary rock, which are well lit on summer mornings. If you're not in a hurry it's worth a trip.

MILE 6.0: Many of the small beaches along this side of the island are made of black sand. Paddle toward the channel between Wilson and Copper Islands known as Swede's Gap. If there are waves and wind out on the lake, you will definitely start to feel it here. Paddle between Wilson and **Barr Islands**. *Caution:* The south side of Wilson Island is extremely exposed to southerly winds (and prone to reflection waves) until you reach the shelter of Minnie Island. Wait for a good, calm day before paddling this stretch.

Rossport Islands Kayak Symposium

In late June there is a symposium in Rossport, offering instruction, interpretive tours of the island group, slide programs, and new kayak demos. Call Superior Outfitters at (807) 824–3314 for more information.

MILE 10.0: The recesses of **Wilson Island Harbor** will provide a break from any weather out on the lake and a chance to stretch on one of the small beaches there.

MILE 11.0: Leave Wilson Island and aim for the gap between **Minnie** and **Salter Islands.** On the northwest corner of Minnie is a cleared campsite, with room for several tents, but this is a popular spot with local fishermen and may not be available. Those with only one tent may be able to find other spots around the harbor, but it can be a challenge because brush generally comes right down to the water.

MILE 13.5: Leave the protected harbor and paddle through the gap between **Harry Island** and Minnie Island. Paddle toward the bay on the north side of **Battle Island (N 48° 45.312' W 87° 33.250')**. *Caution:* Once again you will be exposed to wind and waves from the open lake.

MILE 14.5: There is a large gravel beach at the west end of the bay. An old road leaving from the beach leads to the lighthouse; it's about a five minute walk. Though the lighthouse is now automated, the former keeper still lives there in the summer and has gathered some good stories from his years tending the light.

MILES 15.0 TO 21.0: By the most direct route back through the islands, it is 6.0 miles back to Rossport. You can go back directly or explore the islands, taking advantage of many possible sidetrips.

Where to Eat & Where to Stay

RESTAURANTS & LODGING A real standout here is the **Rossport Inn**, recommended for both lodging and dining. The owners are kayakers and very familiar with the islands and their history. The inn has rooms in the main building (built in 1884) or cabins that are handy for a group of kayakers doing day trips out from Rossport. Call (807) 824–3213 for information and reservations. There are a few other bed and breakfasts located in town; call the Rossport Tourist Association at (807) 824–3389 for more information. **CAMPING** The closest campground is at **Rainbow Falls Provincial Park**, which has two separate sections, one on Lake Superior (about 3 miles east of the Rossport dock), and the other located on an inland lake. Call (807) 824–2298.

Route 26:

━━ ━━ ━━ ━━ ━━ ━━ ━━ ━━ ━━ ━━ ━━ ━━ ➡

Slate Islands

The Slate Islands are an almost circular group about 6 miles offshore at Terrace Bay. There are currently no charter boats to take kayakers out to the islands, so there is no alternative to making the crossing. Once there, however, the scenery is excellent, and the channel between Mortimer and Patterson Islands provides bombproof protection. A good plan is to set up a base camp somewhere in this channel and make day trips to the more exposed parts of the islands. There is no slate on the Slate Islands, but there are large beaches of flattened shinglelike stones on the south of Patterson Island. The Slate Islands may have been the site of a meteor impact millions of years ago, but the evidence of this will not be obvious except to geologists, some of whom think that the islands are the remnants of a crater formed by the meteor's impact. The Slates are also well known for having the largest herd of woodland caribou in the area, currently back up at 600 animals from 100 in 1997. With so many caribou in such a small area, your chances of seeing one are pretty high. Fishing is good here, too, and lake trout can be caught on the shoals and in the shallows in June. Later in the year they are hard to catch without trolling in deep water.

TRIP HIGHLIGHTS: Caribou viewing, fishing.

TRIP RATING:

Intermediate/Advanced: 30-mile (minimum) trip from Terrace Bay around the islands and back.

TRIP DURATION: 3 to 5 days.

NAVIGATION AIDS: Canadian topographic maps: *Schreiber* (42 D/14), *Slate Islands* (42 D/11), and *Pic Island* (42 D/10) at 1:50,000.

CAUTIONS: Long, exposed crossing, extremely cold water (wet suit or dry suit strongly recommended).

TRIP PLANNING: The sticking point here is really the crossing to the islands; there is sheltered paddling once you get there. Plan your trip in June or July (before the winds pick up in August and September) and start your crossing as early in the morning as possible to avoid afternoon winds. And, as always, check the marine forecast before setting out. Plan one or two wind days into your itinerary to avoid the "I have to get back to work even if it kills me" syndrome. The Slate Islands were designated a Provincial Park in 1985, and a Crown land permit is required for non-Canadian residents camping there. You can pay the fee at the Ministry of Natural Resources office in Terrace Bay before you go. Call (807) 825–3205 for more information. Aside from a few old cabins, there are no facilities on the island and no park rangers to go to if you need help, so a VHF marine radio is strongly recommended.

LAUNCH SITE: From Highway 17, just west of the tourist information center, turn south onto Lakeview Road (look for a small sign saying TO BEACH). Go 0.1 mile, turn left onto Kenogami Street, and go 0.2 mile. Turn right onto Beach Road, then follow it down the hill and through the golf course to the end of the road at Terrace Bay Beach. There is plenty of room for parking and no charge for leaving your car there. A small dock has been put in near the mouth of the Aguasabon River for use by motorboats; kayakers will have an easier time launching from the beach.

DIRECTIONS

START: Leave from **Terrace Bay Beach (N 48° 31.619' W 087° 00.041')**, aiming for the north side of **Mortimer Island**.

MILE 6.5: There are some cobble beaches along the shore that are fine for rest stops as long as it is reasonably calm.

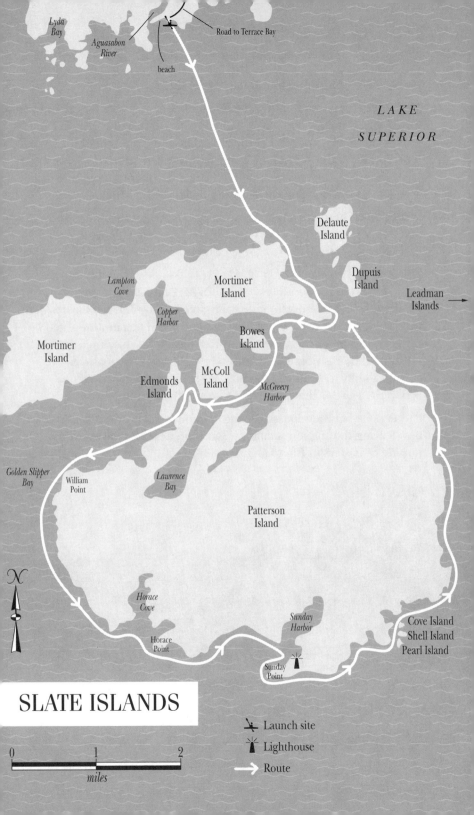

Lyda
Bay

Aguasabon
River

Road to Terrace Bay

beach

LAKE

SUPERIOR

Delaute
Island

Dupuis
Island

Leadman
Islands

Lamplon
Cove

Mortimer
Island

Copper
Harbor

Bowes
Island

Mortimer
Island

McColl
Island

McGreevy
Harbor

Edmonds
Island

Golden Slipper
Bay

William
Point

Lawrence
Bay

Patterson
Island

Horace
Cove

Sunday
Harbor

Horace
Point

Cove Island
Shell Island
Pearl Island

Sunday
Point

SLATE ISLANDS

N

⚓ Launch site

🗼 Lighthouse

→ Route

0   1   2

miles

MILE 7.5: There is a tombolo that makes a good resting spot because you can land on either side of the point. Turn south and enter the passage between **Mortimer** and **Delaute Islands**.

MILE 9.0: Turn west and into the channel, then south between **Patterson Island** and **Bowes Island**. Take some time to explore the channel and the great scenery. *Sidetrip:* Paddle along the south shore and then north into Copper Harbor. The northwest part is called Lampton Cove, and it has a mooring dock for boats and a fire pit. Look for an old mine shaft across from the dock on the east side of Copper Harbor.

MILE 10.0: There are a total of three old cabins on the east end of **McGreevy Harbor**. They are now available on a first-come, first-serve basis, although in past years some of them have been in a fairly disgusting state. But at least the clearings around them make good tent sites.

MILE 11.0: On the southwest corner of **McColl Island** is the Comeandrest, a wonderful little cabin fixed up by Terrace Bay residents for use on fishing trips. For a few years the cabin was monopolized by caribou counters from a western university, but because their grant was not renewed, it is now available to others. Please keep it as clean or cleaner than you found it. You may see some decaying corrals in McGreevy Harbor that were used to round up caribou for study.

Paddle west between **Patterson** and **Edmonds Islands**. *Caution:* You are now leaving the sheltered channel, and the next 12.0 miles around the outside of Patterson Island are exposed to south and west winds. Wait for

a calm day before attempting it. If you are doing this stretch as a day trip, bring enough supplies and equipment to see you through the night if you get caught by unexpected bad weather.

MILE 13.0: Round **William Point** and turn south. The outside of Patterson Island is one of the scenic highlights of the trip.

MILE 15.0: **Horace Cove** extends north. There are a few cobblestone beaches available for stops. Only the back of the harbor (the "hook") will offer any protection against southerly winds.

MILE 16.0: A trip to the **Slate Islands Lighthouse** is highly recommended, and the most-sheltered access to it is at **Sunday Harbor**. Look for a dock and small beach in the first bay on the eastern side of Sunday Harbor. There is a trail leading up the lighthouse. Although the building itself is a standard-issue red and white structure, the payoff here is the terrific view, as the light is set on a high cliff.

MILE 18.0: On the south side of Sunday Point is another dock for the lighthouse and keepers' cottages. It is landable on a calm day, but there is only a boulder "beach" next to the dock.

MILE 19.5: Turn north between **Patterson** and **Pearl Islands**. This nameless cove is fairly sheltered and has a large terraced beach that goes far back into the woods.

MILE 20.0: There are no more sheltered landing spots until you reach the Mortimer-Patterson Island channel.

MILE 23.5: You have circled back to Mile 9.0 (see earlier).

MILES 24.0 TO 33.0: Paddle back to the north side of Mortimer and choose your moment for crossing back to Terrace Bay.

Where to Eat & Where to Stay

RESTAURANTS & LODGING Contact the Terrace Bay Tourist Information Center at (807) 825–9721 for information about restaurants and lodging. **CAMPING** Camping is not prohibited or officially allowed at the Terrace Bay Beach, according to one town official, but though it's convenient, it's not especially peaceful, and you may hear some late-night carousing or see some people testing their four-wheel-drive vehicles on the beach. One alternative is to camp at the RV park at the west end of town (at the Aguasabon Falls exit on Highway 17). Another is to stay at Lyda Bay, about 1.5 miles west of Terrace Bay. Lyda Bay has a great sand beach, islands at the south end to break up incoming waves, and no road access. The Casque Isles Trail does come through here so there may be some foot traffic.

Route 27:

━ ━ ━ ━ ━ ━ ━ ━ ━ ━ ━ ━ ━ ━ ━ ➤

Neys Provincial Park

Neys Park, with its 1-mile-long sand beach and great views of Pic Island is already known to many campers and travelers who stay at the campground, but the best parts of Neys are only accessible by boat. The scenic, weathered and rounded gray or pink rock along the western side of the Coldwell Peninsula is syenite, similar to granite in appearance. At the end of the peninsula are a number of small islands, in addition to Pic Island, and two beaches. As there is no road or trail access, it's a quiet and pretty place to spend an afternoon. Currently there are no backcountry facilities for camping, so reaching the islands makes for a long day trip. Pic Island,

although not part of the park, has only one landing spot (Windy Bay), and the beach there is covered with driftwood logs. Overnight camping is possible on Crown land west of the Pic River, however.

TRIP HIGHLIGHTS: Good scenery, remote beaches and islands.

TRIP RATING:

> *Beginner:* 2-mile day trip from Prisoner's Cove to beach on west side of Coldwell Peninsula and back
>
> *Intermediate:* 11-mile trip from Prisoner's Cove to the beach on the south side of the peninsula and back.
>
> *Advanced:* Add a circumnavigation of Pic Island to the intermediate route for a total distance of 31 miles, or add a trip to Detention Island and back for a total distance of 18 miles.

TRIP DURATION: Part or full day.

NAVIGATION AIDS: Canadian topographic maps: *Coldwell* (42 D/15) and *Pic Island* (42 D/10) at 1:50,000.

CAUTIONS: Exposed rocky shoreline with potential for reflection waves and few good landing spots. Be especially wary of south and southwest winds: Check marine forecast before going.

TRIP PLANNING: To have calmer weather, plan this trip early in the season and early in the morning. Most of the shoreline consists of bare, sloping rock or steep cobble beaches with numerous shoals; should the weather turn bad, there are few "outs," so be aware of the weather and plan accordingly.

LAUNCH SITE: The Neys Park entrance is directly off Highway 17 west of Marathon. From 17 turn south onto the park entrance road, drive 1.6 miles to the entrance. The Prisoner's Cove's picnic area is on the left. The park requires a $5.50/day-use fee. An alternative launch site is the Little Pic River boat launch at the west end of the park. Launching here allows a great view of Pic River Canyon, but adds 2 miles to all trips and means that you may have to deal with the combination of current, wave action, and a sandbar at the river mouth.

DIRECTIONS

START: Launch from **Prisoner's Cove**, named for the WW II German POW camp located here in the 1940s. Due to the shallow area extending out from the beach, it is not unusual to launch through small surf. Paddle south along the distinctive rock shoreline.

Neys Provincial Park

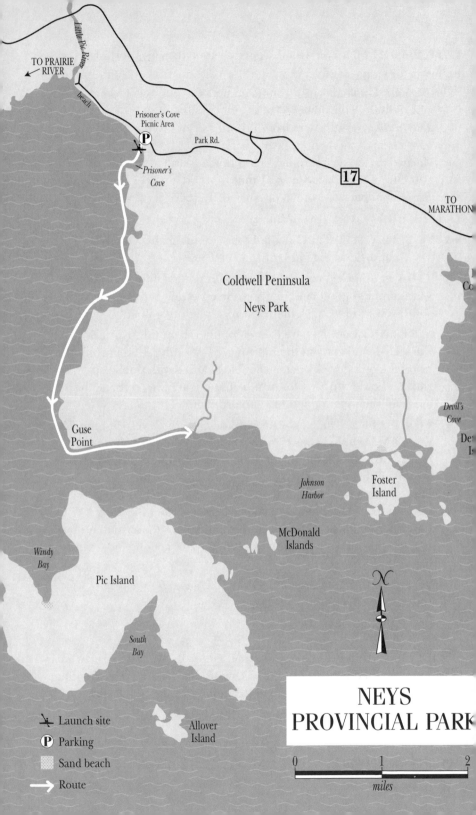

TO PRAIRIE
RIVER

Little Pic River

beach

Prisoner's Cove
Picnic Area

P

*Prisoner's
Cove*

Park Rd.

17

TO
MARATHON

Coldwell Peninsula

Neys Park

Co

*Devil's
Cove*

De
I

Guse
Point

*Johnson
Harbor*

Foster
Island

McDonald
Islands

*Windy
Bay*

Pic Island

*South
Bay*

Allover
Island

N

✈ Launch site

P Parking

▦ Sand beach

→ Route

NEYS
PROVINCIAL PARK

0   1   2

miles

MILE 1.0: Look for a sand beach with a picnic table on the left, the terminus of the newly completed Under the Volcano Trail, with interpretive signs about the geology of the area. If going on, continue south past cobble beaches and shoals. Landing spots will be difficult to find from here on if there is any kind of wave action.

MILE 3.5: When you reach **Guse Point**, turn and paddle east. **Pic Island** is only 0.5 mile away, but because the trees come right down to the water, there is not much to see close up, and the view is better from the peninsula.

MILE 5.5: Look for a small river in the middle of a valley and a sand beach. This is a good spot to take a break before turning around.

MILES 5.5 TO 11.0: Return by the same route.

Sidetrips: Pic Island circumnavigation: It is about 10 miles around the island, more if you go down into the bays. On most of the island, trees come right down to the water, though there may be narrow beaches for landing, depending on fluctuations in water level.

Foster Island: Continuing east look for another beach along the narrow passage between Foster Island and the mainland.

Detention Island: From the beach at Mile 5.5, paddle east past Foster Island and by the southeastern tip of Coldwell Peninsula. It is about 0.5 mile across to Detention Island. This is a tough place to land in surf, and in rough weather, you may want to skip the landing and return to Prisoner's Cove the way you came. There are some Pukaskwa pits on the raised cobble beaches here. These rock hollows may be thousands or at least hundreds of years old, and their purpose is not known. Some suggest that they may have been used for vision quests by the Anishinabe (Ojibwa). Please do not disturb these sites.

Where to Eat & Where to Stay

RESTAURANTS There is a small store that serves some food directly opposite the park entrance on Highway 17, but there is a greater selection of restaurants in Marathon. For more information, contact the Marathon Chamber of Commerce at (807) 229–2151. **LODGING** There are several motels near the Peninsula Road exit into Marathon on Highway 17. For more information, contact the Marathon Chamber of Commerce at (807) 229–2151. **CAMPING** There are nearly 150 RV/tent sites in the park campground, but it may be full on weekends during July and August. For more information, contact Neys Provincial Park at (807) 825–3205.

Route 28:

━━ ━━ ━━ ━━ ━━ ━━ ━━ ━━ ━━ ━━ ━━ ━━ ━━ ━━ ━━ ▸

Hattie Cove to Horseshoe Bay

Pukaskwa National Park has some of the most striking
wilderness shoreline on Lake Superior, but this roadless
park can be difficult to see for those who have days and
not weeks to spend. This short and mostly sheltered day trip
is a good introduction to the scenery of Pukaskwa Park. The
sheltered recesses of Pulpwood Harbor have the classic
north shore look: gray granite bluffs streaked with lichen
and other hardy vegetation. Horseshoe Bay is reminiscent of
beaches of the south shore of Lake Superior.

TRIP HIGHLIGHTS: Sheltered paddling.

TRIP RATING:

> *Beginner:* 4.5 mile paddle from Hattie Cove to Horseshoe Bay
> (weather permitting).

TRIP DURATION: Part day.

NAVIGATION AIDS: Canadian topographic map: *Marathon*
(42 D/9)

CAUTIONS: Reflection waves, westerly winds, fog, cold water.

TRIP PLANNING: Though relatively sheltered, Pulpwood Harbor
is open to west winds, and strong southerlies can create very difficult
conditions in the harbor. Check the marine forecast before starting
(available in the visitor center if you do not have a weather or VHF
radio). Hattie Cove itself is extremely sheltered, and weather conditions outside the cove can be completely different. Take the shoreline trail to the outer side of the point for a look if you are unsure,
and/or stop for a reality check outside the entrance to Hattie Cove
before going on: If the weather is bad there, it will get much worse
the farther west you go. Plan your trip early in the day and before
mid-August, when the winds pick up.

LAUNCH SITE: There is a narrow beach just behind the park's visitor center. From the Marathon exit on Highway 17, go 4.1 miles east and take 627 south. Follow 627, 9.3 miles to its end at the park's entrance gate. Continue past the gate, taking the first left to the visitor center parking lot. The beach is a short carry down the trail and behind the visitor center. Day-use fees apply if not staying at the campground and are $3.00/adult, $7.00/family, $1.50/child.

DIRECTIONS

START: Hattie Cove appears at first to be a small lake, but look for its exit at the west end. Wind and atmospheric pressure changes can cause the water to flow in or out of the cove, sometimes creating a strong current. If the weather is foul, stay in this sheltered area and paddle to the end of the cove; the scenery is pretty and the paddling relaxed. Otherwise, paddle out of **Hattie Cove**, there turn left/east into **Pulpwood Harbor**.

MILE 0.5: Paddle down the first inlet and out again or continue on to Pulpwood Harbor proper.

Hattie Cove to Horseshoe Bay

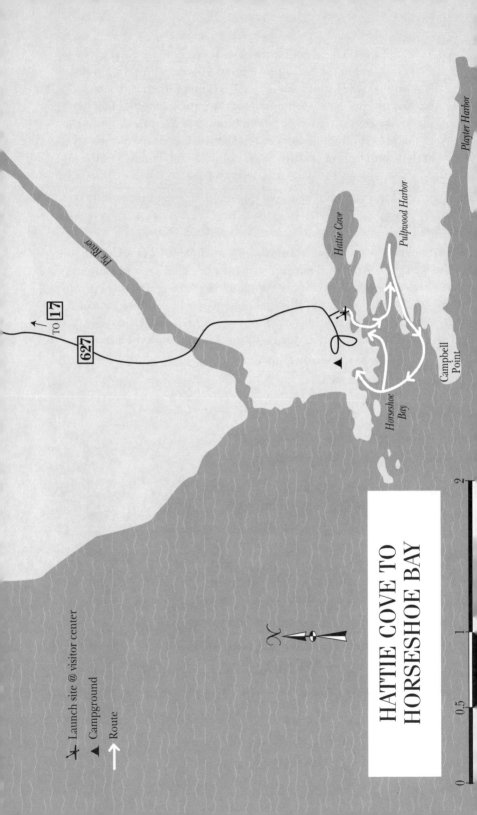

Plater Harbor

Pic River

TO 17

627

Hattie Cove

Pulpwood Harbor

Campbell Point

Horseshoe Bay

Launch site @ visitor center

Campground

Route

HATTIE COVE TO HORSESHOE BAY

0   0.5   1   2

MILE 0.75: Paddle behind the small islets at the entrance to Pulpwood Harbor. The channel between the steep bluffs opens out to flat, low rock shelves, with a narrow beach at the far east end (hardly any sand is visible because of the huge amount of driftwood there). Old boom logs, used to gather up other logs to be towed to their destination, are still chained to the south side of the harbor along the rock walls. Follow the south wall out of the harbor.

MILE 2.0: If weather permits, paddle beyond the larger islands west of the harbor. Cross north to the point marking the entrance to **Horseshoe Bay**. *Caution:* Be wary of **Campbell Point**. This long rock finger sticks well out into the lake and is famous for bad reflection waves on its south side. Do not go near or around it except in calm conditions. The two points on either side of Horseshoe Bay can also be difficult in this respect. In south or southwest winds, reflection waves will bounce back and forth between the two arms, making it difficult to approach the entrance.

MILES 2.5 TO 4.5: Take a break on the beach before heading back, paddling out of Horseshoe Bay and along the north side of the harbor back to the Hattie Cove entrance.

Where to Eat & Where to Stay

RESTAURANTS There are numerous restaurants around the Marathon exit and along Peninsula Road, which runs from Highway 17 into town. For more information, contact the Marathon Chamber of Commerce at (807) 229–2151. **LODGING** There are several motels near the Peninsula Road exit on Highway 17. For more information, contact the Marathon Chamber of Commerce at (807) 229–2151. **CAMPING** There is camping at Hattie Cove; sites are $15 (or $18 for sites with electricity) per night. Call (807) 229–0801 (ext. 229) for more information.

Route 29:

Hattie Cove to Michipicoten River

Many kayakers feel this section of shoreline is the best paddling on Lake Superior, if not the Great Lakes. Over 100 miles of roadless wilderness with beautiful rock shoreline, clear turquoise water, wonderful sand beaches, and white-water rivers with spectacular waterfalls. It just doesn't get any better than this! About one-third of the route passes along Crown land; the remainder along the shores of Pukaskwa National Park, which receives relatively little use compared with parks stateside. Even if you don't have time to do the whole thing, the shorter trip from Hattie Cove to Oiseau Bay and back is an excellent introduction to the park. Keep in mind, however, that the shoreline is not regularly patrolled, and that other people may not be nearby if you need help, so use caution and good judgment when paddling.

TRIP HIGHLIGHTS: White-water rivers, prime wilderness paddling, and good hiking.

TRIP RATING:

Beginner: See Route 28: Hattie Cove to Horseshoe Bay.

Intermediate: 32 miles from Hattie Cove to Oiseau Bay and back; or, starting from Michipicoten River, paddle west for a few days. The shoreline is scenic and has many good beaches and possible camping sites.

Intermediate-Advanced: Hattie Cove to Michipicoten River: 100 miles each way.

TRIP DURATION: Part day to two weeks.

NAVIGATION AIDS: Canadian topographic maps: *Schreiber* (42 D), *White River* (42 C; this map has a tiny corner of shoreline right around the Pukaskwa River), and *Michipicoten* (41); Canadian Hydrographic Services charts 2304, 2308, and 2309. The park also has a map that shows the park campsites and hiking trails.

CAUTIONS: Exposed shoreline, remote area, cold water (wet suit or dry suit recommended).

TRIP PLANNING: Those wishing to avoid the excitement of 6-foot surf should schedule their trip before the winds pick up in August, and try to paddle in the calmer morning hours. Westerly and southerly winds are especially problematic and can kick up big waves in no time. Be alert to changes in the weather, and check the marine forecast daily (after you pass the Pukaskwa River, you may only be able to get the Thunder Bay open-waters forecast). This is a wilderness park with no facilities outside the main campground, so come prepared to be self-sufficient and to deal with emergencies and difficult situations on your own. You must register with the park office before heading out, pay a small fee for backcountry camping, and give the park

office your itinerary. When you are done with your trip, be sure to hand in your permit or call the office: They do send helicopters looking for people who don't check in. Schedule enough wind days into your plans (one out of every four days is a good rule of thumb), and, if possible, allow extra time for exploring and walking the trails. For those who want to do a one-way trip but don't have time to do the whole thing, there is the option of being dropped off by boat along the shore and kayaking back north to Hattie Cove. Call Bruce McCuaig at (807) 229–0605 for charters from/to the northern end of the park or Buck's Marina on the Michipicoten River (705) 856–4488. The portion of this trip between the Pukaskwa and Michipicoten Rivers is Crown rather than park land. Non-Canadian residents are required to have Crown land camping permits (this fee is waived if you are using a Canadian outfitter or guide). Permits can be obtained in Wawa or Marathon at MNR offices, or at any store that sells fishing licenses.

LAUNCH SITE: There is a narrow beach just behind the park visitor center. From the Marathon exit on Highway 17, go 4.1 miles east and take 627 south. Follow 627, 9.3 miles to its end at the park's entrance gate. Continue past the gate and take the first left to the visitor center parking lot. The beach is a short carry down the trail and behind the visitor center. Day-use fees apply if you are not staying at the campground. For those starting from the Michipicoten River, try Buck's Marina (705–856–4488) for launch and parking (currently there is no fee for either), or try Naturally Superior Adventures at (800–203–9092). Both are located on the river. To reach Buck's, take the Michipicoten River Village exit from Highway 17, turn left at the first intersection, and follow the signs to the marina. For Naturally Superior Adventures, take the Michipicoten River Village exit, turn left at the first intersection, and then follow the green-and-white signs saying VOYAGEUR ADVENTURES, or call for directions.

DIRECTIONS

START: Paddle south from the **Hattie Cove (N 48° 35.33' W 86° 17.486')** entrance toward **Campbell Point**.

MILE 1.0: *Caution:* Campbell Point is a real trouble spot. South or southwest winds can cause difficult reflection waves, and the bigger the waves, the farther out this can happen. Wait for good weather before going around.

MILE 2.5: There are a few possible tent sites in and south of **Picture Rock Harbor**.

MILE 4.0: *Caution:* During high water the entrance to the **White River** may have standing waves and strong currents at the river mouth, and if

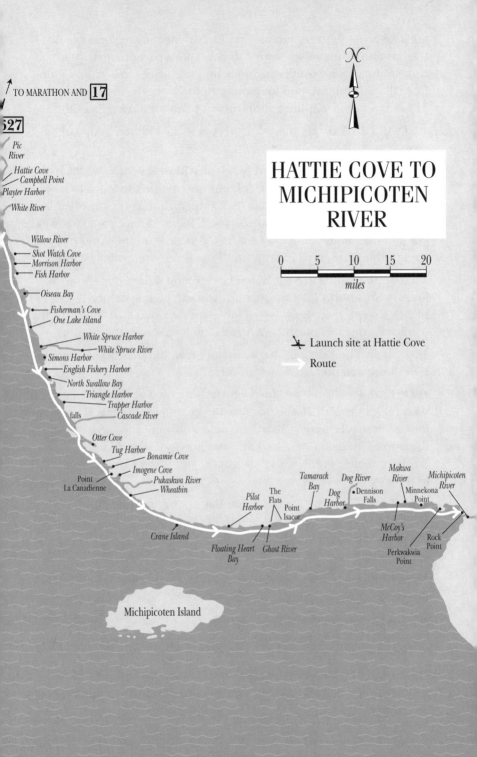

TO MARATHON AND 17

527

Pic
River

Hattie Cove
Campbell Point
Playter Harbor

White River

Willow River
Shot Watch Cove
Morrison Harbor
Fish Harbor

Oiseau Bay

Fisherman's Cove
One Lake Island

White Spruce Harbor
White Spruce River
Simons Harbor
English Fishery Harbor
North Swallow Bay
Triangle Harbor
Trapper Harbor
falls   Cascade River

Otter Cove
Tug Harbor
Bonamie Cove
Imogene Cove
Point   Pukaskwa River
La Canadienne   Wheatbin

Crane Island

Pilot   The
Harbor   Flats
           Point
           Isacor

Floating Heart   Ghost River
Bay

Tamarack
Bay   Dog River

       Dog
       Harbor

Dennison
Falls

McCoy's
Harbor

Perkwakwia
Point

Makwa
River
     Minnekona
     Point   Michipicoten
                  River

                  Rock
                  Point

Michipicoten Island

HATTIE COVE TO MICHIPICOTEN RIVER

0   5   10   15   20
miles

⚓ Launch site at Hattie Cove

→ Route

the lake is rough the combination of waves meeting current can make the entrance impassable. *Sidetrip:* If conditions permit, the trip up the river to the falls is worth doing. Pick up the trail at the bottom of the first falls and continue up to the suspension bridge crossing the river. There is a good campsite a short distance from the river's mouth.

MILES 4.5 TO 7.0: The shoreline here is rocky with few good landing spots.

MILE 7.5: There is a nifty sand beach at **Willow River (N 48° 29.963' W 86° 14.578')** with a fair number of tent sites, but it also tends to be one of the busier spots. In past years the campground has been visited by a bear that is learning to like human food. Please do *not* leave your food out and unattended; use the bear box. A paddle up the Willow River is a very pleasant evening activity. Continue this route, paddling south.

MILE 10.0: Starting at **Shot Watch Cove** (named for a pocket watch found with a bullet hole through it), you can paddle behind a series of islands that provide shelter from waves on the open lake and provide a scenic channel. Follow the mainland closely to stay in the channel.

MILE 11.5: The campsites here are not great, but they do have a pretty view of the well-protected Morrison Harbor.

MILE 12.0: Paddle out of **Morrison Harbor** past a gap in the islands, and then back in to **Fish Harbor**. Follow the channel into **Cave Harbor** and look for a small cave just above the waterline, opposite the big island at the north entrance to the harbor. The shoreline from here to Oiseau Bay is extremely pretty, with pink granite swirls and black diabase dikes in the worn rock shore.

MILE 15.0: The entrance to **Oiseau Bay** opens up, and behind the sprinkling of islands are miles of beach to explore. The official campsite is on the peninsula in the north part of the bay, but there are many possible places to camp.

MILE 13.5: There are good tent sites at the southern arm of **Fisherman's Cove**.

MILE 15.5: Continue south and pass through the scenic channel next to **One Lake Island**, which is sometimes used as a calving ground by woodland caribou.

MILE 17.5: The long beach at the mouth of the White Spruce River is another pretty spot. *Caution:* Beware of currents and standing waves at high water.

MILE 19.5: **White Spruce Harbor** is extremely sheltered, but the campsite is small.

MILE 22.5: *Caution:* The string of islands peters out and the coastline is more exposed from **English Fishery Harbor** to **Otter Island**, and though there are small bays to duck into if the wind picks up, not many provide comfortable camping.

MILE 24.5: **North Swallow Bay (N 48° 12.717' W 86° 08.868')** has good beach and campsite. If you hear something walking around at night, it's probably the camp porcupine(s), so make sure to use the bear/porcupine box for food storage. The coastal hiking trail ends here; for the remainder of the trip, there are no more trails or official campsites.

MILE 31.0: Look for **Cascade Falls**, a beautiful spot where the Cascade River spills directly into the lake. There are a few level spots for tents, but the gravel beach is small. This place was a favorite of Bill Mason, canoeist, filmmaker, and painter. *Sidetrip:* If weather permits cross from the mainland to the north end of Otter Island. There is a small channel between Otter Island and the smaller island to the north, called Old Dave's Harbor. There are some private buildings on the north side, but on the south side of the harbor is the old lightkeeper's house (N 48° 06.789' W 86° 03.696'), now unused. There is a short trail leading west from there to the Otter Island lighthouse, from which there is a good view looking north along the coast. There are Pukaskwa pits on Otter Island, but please leave these undisturbed.

MILE 34.0: Deep in Otter Cove are a park warden station's buildings, but there is no camping.

MILE 35.0: *Caution:* Once past the islands south of Deep Harbor, be careful: There are no good sheltered landing spots until Tug Harbor and Bonamie Cove.

MILE 39.5: Paddle into **Tug Harbor** between Richardson Island and the mainland. The hills are close to the shore, making this a very pretty area. You may find a few marginal tent sites along the channel.

MILE 40.5: **Bonamie Cove** will provide a softer landing on the beach at the south end.

MILE 41.5: *Caution:* **Pointe La Canadienne** is another bad area for reflection waves in south or southwest winds.

MILE 43.0: Imogene Cove has a long sand beach, with a well-established campsite at the north end. This is a very pleasant spot at which to spend a night. On the opposite side of the **Imogene River** are some old cabins falling into ruin.

MILE 46.0: There is a large gravel bar at the mouth of the **Pukaskwa River (N 48° 00.159' W 85° 53.534')** that seems well used, possibly by white-water canoers and kayakers running the river. The shoreline begins to turn east here, and the shore becomes flatter. *Caution:* At high water the Pukaskwa River may have strong currents and/or standing waves at the river mouth. Approach with care.

MILE 49.5: Past Chimney Point you find the **Wheatbin**, a huge, pale gravel beach with plenty of space for tents. Past this point, good campsites will be harder to find (depending on how picky you are), but the best technique is to look for bays where rivers empty into the lake, which may have cobble or sand beaches. Also be warned that it is not uncommon to have big waves roll in from some other part of the lake even when your local weather is calm.

MILE 53.5: Turn into the shallow cove with a small beach at the back, a well-protected site, good for refuge from south or west winds.

MILE 55.5: At the back of **False Ganley Harbor**, there is a cobble beach, and just around the next point is **Ganley Harbor**, a popular anchorage for boaters, marked by a day beacon.

MILE 57.0: Redsucker Cove is sheltered but not an appealing place to stay the night. *Caution:* For the next 7 miles the shoreline is rocky, inhospitable, difficult to negotiate in rough weather, and without good sheltered landing spots.

MILE 63.0: Pilot Harbor (also marked with a day beacon) is another anchorage for boaters, but not an especially comfortable one for landing or camping.

MILE 64.5: Floating Heart Bay (N 47° 55.305' W 085° 32.534') provides the first good beach in a while and is scenic and comfortable. There is an area north of the river that has a flat grassy area; it's a little weedy but has plenty of room for tents. *Caution:* After Floating Heart Bay comes **The Flats,** another rubble-strewn, rocky, and difficult section.

MILE 69.5: Look for a beach in a broad bay. At the east end near the **Ghost River** is a spot that makes a good stopping place, though the bay is not particularly sheltered. If you are not sure about the weather, this may be the best place to wait before going around Point Isacor.

MILE 71.0: *Caution:* **Point Isacor** and the cliffs east are truly spectacular in calm weather, but do *not* attempt this stretch of water in anything but good weather. The shear cliffs breed deadly reflection waves, and in rough weather you will have to stand well offshore. There are a few places to land in calm conditions, but none that will be usable in surf. There are no good places to land for about 5 miles.

MILE 76.0: The small islets in **Tamarack Bay** will break up waves a little, but in really rough conditions, it will be difficult to land among the boulders or on the sloping rock.

MILE 80.5: False Dog Harbor is well protected and has a good sand beach and plenty of tent space. It does see some motorboat traffic, though. Check out the narrow entrance leading into **Dog Harbor**, just east of False Dog Harbor. From here to the Michipicoten River, there are many good sand beaches; finding a campsite will not be so difficult.

MILE 81.5: Look for a huge gravel bar at the mouth of the **Dog River**. *Caution:* Beware of strong currents at the river's mouth. It is certainly possible to camp on the gravel bar, though it is a bad place to launch or land in waves.

Sidetrip: Not far up the river is one sight you shouldn't miss: Dennison Falls. Paddle or portage past the gravel bar, then paddle up river until you see a hideous camp shelter covered with shredded plastic on the east bank. You should be able to pick up a path running along the river. It is about an hour walk to the falls. There is a lower falls over a rock shelf; to the east you may see a rope dangling down a small cliff. The Dog River is a well-known white-water river, and paddlers use the rope to portage their boats around the falls (look for gel coat, plastic, and Royalex trails on the rocks). Unfortunately it's also the main way up to see the high falls. It may be possible to climb up the rocks next to the lower falls if the water is low. Neither route is especially convenient or safe, so please be careful. The falls are worth the hassle, though—300 feet of cascades over black rock. Again, at low water it may be possible to climb up the rock next to the falls, but there is also a portage trail on the east side.

MILE 85.0: Look for a tombolo (an island joined to the mainland by a sandspit or gravel spit). The east side is **McCoy's Harbor**, but there are good beaches on both sides. There is a tent site with a makeshift kitchen back in the woods.

MILE 89.0: There is a good and somewhat sheltered beach between the two arms of **Minnekona Point**.

MILE 90.0: You'll find a gravel beach at the mouth of the **Makwa River**. You are reentering civilization, and it will be harder to find a good quiet site any closer to the mouth of the **Michipicoten River**.

MILE 93.0: **Perkwakwia Point** is your last hurdle. Be cautious and wait for good conditions before attempting to round this peninsula.

MILE 97.0: *Caution:* There may be strong currents at the mouth of the Michipicoten River, and if the wind is off the lake, standing waves as well.

FINISH: If you are shuttling with the outfitter at Rock Point, paddle into the river mouth and look for a boathouse and beach on the north bank, just inside the river mouth. Those going to Buck's Marina should paddle another 1 mile upstream to the boat launch there.

Where to Eat & Where to Stay

RESTAURANTS Try the **Cedarhof** (705–856–1136) on Highway 17 just south of Wawa, or contact tourist information for Wawa (800–367–9292) or Marathon (807–229–2151). **LODGING** Contact tourist information offices for Wawa (800–367–9292) or Marathon (807–229–2151). **CAMPING** The **Hattie Cove Campground** is at the north end of the park, call (807) 229–0801 (ext. 229) for more information. If you are starting from Michipicoten River, the closest camping is at **Naturally Superior Adventures**, an outfitter on the river, or at **Lake Superior Provincial Park**; call (705) 856–2284 for more information.

Hattie Cove to Michipicoten River

Route 30:

Michipicoten Island

T his isolated, seldom visited island offers true solitude, striking scenery, and plentiful caribou and beaver. Designated as an Ontario Provincial Park in the 1960s, it has seen little development of any kind except for a few private inholdings, or patent lands, in Quebec Harbor. The north side of the island consists primarily of bluffs or cliffs set back from boulder beaches, while the south shore has alternating sand and raised cobble beaches. Located 10 miles off the Ontario coast, it can be reached by charter boat or by paddling from Wawa and crossing to the island from the mainland. Apart from Quebec Harbor, the shoreline of the island is extremely exposed and offers relatively few good landing beaches, making this a challenging paddle.

TRIP HIGHLIGHTS: Little development, very lightly used area, caribou herd.

TRIP RATING:
Intermediate: 40-mile paddle around the island.
Advanced: Approximately 140 miles: Paddle from Wawa along the Pukaskwa shore, then cross from either Redsucker Cove or Floating Heart Bay (see Rte. 29 for the description of this section).

TRIP DURATION: Allow a minimum of seven paddling days, with extra wind days depending on time of year and tolerance for large, steep seas.

NAVIGATION AIDS: Canadian topographic maps: *Bonner Head* (41 N/13) and *Michipicoten Island* (41 N/12) at 1:50,000.

CAUTIONS: Extremely exposed shoreline in a section of Lake Superior known for sudden squalls and large waves. Be especially wary of west and south winds. This is a wilderness park with no facilities, so come prepared to be completely self-sufficient. A wet suit or dry suit is recommended because water temperatures here are cold (< 50° F) year-round.

TRIP PLANNING: Charter boat service is available to take paddlers and their boats to Michipicoten Island. (Check with Buck's Marina [located 1 mile up the Michipicoten River] or Horst Anderson and Sons at 705–889–2126.) This is a long (three-hour minimum) and hazardous crossing, and we recommend taking a charter boat out because it leaves more time to paddle the island and reduces the risk of being windbound on the island, not to mention the chance of sudden weather changes in the middle of a crossing. If crossing from the mainland, choose your day carefully: Wait for a fair, calm day before attempting to cross and allow three hours for the trip. To avoid rough weather, plan to take your trip early in the summer, and try to finish up by early afternoon each day. Fog is most common in May and June, but it can occur at any time. The Ontario MNR requires nonresidents of Canada to pay a $10/night fee to camp on Crown land, such as Michipicoten Island, and the fees can be paid at any MNR office or at any store that issues fishing licenses. The fee is waived for those using a Canadian outfitter or guide.

LAUNCH SITE: The easiest access is from the Michipicoten River. From Highway 17 south of Wawa, take the Michipicoten River Village exit going west. If you are going to the outfitters, follow the green and white **Voyageur Adventure** signs or call for directions to Rock Island.

DIRECTIONS

If launching from Wawa, see Route 29 for a description of the first 30 miles. Floating Heart Bay has one of the few sand beaches in the area and makes a good point to start your crossing to the island. The trip description proceeds counterclockwise around the island, but can be done in reverse if desired.

START: Begin your crossing at **Floating Heart Bay (N 47° 55.305' W 85° 32.534')**, cross to lighthouse at **Point Maurepas (N 47° 47.762' W 85° 44.182')**. The crossing is 11.8 miles. There are small rocky beaches on either side of Point Maurepas and numerous shoals that could make

Michipicoten Island

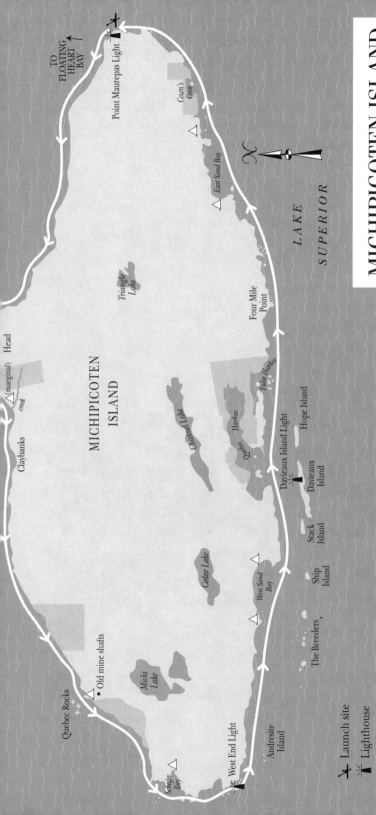

MICHIPICOTEN ISLAND

MICHIPICOTEN ISLAND

LAKE SUPERIOR

TO FLOATING HEART BAY

Point Maurepas Light

Cozen's Cove

East Sand Bay

Triangle Lake

Head

(marginal)

creek

Claybanks

Channel Lake

Harbor

Quebec Harbor

Four Mile Point

False Harbor

Hope Island

Davieaux Island Light

Davieaux Island

Stack Island

Cedar Lake

West Sand Bay

Ship Island

The Breeders

Old mine shafts

Quebec Rocks

Michi Lake

Schafer Bay

West End Light

Andresite Island

0 1 2 3 4

miles

✈ Launch site

✻ Lighthouse

△ Good camping area (no campsites)

▢ Private land, closed to camping

⬆ Route

✛ Rocks

landing tricky in rough conditions. The lighthouse and outbuildings are locked, but the grounds make a good spot to rest after the crossing.

MILE 1.0: West of the lighthouse, cobble beaches line the shore. The land rises to form a series of striking bluffs and cliffs. Small patches of gravel or smaller rocks may be found, but most of the beaches are of large, round stones.

Michipicoten Island

MILE 7.0: At **Bonner Head** the cliffs come right up to the shoreline, and although there are a few gravel beaches, this spot is not recommended for overnight camping.

MILE 9.0: Though the beach will not be easy to land on in rough weather, the bay west of Bonner Head provides some shelter from east and south winds, and there are a few small patches of gravel by the creek. This area can be used to set up tents. On the north side of the creek are the unusable remains of a cabin.

MILE 10.0: The topography becomes steeper at the **Claybanks**, named for the red clay soil that can be seen under the trees.

MILE 16.0: Opposite the **Quebec Rocks** is one of the better landing beaches on this end of the island. The beach is also near the site of an old copper mine, operating until the 1920s. Find the gap in the rock cliffs at the northeast end of the beach, and walk about 200 feet into the woods to find the old, stone miners' cottages. The mine shafts themselves and pieces of old machinery are about 0.25 mile back in the woods. *Caution:* Be on the lookout for shaft openings and give them a wide berth. The copper ore was transported by rail to **Quebec Harbor**, where it was then taken by boat to the mainland. The trails winding all through the forest and brush are caribou tracks—look for discarded antlers along the way.

MILE 17.0: About 1 mile past the mine beach, look for a large cave set midway in a cliff, formed when the lake was higher and the land lower. Land at the beach just southwest of the cave to climb into it and walk about 50 feet back.

MILE 18.0: Two long rock fingers form the entrance to **Schafer Bay**, a very pretty spot with a nice gravel beach at the end and some small sea caves on the south side. It is open to the west, but offers good shelter from other wind directions.

MILE 19.0: Look for a gravel tombolo. Depending on conditions either side can be used for landing and camping. Behind the beach area, walk through large, mossy, crevasses up to the rock overlooking the beach for a good view.

MILE 21.0: Paddle through rock shoals around the **West End Island** light, then turn east, past low cobble beaches. *Sidetrip:* For a change of pace, paddle out to the chain of islands starting with Antelope Rock, formed of pale gold or orange rock.

Woodland Caribou

There are two subspecies of Caribou: Arctic and Woodland. Woodland caribou are virtually extinct in the lower forty-eight states (except for a small herd in the northern Idaho panhandle), and their main habitat is now in northern Canada. A few herds remain in the more southern regions around Lake Superior. For those who want to see this increasingly rare animal without venturing too far north, Michipicoten and the Slate Islands provide the best opportunities for caribou viewing. In 1967 a single caribou was sighted on Michipicoten Island, and the Ontario Ministry of Natural Resources decided to introduce additional animals and establish a herd. As of 1992 an aerial survey estimated a population of approximately one hundred caribou. Unlike the caribou of Pukaswa Park and the Slate Islands, they are not subject to predation by wolves, because wolves have not made the crossing to the island. Caribou live mainly on the abundant mosses and lichens found in the northern forests, in particular the spongy, pale green lichen called reindeer moss. Both males and females grow antlers each year, and it's not uncommon to find discarded antlers along the intertwining maze of trails that cross Michipicoten.

MILE 25.0: Look for a broad sandy point—take a break from all the rocks and enjoy the sand! This spot is fairly level and has plenty of room for tents.

MILE 26.0: **West Sand Bay** is another good lunch or camping spot, which offers protection from north and east winds. Look for beaver and caribou in the evenings.

MILE 28.0: Paddle to the entrance of **Quebec Harbor**. Much of the harbor is privately owned and offers poor camping sites in any case. But, if you have the time, paddle in to see the old fishery at the northeast end of the harbor and the three shipwrecks clustered at the southeast corner: two partially submerged tugboats and one completely submerged ship.

MILE 28.5: Paddle from the entrance of Quebec Harbor to **Davieaux Island**. The dock is not particularly easy for kayakers to use, but if the weather is relatively calm, it is possible to land at a very small **cobble beach (N 47° 41.642' W 85° 48.427')** west of the dock. Follow the trail up to the lighthouse for a view of Quebec Harbor and the hills beyond.

MILE 31.0: False Harbor has a few narrow, buggy beaches, and the entrance island has one small gravel spit that would be comfortable for one tent. Watch for shoals on either side of the island.

MILE 32.0: The next stretch of shoreline is fairly rocky, with raised cobble beaches. *Caution:* Beware the rocky points along this section, particularly in southwest winds, as there is potential for bad reflection waves.

MILE 36.0: There is another large sand beach in **East Sand Bay** with possible campsites.

MILE 37.0: Another sand beach with possible campsites east of the small peninsula.

MILE 38.0: Cozen's Cove is patent or private land, but the red stone beaches are worth a visit.

MILE 40.0: Maurepas Point: Return to the mainland by the same route.

Where to Eat & Where to Stay

RESTAURANTS See Rtes. 30 and 31 for dining options. **LODGING** There are several motels on Highway 17 opposite the exit to Michipicoten River Village, and many more in and around Wawa. Contact the Wawa Chamber of Commerce at (800) 367–9292 for more information. **CAMPING** There is camping at the **Rabbit Blanket Lake Campground**, located at the north end of Lake Superior Provincial Park. Call (705) 856–2284 for more information.

Route 31:

━━ ━━ ━━ ━━ ━ ━━ ━ ━━ ━ ━━ ━ ━━ ━━ ➤

Lake Superior Provincial Park

This route contains many well-known and impressive land-marks, such as the cliffs at Old Woman Bay, the Devil's Chair, and the Agawa Rock Pictographs. The shoreline is varied; sections of sheer cliffs plunging into the water, peaceful sandy harbors, and striking, patterned rock. Parts of the coast appeared in Bill Mason's film about canoeing on Lake Superior, *Waterwalker.* This route, which describes the whole park shore, can be done in five to seven days, but several road access and launch points make it easy to see some of the better scenery in weekend or day trips.

TRIP HIGHLIGHTS: Excellent scenery and backcountry camping, with good trail system and many day-hiking options.

TRIP RATING:

Beginner: 2-mile, part day trip from Sinclair Cove to Agawa Rock and back; 10-mile, 2-day trip from Gargantua Bay to Cape Gargantua and back with stops at Gargantua Harbor, Warp Bay, and Devil's Warehouse.

Intermediate: 12-mile round-trip from Gargantua Bay to the Devil's Chair and back; 8-mile day trip from Old Woman Bay to Brulé Harbor and back.

Advanced: 60-plus miles: five-day, one-way trip from Agawa Bay to Michipicoten River.

TRIP DURATION: Part day to five days.

NAVIGATION AIDS: Canadian hydrographic charts 2309 and 2307; Canadian topographic maps 41 N/15, 41 N/10, and 41 N/7; or the official park map, which is inexpensive and quite good.

CAUTIONS: Exposed shoreline, stretches where landing isn't possible, cold water (wet suit or dry suit is recommended), and remote sections with no facilities and few people.

TRIP PLANNING: As with all trips on the east end of the lake, June and July have the calmest weather, and paddling in the early morning will help you avoid afternoon winds. For longer trips allow about one day in three as a wind day. With all the access points along the shoreline, there are many possible trips within the park. Check the marine forecast before paddling, and be especially cautious when west winds are predicted.

LAUNCH SITE: Parking and launching sites are available within the park at Old Woman Bay, Katherine Cove, Sinclair Cove, Gargantua Bay, and Agawa Bay. All parking areas can be reached from Highway 17 via well-marked exits, and all are close to the highway except for Gargantua Harbor. Permits are required for parking and overnight camping. Call the park office at (705) 856–2284 for more information. For those doing the whole park shoreline, parking and shuttle service are available from Naturally Superior Adventures, located at the mouth of the Michipicoten River (800–203–9092). Because of the rather steep day-use fees at the park, it may be cheaper to leave your vehicle at the outfitters and have them shuttle your car to the end of your trip than to leave it in the park during the time you are gone. Call ahead for prices. The Michipicoten Post Provincial Park is located on the south bank of the Michipicoten River but is a day-use only park.

DIRECTIONS

These directions are given for the entire shoreline. Refer to the appropriate locations and mile points for the shorter trips.

START: Launch at **Agawa Bay (N 47° 19.562' W 84° 36.647')** campground. This pebble beach is fairly steep, and launching and landing can be challenging in large seas.

MILE 3.5: The first campsite is on **Agawa Point**, but unless you are desperate, keep going (the landing next to the site consists of large boulders). Follow the channel between the **Agawa Islands** and the mainland to the vertical face of **Agawa Rock**. *Caution:* Reflection waves in rough weather will make viewing the pictographs from the water difficult, but if the water is calm, the view from the water is best. Near the beginning of the rock ledge, there is a description of the individual pictographs and

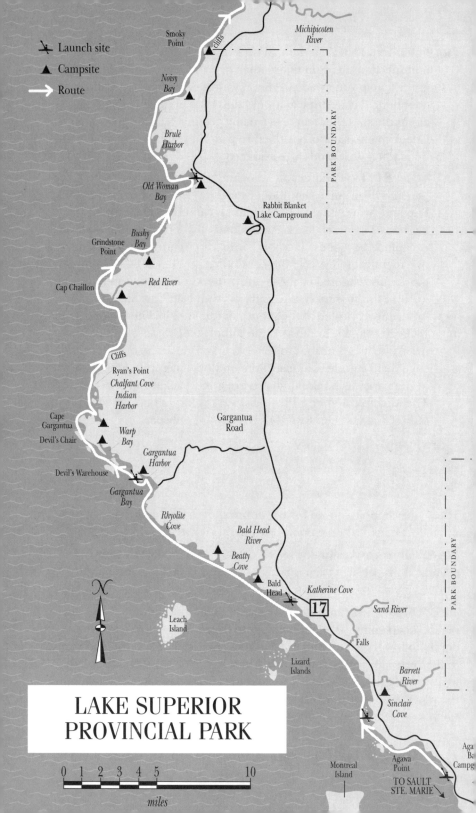

LAKE SUPERIOR
PROVINCIAL PARK

✈ Launch site
▲ Campsite
→ Route

Smoky Point
Michipicoten River
cliffs
Noisy Bay
Brulé Harbor
PARK BOUNDARY
Old Woman Bay
Rabbit Blanket Lake Campground
Bushy Bay
Grindstone Point
Cap Chaillon
Red River
Cliffs
Ryan's Point
Chalfant Cove
Indian Harbor
Gargantua Road
Cape Gargantua
Devil's Chair
Warp Bay
Gargantua Harbor
Devil's Warehouse
Gargantua Bay
Rhyolite Cove
Bald Head River
Beatty Cove
Bald Head
Katherine Cove
17
Sand River
PARK BOUNDARY
Leach Island
Falls
Barrett River
Lizard Islands
Sinclair Cove
Montreal Island
Aga Ba Campg
Agawa Point
TO SAULT STE. MARIE

N

0 1 2 3 4 5   10
miles

their significance (you will need to get out to read these). This is a tough spot to land so continue on to **Sinclair Cove** if you want to walk the trail to the pictograph wall.

MILE 5.5: Next to the boat launch, there is a small beach that provides a sheltered launch/landing spot. Follow the road about 200 feet up the hill to the trailhead to the pictographs.

MILE 6.0: There are two small campsites on a gravel beach in the bay opposite Barrett Island, but there is a more comfortable place to camp around the corner at the **Barrett River**.

MILE 9.5: Sand beaches are the rule from the Barrett River to Bald Head. There is a trail on the north side of the **Sand River** that runs along a series of waterfalls. Rumor has it that the trout fishing on the river is good.

MILE 16.0: After **Bald Head**, the highway and shoreline diverge, making for a more quiet paddle. There is a trail along the Bald Head River, leading to another series of waterfalls. Look for it on the south side of the river, just inside the gravel bar at the river mouth.

MILE 18.0: Beatty Cove (N 47° 30.189' W 84° 52.948') is a good spot for camping; it has a good sand beach and plenty of tent sites.

MILE 21.5: Rhyolite Cove is formed of distinctive red rock or rhyolite, composed of fused volcanic ash. Walk south on the coastal trail to the next rock point for a clear view of this peculiar rock.

MILE 24.0: For those wanting to visit the Cape Gargantua (pronounced locally "gar-gan-twa") area for a few days, this is the access point to the scenic area. Gargantua Road winds west from Highway 17 and ends in a small parking lot with beach access at the south end of **Gargantua Bay**. The shore is steep and lined with medium-sized rocks here, making this a bad place to launch in strong west or southwest winds.

MILE 25.0: Gargantua Harbor is a good camping spot, although it is a popular spot for day hikers. As you paddle towards the beach, look for the submerged wreck of the Columbus, which burned and sank in the early 1900s.

MILE 27.0: Paddle out to **Devil's Warehouse** from the point. The northeast side of the island has sheer cliffs, which have recently become home to nesting peregrine falcons (hard to see, but listen for the sound of the chicks during nesting season). Follow the cliffs north and land at the small beach where the cliffs move back from the waterfront. Look for a large cave in the cliffs: The fallen pieces of rock are hematite, thought to be one ingredient of the red ochre used to make the pictographs at Agawa Rock.

MILE 28.0: **Warp Bay (N 47° 35.224' W 85° 00.475')** is one of the more popular spots for kayakers, boaters, and hikers, and it's easy to see why. The grassy dune campsites have a terrific view of the island group, including Devil's Warehouse, which also shelters the bay from strong winds. Trails leave from the west side of the beach (leading eventually to a small black sand beach offering a view of the Devil's Chair) and the east side of the beach (look for a small spur trail where the main trail crosses the Gargantua River, then follow the river up to a nice swimming hole under the falls).

MILE 29.0: Follow the Tugboat Channel between a chain of islands and the mainland. Look for a string of low black shoals ending in several spiky rock formations, the **Devil's Chair**.

MILE 30.0: Round **Cape Gargantua's** north side. To the east is the entrance to Indian Harbor, a very sheltered spot with several tent sites. The coast north of **Chalfant Cove** offers no good harbors until Brulé Harbor.

MILE 38.0: From **Ryan Point** on there are stretches of cliffs followed by a long cobble beach. Look for a large red outcropping at the northwest end of the beach, Red Rock River, and a few tent sites. *Caution:* Potential for reflection waves at **Cap Chaillon**.

MILE 41.0: Look for shoals of soft sandstone just off Grindstone Point, which is riddled with potholes and their "grinding stones." The campsite marked on the park map is not there, and the boulder beach makes a poor landing spot in any case.

MILE 42.5: There is a small gravel beach at **Bushy Bay** that has a tent pad.

MILE 46.0: The cliffs at **Old Woman Bay** are named for the face of an old woman that can be seen (with a little imagination) in the rock.

MILE 49.0: Look for terraced beaches just before passing between Entrance Island and the mainland. Pukaskwa pits can be found on many of the terraces. Please do not move the rocks or disturb the pits in any way.

MILE 50.0: **Brulé Harbor (N 47° 48.359' W 84° 56.598')** is very sheltered from any kind of weather, and the hills around it make it a pretty spot for a lunch break or overnight stay.

Places of Legend

Many places within the park are important to the Ojibwa and considered sacred. The image of the manitou Mishipeshu on Agawa Rock is also well known to kayakers in the region. Taking the form of a horned lynx, Mishipeshu was thought to cause wind and waves on Superior by lashing his tail. The Ojibwa made offerings of tobacco at the Devil's Chair to appease Mishipeshu and for safe passage, a custom that many paddlers continue today. On the days when the waves and wind make the lake seem alive, it is easy to imagine Mishipeshu roaming the lake floor in a restless mood and whipping up bad weather. The Devil's Warehouse and Devil's Chair were so named by white missionaries who wanted to discourage the Ojibwa from visiting these places and honoring the spirits associated with them. The spirit places were not considered evil by the Ojibwa, but rather places of great power. The Devil's Chair was thought to be the resting place of the Nanibozoo, a demigod and teacher of the Ojibwa people. According to tradition he stopped to rest at this spot after jumping across Lake Superior. The cave on Devil's Warehouse may have been the source of the hematite used to make the pictographs on Agawa Rock.

MILE 54.0: Noisy Bay, named for the small noisy falls at the river mouth, offers some rocky campsites.

MILE 56.5: Smoky Point is the last good landing/camping spot before Michipicoten River. The north side of the point is the best place to land, and there are trails going to the other side of the point and northward along the shore. This is the park boundary; the land north of here is Crown land. *Caution:* The next 3 miles of shore are mostly cliffs prone to reflection waves in high winds.

MILE 59.5: The large sand beach at the mouth of the Michipicoten River is the former site of a fur trading post, and was on a Voyageur

Gales of November Rendezvous

Lake Superior's November gales are legendary, but not everyone dreads their arrival. Since 1985, a kayaking get-together has been held every November just south of Agawa Bay near Lake Superior Provincial Park. In past years paddling conditions have been so rough that some kayaks were snapped in two, but paddling isn't mandatory. Some folks opt for paddling in the more protected areas of the park, or even hiking instead of pushing the kayaking envelope. At the end of the day, everyone gathers in the big (heated) tent to socialize and tell tall tales. Come prepared for some very, very bad weather indeed, and enjoy! Contact Stan Chladek at Great River Outfitters for more information (248–683–4770).

Route to Hudson Bay. Currently it is a provincial park, but it is for picnic and day use only.

MILE 61.0: The route ends at the mouth of the **Michipicoten River (N 47° 55.995' W 84° 51.115')** (see Trip Planning about parking and shuttles). *Caution:* Strong west and south winds combined with heavy current at the river mouth can produce very large standing waves.

Where to Eat & Where to Stay

RESTAURANTS   There are several Greek restaurants that serve gyros on the main street in Wawa. See also Rte. 30 for another dining option. **LODGING**   Wawa has many motels located on or near Highway 17. Call (800) 367–9292 for more information. **CAMPING**   There are several campgrounds in the park at Agawa Bay, Rabbit Blanket Lake, and Crescent Lake. The free park brochure will show the locations. All are within easy distance of Highway 17. Call (705) 856–2284 for more information.

Lake Michigan
Michigan

Route 32:

━━ ━━ ━━ ━━ ━ ━ ━ ━ ━ ━ ━ ━ ━ ━ ➤

The Garden Peninsula: Sac Bay to Fayette State Park

This route includes beautiful limestone bluffs, sand beaches, a gull and cormorant rookery, and a historic iron smelting townsite. The west side of the Garden Peninsula, within Big Bay De Noc, provides a relatively sheltered route for beginning to intermediate paddlers. In addition to sheltered waters and beautiful coastal scenery, the Fayette State Park includes a historic townsite and museum on the iron smelting industry, which was active in Snail Shell Harbor during the 1800s.

TRIP HIGHLIGHTS: Excellent historical site, bird watching, scenic limestone bluffs.

TRIP RATING:

Intermediate: An 8-mile trip from Sac Bay to Snail Shell Harbor and back to the Fayette boat landing, or a 13-mile trip adding the loop around the Snake Island bird rookery.

TRIP DURATION: Part or full day.

NAVIGATION AIDS: NOAA chart 14908, USGS: *Fayette* (7.5 minute).

CAUTIONS: Possible clapotis off the cliffs, some steep rock or cobble shoreline could make landing difficult in rough seas.

TRIP PLANNING: Although sheltered by both the Garden Peninsula and the Door Peninsula, winds from the southwest have the full 80-mile fetch from Green Bay. From Sac Bay to Sand Bay, with a strong southwest wind, landing in rough seas may not be possible because of the rocky coast and cliffs.

LAUNCH SITES:

Sac Bay County Park: From the turnoff for the picnic area and boat ramp continue south on Highway 183, which becomes County Road 483 south of Fayette for about 4 miles. Watch for a tiny sign for Sac Bay County Park and turn right on County Road 438. Follow the signs to the small county park and beach. The park has outhouses but no potable water.

Fayette boat ramp: From Garden Corners on Highway 2, turn south on Highway 183 and drive 17.5 miles. Watch for the state park turnoff. One mile past the state park turnoff watch for a small sign for a picnic area and turn right. The boat ramp is located just north of the swimming beach on the south edge of the park. Potable water and bath-rooms are available in the campground just north of the boat ramp (**N 45° 42.55' W 086° 40.05'**).

START: From the **Sac Bay County Park (N 45° 39.38' W 086° 42.22')**, head west along the park's sandy shores, then around the point and north up the coast.

MILE 2.0: As you head north up the coast, the cobble and rock coastline rises up into limestone bluffs.

MILES 2.5 TO 4.0: You pass beautiful limestone cliffs that rise 100 to 150 feet from the water. Small sea caves and huge slabs of rock perch along the shore. Near Mile 4.0 there is a dock and old machinery from an old quarry.

MILE 4.5: At about Mile 4.5 you come to an old resort with a private breakwall and harbor. The resort and harbor is privately owned, so you should only use the harbor in an emergency. Above the resort is a high cliff and limestone rock outcrop called **Burnt Bluff**.

MILES 5.0 TO 6.0: From Mile 5.0 to Mile 6.0, the shoreline changes from cliffs to cobbles and then becomes a gravel beach.

MILE 7.5: From Mile 6.0 to Mile 7.5, the shore of **Sand Bay** becomes a fine sand beach. You pass the swimming beach, then reach the boat ramp and take-out point. You can end the trip here or continue on to the Fayette State Park and Snake Island, then back to the boat ramp.

MILE 8.0: About 0.5 mile past the boat ramp, you pass red buoy 2, marking the entrance of **Snail Shell Harbor**. Paddling into the harbor, you see the old iron works and the numerous restored buildings of the reconstructed townsite. On the northeast side of the harbor are high limestone bluffs.

MILE 9.5: At Mile 9.5 you come to a low gravel and cobblestone island about 0.5 mile offshore called **Snake Island**. This island is a gull and cormorant rookery, having large numbers of birds. You can circle the island for some good bird watching, but keep far enough offshore to keep from disturbing the nesting birds.

MILE 12.0: Rounding the island and heading south to return to the boat ramp you complete the trip at about Mile 12.0.

Sac Bay to Fayette State Park

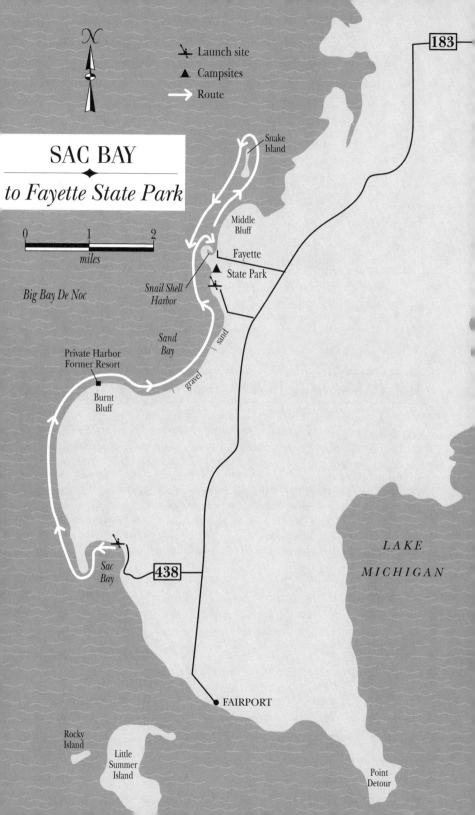

N

Launch site
Campsites
Route

SAC BAY
to Fayette State Park

0   1   2
miles

Big Bay De Noc

183

Snake Island

Middle Bluff

Fayette
State Park

Snail Shell Harbor

Sand Bay

sand

gravel

Private Harbor Former Resort

Burnt Bluff

438

Sac Bay

LAKE MICHIGAN

FAIRPORT

Rocky Island

Little Summer Island

Point Detour

Fayette Historical Townsite

In 1867 Fayette Brown, the manager of the Jackson Iron Company, arrived at Snail Shell Harbor, a fine deep-water harbor. Without the massive bulk freighters of today, the shipping costs of raw ore by barge and rail was substantial. Recognizing the potential of smelting iron at Snail Shell Harbor and then shipping the finished iron pigs, the Jackson Iron Company constructed a smelting facility at Fayette. Iron ore was shipped by rail to Escanaba, then shipped by barge to the harbor. Using charcoal from local timber and limestone from the cliffs, the Fayette townsite was a busy smelting and shipping center until the furnaces were finally shut down in 1891.

Where to Eat & Where to Stay

RESTAURANTS Just south of the boat ramp launch site is **Sherry's Port Bar and Restaurant** (906–644–2545). There are also a few restaurants in Garden just north of Fayette. Within an hour's drive there are numerous dining options in Escanaba or Manistique. **LODGING** Lodging options are limited on the Garden Peninsula. One option is **Summer House Bed and Breakfast** in Garden, Michigan (906–644–2457). There are numerous lodging options available in Escanaba or Manistique. More information is available at the **Upper Peninsula Travel Planner** (800–562–7134). **CAMPING** The **Fayette State Park** has eighty campsites. For information call (906) 644–2603. There is also camping available at a state forest campground 4 miles north of the state park.

Route 33:

▬ ▬ ▬ ▬ ▬ ▬ ▬ ▬ ▬ ▬ ▬ ▬ ▬ ▬ ▬ ▬ ▬ ➤

Wilderness State Park:
Waugoshance Point

The long narrow Waugoshance Point and the chain of small rock and gravel islands at its tip reach 7 miles west into Lake Michigan. The point and the islands consist of low rock and gravel beaches covered with a mixed ever-green and hardwood boreal forest. The islands are sur-rounded by a large shoal, and with even small changes in the water level, the shoreline changes and small islands appear and disappear. Part of the charm of this area is that you can visit year after year, and it will never look exactly the same. The Wilderness State Park is home to a variety of wildlife and interesting plant life including all of the wild orchids native to Michigan. The miles of gravel and rock beach and the many small islands are an ideal habitat for gulls and wading shore birds, including the endangered piping plover.

TRIP HIGHLIGHTS: Excellent bird watching, countless small shoals and islands to explore, an unusual abandoned lighthouse.

TRIP RATING:
Beginner: 4 miles round-trip to the tip of Waugoshance Point and back.
Intermediate: 9 miles round-trip to Crane Island and back.
Advanced: Paddle to Crane Island, around the offshore abandoned lighthouse, then back: 12 miles round-trip.

TRIP DURATION: Part or full day.

NAVIGATION AIDS: NOAA chart 14911, USGS: *Big Stone Bay, Waugoshance Island*, state park visitors map.

CAUTIONS: Shoals and shallow boulders even far offshore; the shoal surrounding the offshore abandoned lighthouse can be very rough, even when calm near shore.

TRIP PLANNING: Small boulders and shoals are everywhere so bring a boat you don't mind scratching and some repair tape. Winds from a northerly direction combined with the shoals and boulders can make for rough conditions; paddle on calm days or on days with a southerly wind. Check with the state park for sensitive nesting areas, such as the piping plover nesting beaches, so you can avoid them.

LAUNCH SITE:

Wilderness State Park is located on Wilderness Park Drive, 9 miles west of Mackinaw City. Take County Road 81 west, then follow the signs to the park. A state park registration sticker is required. The fee: $4.00 per day or $20.00 for an annual permit. Once you are in the park, follow the park drive road west to a gravel road marked SCENIC DRIVE. The best put in is the second to last lot at the western end of the drive. There are no toilet facilities or potable water at the parking lot so use facilities at the state park campground.

DIRECTIONS

START: You put in at a **sand and gravel beach (N 45° 45.50' W 084° 58.13')**, then head west along the shore of **Waugoshance Point.**

MILE 1.75: After about 1.75 miles of paddling, you come to the end of Waugoshance Point and can paddle on to **Temperance Island.** At high lake levels the island may actually break out into several smaller islands,

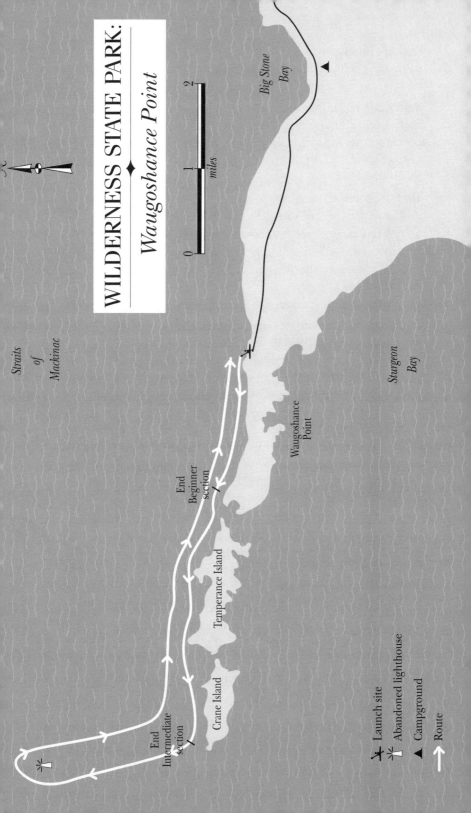

WILDERNESS STATE PARK:
Waugoshance Point

Straits
of
Mackinac

Big Stone
Bay

Sturgeon
Bay

Waugoshance
Point

End
Beginner
section

End
Intermediate
section

Temperance Island

Crane Island

0   1   2
miles

⌖ Launch site
✦ Abandoned lighthouse
▲ Campground
↑ Route

so don't be surprised if the shoreline does not appear as drawn on the route map. The beginner route ends here; simply retrace your route back.

MILES 2.0 TO 3.5: Pass the shores of Temperance Island. This is a low rock and gravel island covered with a mixed evergreen and hardwood boreal forest. Watch for shore birds and avoid the sensitive nesting areas noted by the park to protect the piping plover and other endangered species.

MILES 3.5 TO 4.5: You paddle along the shores of **Crane Island**, which is similar to Temperance Island in shoreline and forest cover. This island may also become several smaller islands when lake levels are up, so don't be surprised if it does not appear as shown on your map or chart. The end of Crane Island is the end of the intermediate route; simply retrace your route back.

MILE 6.5: If weather permits and you have advanced paddling skills, you can make the 2.0-mile crossing north to the crib work and **abandoned lighthouse (N 45° 47.28' W 085° 05.48')**. This haunted old relic of a lighthouse was put into service in 1851 and features a "birdcage" style lantern; it was the first crib mounted light on the Great Lakes. It was rebuilt in 1867 and again in 1896, when the support structure was converted to massive limestone blocks. The light was kept in service until 1912. It was abandoned after modern lights were placed farther offshore. *Caution:* Conditions may be calm along the point and islands, especially with a southwest wind, but very rough 2 miles offshore on the shoal surrounding the lighthouse. This is the end of the advanced route. Retrace your route back.

Where to Eat & Where to Stay

RESTAURANTS   Mackinaw City is a resort town with many dining options. For information call the Mackinaw Area Tourist Bureau (800–666–0160). **LODGING**   Mackinaw City also has numerous motels and lodging options. Prices can be a bit high during the height of the tourist season. For information call the Mackinaw Area Tourist Bureau (800–666–0160). **CAMPING** Camping at the **Wilderness State Park** is your best option—with 250 campsites available in all. Phone (800) 44–PARKS for state park reservations, or call (616) 436–5381 for Wilderness State Park information.

Route 34:

━━ ━━ ━━ ━━ ━━ ━━ ━━ ━━ ━━ ━━ ━━ ➤

Beaver Island

Beaver Island and the nearby islands of High Island and
Garden Island are fascinating areas to explore by
kayak. Beaver Island, the largest island, has 350 year-
round residents, two historic lighthouses, beautiful sand
beaches, and a fascinating history that includes the self-
declared "King of Beaver Island." Much of the main island is
private land, but there are still large tracts of wild state lands
to explore. High Island and Garden Island have almost no
private land holdings and offer a true wilderness camping
experience. The smaller islands have abundant wildlife,
including many gulls and shore birds, and a significant population of large but harmless water snakes.

TRIP HIGHLIGHTS: Lovely sand bays and beaches, bird watching,
scenic lighthouses, unusual history.

TRIP RATING:
Intermediate: A 30-mile circumnavigation of Beaver Island.
Advanced: Paddlers with advanced skills can also add sidetrips to
High Island and Garden Island. The sidetrips and Beaver Island
circumnavigation total about 50 miles.

TRIP DURATION: Multiday; a full week for the tour of all three
islands.

NAVIGATION AIDS: NOAA chart 14911, USGS: *Beaver Island*
(45085-E1).

CAUTIONS: Potential for large seas with up to 300 miles of fetch with
south-southwest winds; shoals surround the islands making breaking waves likely even far off shore.

TRIP PLANNING: Plan to be at the ferry dock at least one hour in advance of the departure time. During the summer months of June, July, and August, there are two trips a day, with three trips a day on Friday and Saturday. Plan on leaving with the earlier 8:00 A.M. departure from Charlevoix to allow for more paddling time on your first day. Round-trip fare for a passenger is $31, and an additional $40 for round-trip transport of a kayak. Long-term parking is available in the summer months for $5.00 per week. The 32-mile crossing takes the ferry about two hours to St. James Harbor. For ferry information call (888) 446–4095. Camping is allowed on any of the state lands (see route map), but much of the land on the north end of Beaver Island is private. With the exception of one small private land holding on Garden Island, most of Garden and High Islands are available for wilderness camping. To wilderness camp on state land, you are supposed to get a free permit from the DNR, but few people do and enforcement is rare.

LAUNCH SITE: The ferry dock is located in the Round Lake Yacht Basin, just southeast of the lift bridge in downtown Charlevoix. At the Beaver Island end, the ferry dock is located in the northeast corner of St. James Harbor at the north end of the island.

DIRECTIONS

START: The ferry arrives in **St. James Harbor** about two hours after the departure time. Camping is available about 1.5 miles from the town of St. James on the north end of the island, but the 100-foot high sand bluffs prevent easy access from the water. Either settle into a motel for the night and head to the Shamrock Bar (the town center for social life) or head south down the coast to get to state lands.

MILE 6.5: As you head south down the coast, you paddle along the low sand beaches of **Sand Bay**, which is composed almost entirely of private land. At about Mile 6.5 you come to **Beaver Island State Forest**, which offers one possibility for staying overnight.

MILE 11.0: At approximately Mile 11.0, you come to **Cables Bay**, where there is a park, picnic area, and public swimming beach, a good place to land and take a break. Unfortunately no overnight camping is allowed.

MILE 14.0: At the south end of the island, you find the **Beaver Head**

Garden
Island

Jensen Harbor

Sturgeon Bay

Hog
Island

Garden Island Harbor

Manitou Bay
Northcutt Bay

St. James
Lighthouse

ST. JAMES

High Island Bay

*St. James
Harbor*

High
Island

Beaver
Island

*Sand
Bay*

▲ Beaver Island
State Forest

Park and
Public Beach

Beaver Head
Lighthouse

*Cables
Bay*

N

⊁ Launch site
☀ Lighthouse
▲ Campground
☐ State lands
→ Route

BEAVER
ISLAND

0   1   2   3
miles

Lighthouse. The first lighthouse was constructed in 1852, but the tower was rebuilt in 1858. The lighthouse keeper's quarters were added in 1866, and the lighthouse operated until it was decommissioned in 1962. The Charlevoix Public School District now owns the land and buildings and uses the site for environmental education.

MILES 16.0 TO 17.5: On the southwest tip of the island, there is a stretch of about 1.75 miles of coast that is state land. You may be able to find a suitable campsite for wilderness camping in this area or continue up the coast to High Island, where there is fine camping on the east side.

MILE 25.0: Continue north along the coast and take note that much of the shoreline is private land. At about Mile 25 advanced paddlers can make a 3.75-mile crossing to the east side of High Island. Intermediate paddlers will want to continue around the island for another 5.0 miles to complete the circumnavigation of the island at St. James Harbor.

MILE 29.0: In **High Island Bay** there is a large sand beach with deep water just offshore. This is a great place to camp. Two cabins are near the beach: one is dilapidated; the other is used by DNR researchers visiting the island. Neither should be used by kayakers. The point on the east end of the bay is a gull rookery, which is not open to the public during summer months.

MILES 33.0 TO 35.0: The west side of High Island has a beautiful coast with large dune bluffs up to 300 feet high. The climb up the bluffs is brutal, but well worth the work because it gives you an unmatched view of all the islands.

MILES 35.0 TO 37.0: Continue around the island, heading east along the north coast. Keep a reasonable distance offshore when passing the point where the gull rookery is located, then head east for the 3.75-mile crossing back to Beaver Island.

MILES 41.0 TO 43.0: After reaching the coast of Beaver Island, turn north and head up the west side of the island to its northwest tip. Heading northeast advanced paddlers can make the 3.5-mile crossing to **Garden Island Harbor**.

MILE 46.5: Please make note of the private land holding within Garden Island Harbor and respect the rights of this property owner. The inner harbor, called **Indian Harbor**, has some relatively good campsites, and there is a cabin nearby that should be used only in emergencies. About

0.5 mile inland from the harbor is a Native American burial ground with above-ground spirit houses. Please respect this sacred area and avoid it if you pass by on one of the trails.

MILE 48.0: Heading southeast along the southern end of the island, you can visit two small sand bays, **Northcutt Bay** and **Manitou Bay**. These are also good potential campsites. From the south end of the island, you can make the 1.5-mile crossing to the northeast tip of Beaver Island.

MILES 49.5 TO 50.5: After reaching the north coast of Beaver Island, head south, then west around **Whiskey Point** and to the St. James Harbor ferry dock. If you have time you can visit the St. James lighthouse, constructed in 1870.

The Mormon King of Beaver Island

James Strang and his Mormon followers arrived on Beaver Island in 1848. The community prospered and grew to a population of over 2,000 at a time when most of northwest Michigan was populated by a few lawless trappers and fishermen living along the coast. Strang had five wives but was very intolerant of such Gentile practices as drinking tea and liquor and the use of tobacco. Conflicts between Gentiles and the island Mormons were frequent. James Strang also declared himself king and claimed sovereignty over Beaver Island. In 1851, accused of piracy and high treason, Strang was brought by U.S. officials to Detroit for trial, but he was acquitted of all charges. In spite of his legal triumph, Strang continued to make enemies, and in 1856 he was ambushed and shot dead outside his home on Beaver Island. The Mormon community did not survive the death of their leader, and all that remains today is a museum of the Mormon print shop.

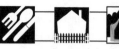

RESTAURANTS   The **Shamrock Bar** (616–448–2278) in St. James is the center of social life on Beaver Island, offering breakfast, lunch, and dinner, in addition to spirits. For more information call the Beaver Island Chamber of Commerce (616–448–2505). **LODGING**   Motels and bed-and-breakfasts are available in the town of St. James. For more information call the Beaver Island Chamber of Commerce (616–448–2505). **CAMPING**   There is a city campground 1.5 miles from St. James, but access from the water is difficult due to high sand bluffs. There is also a state forest campground about 7 miles south of the town of St. James that does have access from the water. Wilderness camping is allowed on state land.

Route 35:

━━ ━━ ━━ ━━ ━━ ━━ ━━ ━━ ━━ ━━ ━━ ➤

Old Mission Peninsula Lighthouse Park

The Old Mission Peninsula divides Grand Traverse Bay into east and west arms. At the northern tip of the peninsula is a township park with great view of Grand Traverse Bay, and a historic lighthouse. The lighthouse began service in 1870 and rests almost exactly on the forty-fifth parallel, halfway between the pole and the equator. The light is no longer in service and has been replaced by a modern lighthouse, located on a concrete pylon about 1.5 miles north of the tip of the peninsula.

TRIP HIGHLIGHTS: A historic lighthouse, township park, nice beaches.

TRIP RATING:
Beginner–Intermediate: No specific route is given—this is just a great area to explore with various out-and-back trips.

TRIP DURATION: Easy day trip.

NAVIGATION AIDS: NOAA chart 14913, USGS: *Grand Traverse County* at 1:100,000.

TRIP PLANNING: Even the tip of the peninsula is well sheltered within Grand Traverse Bay from all but northerly winds. The water is very shallow far offshore, with some cobbles and rounded boulders mixed in with the sand

The Old Mission Peninsula

Just north of Traverse City Michigan, the Old Mission Peninsula extends over 15 miles out into Grand Traverse Bay. The waters of Grand Traverse Bay provide this long, narrow peninsula with the ideal climate for growing fruit trees; much of the area is planted in cherries and apples. Over half of the nation's tart cherries come from the Traverse City area. This is also wine country with many vineyards and four wineries on the peninsula, producing some excellent chardonnay and Riesling wines. There is no reason to dread the drive to the launch sites—your drive on M37 includes beautiful views of orchards and west and east Grand Traverse Bay as you climb up a high ridge in the middle of the peninsula. Best of all each of the four wineries (Chateau Grand Traverse, Bowers Harbor Vineyard, Chateau Chantal, Peninsula Cellars) offers free wine tasting, so pick a designated driver before you start out. In addition to grand views of maple/beech forests, orchards, and vineyards, Grand Traverse Bay offers lovely sand beaches in a protected bay for novice paddlers.

bottom. Take care not to run onto a boulder, and avoid this area when winds and seas are coming from the north.

LAUNCH SITE: Directions could not be any easier. Simply head north on Highway 37 from Traverse City, following it up the peninsula about 17 miles until you run out of road—at the park. Free parking is available at the park. The beach (**N 44° 59.52' W 085° 28.80'**) is about 200 feet from the parking lot, and it is an easy carry over level ground.

TRIP DESCRIPTION: No specific route is described. This is really just a great place to put in your kayak or just wade and play at the beach. Outside of the lighthouse park, most if not

N

Mission Point Light

Grand Traverse Bay

OLD MISSION PENINSULA
Lighthouse Park

0   1   2   3
miles

⚓ Launch site
🗼 Lighthouse
■ Winery

37

OLD
MISSION   swimming
beach
*Old Mission
Harbor*

Old Mission Rd.   ■ Peninsula Cellars

37

Chateau
Chantal
■

*West
Arm*

*East
Arm*

Bowers Harbor
Vineyard

*Bowers
Harbor*   ■

The Cherry Festival

Years ago this festival started out as a small celebration of the cherry harvest. Now it has become a huge corporate entity that can either be great fun or your worst nightmare. If your goal is to watch the air show, with the Navy's Blue Angels, and the fireworks, parades, and other events, then you and the 500,000 other people who invade this little town of less than 16,000 people are in for a treat. If your goal is to enjoy a quiet weekend at the beach or on a nice kayak trip, do not even think of visiting this area for the two weeks that follow the fourth of July.

all of the waterfront land is privately owned so please respect property rights and do not land unless invited. Kayakers who insist on having a destination can shuttle a car to Bowers Harbor (see Rte. 36 for Launch Site information) for an 8-mile paddle down the west side of the peninsula, or you can head down the east side for 3 miles to the swimming beach at Old Mission. I prefer to just do short out-and-back trips and enjoy the scenery, which is best at the tip of the peninsula. Advanced paddlers can also head out about 1.5 miles offshore to check out the more modern Mission Point Light, which is not nearly as scenic or historic as the old lighthouse on shore.

Where to Eat & Where to Stay

For information on restaurants, lodging, and camping, see Route 36: Bowers Harbor to Power Island.

Old Mission Peninsula Lighthouse Park

Route 36:

▬ ▬ ▬ ▬ ▬ ▬ ▬ ▬ ▬ ▬ ▬ ▬ ▬ ▬ ▬ ▬ ▬ ➤

Bowers Harbor to Power Island

Power Island, also known as Marion or Ford Island, is a 200-acre island that is maintained as a park by Grand Traverse County. The island has a dock, swimming beach, hiking trails through a maple/beech forest, and a small islet on the northeast tip that has five campsites. Sheltered deep in the west arm of Grand Traverse Bay, this route provides a great day trip or overnight trip for beginner paddlers.

TRIP HIGHLIGHTS: Sand beaches and maple beech forests on a wild 200 acre island.

TRIP RATING:
Beginner: Easy 5-mile round-trip.

TRIP DURATION: Day trip or overnight trip.

NAVIGATION AIDS: NOAA chart 14913; USGS: *Grand Traverse County* at 1:100,000.

TRIP PLANNING: This is a very well-sheltered area except with northerly winds. If you plan to camp on the island overnight, you may want to reserve a campsite by calling the Grand Traverse Parks and Recreation Department (616) 922–4818. Camping fees are $15/night per campsite.

LAUNCH SITE: To get to the launch site, head north on Highway 37 about 5 miles out from the base of the peninsula. Follow the signs to Bowers Harbor, turning left on Seven Hills Road, then left again onto Peninsula Drive. The boat ramp is just off Peninsula Drive on Neah-ta-wanta Road.

Power Island & Bassett Island History

The island was privately owned in the 1800s and was named Marion Island in 1881, when the island was given to the owner's daughter, Marion. Many still call it Marion Island. On the northeast tip of the island is a small islet, Bassett Island, which is connected to Power Island at low water levels. In 1906 there was a 50-x-100-foot dance hall on Bassett Island, which was called the "haunted island" or the "island of the dead" because local lore told a story of a Native American woman who was decapitated for "misbehaving." From 1917 to 1944 Henry Ford owned the island, and many called it Ford Island. The most recent owner's last name was Power, and at his request he had the island's name changed to Power Island after his death in memory of the donation of the island to Grand Traverse County.

DIRECTIONS

START: You begin your trip at the **public boat ramp (N 44° 53.72' W 085° 31.47')**. Adequate parking and a porta-john toilet are available at the site. From the boat ramp head southwest to Power Island.

MILE 1.0: After about 1.0 mile you exit the shelter of **Bowers Harbor** and head into the west arm of Grand Traverse Bay. If you follow the north shore of the harbor rather than heading straight to the island, watch out for the shallow sand- and boulder bar that extends out from **Tucker Point.**

MILE 2.5: Crossing to the west side of **Power Island**, you come to a dock and sand **beach (N 44° 51.92' W 085° 34.27')** that is very popular with other boaters for day use. After exploring the island, you can retrace your path or camp overnight on **Bassett Island.**

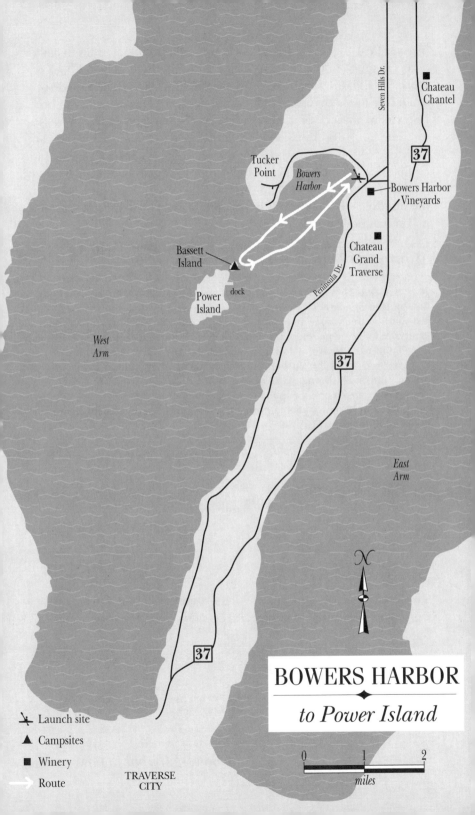

Chateau
Chantel

37

Seven Hills Dr.

Tucker
Point

*Bowers
Harbor*

Bowers Harbor
Vineyards

Bassett
Island

Chateau
Grand
Traverse

Power
Island

dock

Peninsula Dr.

West
Arm

37

East
Arm

N

⚓ Launch site

▲ Campsites

■ Winery

➜ Route

BOWERS HARBOR
◆
to Power Island

TRAVERSE
CITY

0   1   2

miles

Sidetrip: Near the Power Island dock, you will find hiking trails that allow access to much of the 200-acre island. North of the beach and dock is Bassett Island, the small islet connected to Power Island by a sandbar, when lake levels are low. Bassett Island has five campsites that can be reserved in advance or used on a first come, first serve basis. There is a full time ranger on the island in summer, and in fall or spring you can leave payment in the pay boxes at the registration board. Campsites are equipped with "raccoon poles" to keep your victuals out of the hands of masked raiders. We'd thought this was a bit of a joke, but judging from the hundreds of muddy foot prints on our kayaks, an army of raccoons had visited our camp in the night.

Where to Eat & Where to Stay

RESTAURANTS   The Boathouse (616–223–4030) is located at the Bowers Harbor marina. For fine dining the **Bowers Harbor Inn** (616–223–4222), just south of the harbor on Peninsula Drive, is a good choice. It's a bit formal and expensive for some paddlers; the adjacent **Bowery Bar and Grill** is more reasonably priced and has a less-formal dining atmosphere. On M37 just past the Seven Hills Road turnoff is **Mollys** (616–223–7200), a bar and restaurant with reasonably priced, informal dining. **LODGING & CAMPING**   The Traverse City area is a very popular tourist destination so there are many options for camping and lodging. For information call the Traverse City Visitors and Convention Bureau at (612) 947–1120.

Route 37:

▬ ▬ ▬ ▬ ▬ ▬ ▬ ▬ ▬ ▬ ▬ ▬ ▬ ▬ ▬ ▬ ▬ ➤

Empire Dune Bluffs to Glen Haven

T he protected park lands of the Sleeping Bear Dunes National Lakeshore include two large islands and approximately 30 miles of mainland lakeshore. Lovely sand beaches and huge coastal sand dunes make this a great area for sea kayakers. Some of the dune bluffs are well over 400 feet high and plunge down to the lake at alarmingly steep angles. Many of the older dunes just inland from the coast have been covered with trees, producing high, rolling hills carpeted with a lush maple/beech forest. Wilderness camping is not allowed along the mainland coast, but excellent day trips are available to kayakers. To the north the Manitou Islands offer exceptional paddling, as well with a rich history, coastal dunes, shipwrecks, and beautiful forests. Several campsites are located on the water, and wilderness camping is allowed on North Manitou, making the Manitou Islands an ideal place for multiday trips. The 7–8-mile crossing to the islands is not to be taken lightly, so we strongly recommend that people take the ferry from Leland, which services both North and South Manitou Islands.

The Empire Dune Bluff section offers novice paddlers a great short trip. The dune bluffs are very steep and rise about 200 feet above the lake. With luck you may get to watch hang gliders taking advantage of the updrafts that a west wind hitting the dune bluffs creates. With its west facing dune bluffs and a safe landing beach along the entire coast, this is also a good choice for a sunset paddle. The national lakeshore does not enforce any strong policy against nudity, and for this reason the beach about 1 mile north of Esch Road is a popular place for nude sunbathers. Most will discreetly cover up as you pass by, but if you are offended by nudity you may want to swing wide of shore for that beach area. Continuing north of the Empire City beach, the dune bluffs become even more spectacular, rising as high as 460 feet above the lakeshore.

Empire Dune Bluffs to Glen Haven

TRIP HIGHLIGHTS: Massive dune bluffs, good bird watching for hawks and eagles, scenic overlook for those willing to make the climb.

TRIP RATING:

Beginner: 7-mile round-trip from Esch Road to Empire Beach and back.

Intermediate: Esch Road to the Glen Haven Cannery, about 11 miles one way.

TRIP DURATION: Day trip or partial day trip.

NAVIGATION AIDS: NOAA chart 14912; USGS: *Crystal Lake* (44086-E1) at 1:100,000.

TRIP PLANNING: Although there are a few small rounded boulders and cobbles along the dune bluffs, most of the shore is a gentle sand beach that allows a safe surf landing. Always check the weather forecast; a west wind could create surf along this exposed coast.

LAUNCH SITES:

Esch Road/Otter Creek: Head south from Empire on Highway 22. The Esch Road turnoff is about 4 miles south of town. Turn right and head west to where the road dead-ends at the lake. Unload your boats at the end of the road, it is a 200-foot carry over sand to the water. There is some parking available on either side of Esch Road, but it can get very crowded in summer. Outhouse toilet facilities are available, but there is no potable water. GPS coordinates for Esch Beach are **N 44° 45.80' W 086° 04.52'**.

Empire City Beach: From the intersection of M 72 and Highway 22, follow the signs from the main street to the city beach. The beach has running water, changing rooms, and bathroom facilities. Ample parking is available. Empire Beach GPS coordinates are **N 44° 48.78' W 086° 04.10'**.

Glen Haven/The Old Cannery: From Empire head north on Highway 22 until you reach Highway 109. Go left on 109 and head north. Follow the signs to Glen Haven by heading north on the paved road where 109 turns east. The old cannery is a red building with an old fishing tug on display on shore next to the building. This popular day-use beach has porta-johns and parking, but no potable water. The beach is located at GPS coordinates **N 44° 54.27' W 086° 01.57'**.

Empire Dune Bluffs to Glen Haven

The Legend of the Sleeping Bear

Native American lore tells of a great forest fire long ago in what is now called Wisconsin. To escape the fire a mother bear and her two cubs tried to swim across Lake Michigan. Nearing the shore the exhausted cubs lagged behind. The mother bear climbed to the top of a bluff to watch and wait for her cubs. The cubs never made it to shore, and their mother can still be seen today as a solitary dune covered with trees—the "Sleeping Bear." Her cubs became the islands of North and South Manitou a few miles offshore.

DIRECTIONS

START: From **Esch Road** the dune bluffs begin less than 1.0 mile to the north. Heading north along the shore, you pass a low sand beach that is very popular for day use by swimmers.

MILE 0.5: About 0.5 mile north of Esch Road, the dune bluffs begin. A west wind hitting the steep dune bluffs creates an updraft so keep your eyes open for hawks, eagles, or hang gliders catching a ride on the wind.

MILE 1.0: About 1.0 mile north of Esch Road, the beach narrows and dune bluffs rise even more steeply from the lake. You are now in the heart of naturist territory, so stand well offshore if you are offended by nudity. If you are not, then this could be your big chance to kayak naked!

MILE 2.0: At Mile 2.0 you reach the end of a point where the beach is very narrow. Here the Empire Dune Bluffs reach their maximum height. Watch out for a few small rounded boulders and cobbles as you land on the beach. This is a great place to stop and enjoy the view of the **Empire Bluffs** to the south and the Sleeping Bear Dune Bluffs to the north.

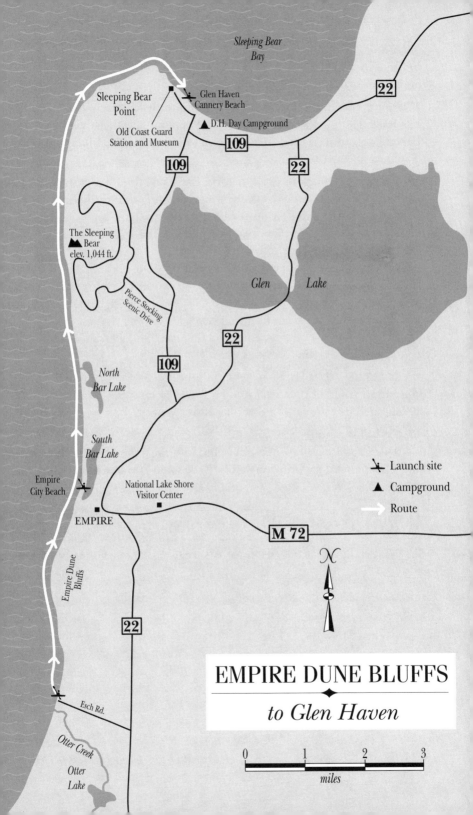

Sleeping Bear
Bay

Sleeping Bear
Point

Glen Haven
Cannery Beach

Old Coast Guard
Station and Museum

▲ D.H. Day Campground

109

109

22

The Sleeping
Bear
elev. 1,044 ft.

Pierce Stocking
Scenic Drive

Glen   Lake

22

North
Bar Lake

109

South
Bar Lake

Empire
City Beach

National Lake Shore
Visitor Center

⤬ Launch site

▲ Campground

⟶ Route

EMPIRE

M 72

Empire Dune
Bluffs

𝒩

22

Esch Rd.

Otter Creek

Otter
Lake

EMPIRE DUNE BLUFFS

◆

to Glen Haven

0   1   2   3

miles

MILE 3.5: After Mile 2.0 the dune bluffs diminish until you reach the low sand beach at Empire. This is a very popular beach for swimming and day use.

MILE 5.5: About 2 miles north of the **Empire Beach**, you come to **North Bar Lake**. Here there is a small stream that connects the small lake with Lake Michigan. It is often blocked by a sandbar. This is also a popular beach for day use by swimmers.

MILE 6.5: As you head north of North Bar Lake, the huge dune bluffs begin to appear. At Mile 6.5 there is a steep, bare sand dune bluff that rises more than 400 feet from the lake. At its top there is an observation platform that is part of **Pierce Stocking Scenic Drive**. The view from the top is excellent but the climb from the bottom is a real killer. Unless you are very fit, take the easy way out and return by car to the scenic drive later. *Caution:* Not only can climbing the steep sand be a physical challenge, but there is also some chance of a landslide. The big slides happen about once every one hundred years, but on my last visit a mass of sand big enough to bury an entire subdivision had fallen off Pyramid Point into the lake the previous week.

MILES 6.5 TO 10.0: The spectacular high dune bluffs continue for a few miles then gradually taper back to become the low dune bluffs—10-to-20-feet high—at the end of **Sleeping Bear Point**.

MILE 11.0: Rounding Sleeping Bear Point and entering Sleeping Bear Bay, you pass along low dune bluffs and sand beaches. Passing the **former Coast Guard station**, you come to the **Glen Haven Cannery Beach (N 44° 54.27' W 086° 01.57')**.

Where to Eat & Where to Stay

See Route 39: North and South Manitou Islands for information on restaurants, lodging, and camping.

Empire Dune Bluffs to Glen Haven

Route 38:

━━ ━━ ━━ ━━ ━━ ━━ ━━ ━━ ━━ ━━ ━━ ━━ ⟶

Pyramid Point: Good Harbor Bay to Glen Haven

The dunes at Pyramid Point are spectacular, rising more than 400 feet from the lake. For those who are fit and foolish enough to climb the steep sand bluff, there is a wonderful view of the dune bluffs and North and South Manitou Islands. Much of the shoreline on either side of Pyramid Point is privately owned so please respect the rights of property owners and do not land without permission.

TRIP HIGHLIGHTS: Massive dune bluffs, good bird watching for hawks and eagles, scenic overlook for those willing to make the dune climb.

TRIP RATING:
Intermediate: An 11-mile one-way trip along a sand beach coast.

TRIP DURATION: Day trip.

NAVIGATION AIDS: NOAA chart 14912; USGS: *Glen Arbor* (7.5 minute).

TRIP PLANNING: The coast consists almost entirely of sand beach, and North and South Manitou provide some shelter from large seas coming from the northwest. Winds from the southwest or from the north can make for very rough seas off Pyramid Point. Check the weather before departing, and plan on spending most of the time in your kayak because of private land holdings east and west of pyramid point.

LAUNCH SITES:
Glen Haven Cannery Beach: See the Glen Haven Cannery trip description, Route 37.

Good Harbor Bay Beach: From Glen Haven follow Highway 109 east, then take Highway 22 north. After about 6 miles on Highway 22, watch for County Road 669 (Bohemian Road). Turn left and head north on Bohemian Road until it dead-ends at the beach. It is about a 200-foot carry from the road to the beach. There is no parking lot so parking is limited to either side of the road. There are no bathroom facilities at this launch site.

DIRECTIONS

START: The **launch site** beach is a popular site for day use by swimmers **(N 44° 56.37' W 085° 52.35')**. Try to avoid swimmers as you head out into the lake and west along the shore.

MILE 1.0: As **Good Harbor Bay** gives way to Pyramid Point, you head north along the coast, passing sand beaches with a low dune bluff edge perhaps 10 to 20 feet high. Most of the land is private so do not land without permission from the land owners.

MILE 3.0: After about 3.0 miles of beach, low sand dunes, and private land holdings, the **Pyramid Point** bluffs begin. Huge dune bluffs continue for about 1.0 mile before tapering down to a lower dune-bluff shoreline or older forest-covered dunes. Here is where you can attempt to climb up the 400 foot or higher dune bluffs, which rise up at about a 45° angle. Those who survive this outrageous climb are rewarded with a fantastic view of the lake and North and South Manitou Islands. *Caution:* Not only can climbing the steep sand be physically trying, there is a chance of a sand slide. A large one occurred here in 1998.

MILES 4.5 TO 7.0: After Mile 4.5 the steep, bare sand bluffs disappear, and the shore consists of wooded dune bluffs that rise about 100 feet above the lake. The shore changes from sand to cobbles and small boulders. As you continue farther west from Pyramid Point, much of the land is private with no public access. After Mile 7.0 the sand beach shore begins again with low wooded dunes behind the beach.

MILE 8.0: You pass the **Homestead Resort**, featuring private beaches and an entire mountain range of condominiums. Looking up the hill, you can see ski slopes and chairlifts.

MILE 11.0: From Mile 8.0 to Mile 11.0, you paddle along the low dune

Pyramid Point

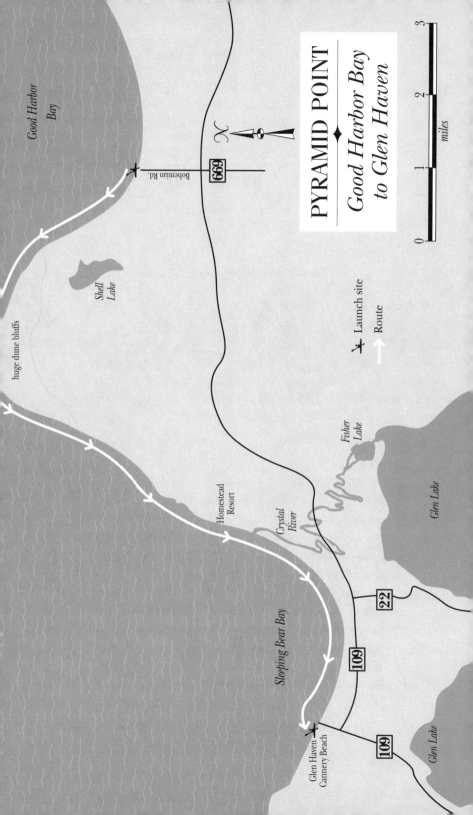

PYRAMID POINT

Good Harbor Bay to Glen Haven

Launch site
Route

miles
0 1 2 3

Good Harbor Bay

Bohemian Rd.

669

Shell Lake

huge dune bluffs

Homestead Resort

Crystal River

Fisher Lake

Glen Lake

Sleeping Bear Bay

22

109

109

Glen Haven Cannery Beach

Glen Lake

bluffs and lovely sand beaches of **Sleeping Bear Bay**. Most of this land is privately held so do not land without permission. At Mile 11.0 you reach **Glen Haven Cannery Beach** where there is public access. End your trip here. *Caution:* There are old submerged dock pilings just off the old cannery that you could hit with your kayak. Small plastic hazard buoys mark the general location of the old dock.

Where to Eat & Where to Stay

See Route 39: North and South Manitou Islands for information on restaurants, lodging, and camping.

Glen Haven Coast Guard Station Museum

Just west of the Glen Haven Cannery Beach is a historical Coast Guard station from the early 1890s. The original lifesaving station was located on Sleeping Bear Point from 1901 to 1930, until shifting dune sands buried the facility. It was moved to its current location in 1931 and operated until 1942. The facility is now operated as a museum, displaying the history of the early lifesaving stations, which used teams of men in open rowboats and various devices like the Lyle gun and breeches buoy to rescue shipwreck victims. Between 1835 and 1960 over fifty ships were shipwrecked in the Manitou Passage area. In 1988 the area was designated as an underwater preserve, which is popular with SCUBA divers who enjoy exploring the many shipwrecks along the coast and near the Manitou Islands.

Route 39:

━━ ━ ━━ ━ ━━ ━ ━━ ━ ━━ ━ ━━ ━ ━━ ━ ━━ ━ ━━ ━ ━━ ➤

North & South Manitou Islands

A crossing of about 8 miles from Sleeping Bear Point across the Manitou Passage takes you to South Manitou Island. The bay at the east end of South Manitou is the only natural deep-water harbor on the east side of Lake Michigan between Chicago and the Straits of Mackinac. In the late 1800s and early 1900s, the island was a refuge for ships during storms and a place to pick up firewood to fuel steam engines. A lighthouse established in 1871 stands 100 feet above the harbor, and the lifesaving station established in 1901 is now used as a ranger station for the park. In addition to the island's maritime history, it offers lovely sand beaches, large dune bluffs on the west side, a stand of virgin old-growth cedars, and large steel-hulled shipwreck that is visible above water. The island has a series of old roads and hiking trails that allow you to explore the island by hiking as well as by kayak.

TRIP HIGHLIGHTS: A historic lighthouse, a large modern shipwreck, abandoned farms, old-growth cedar trees, high dune bluffs, and excellent bird watching for gulls and shore birds.

TRIP RATING:
Beginner/Intermediate: A 12-mile trip around South Manitou.
Advanced: 28 miles round-trip—an 8-mile crossing, plus 12 miles around South Manitou.

TRIP DURATION: Overnight or multiday trip.

NAVIGATION AIDS: NOAA chart 14912, USGS: *South Manitou* (7.5 minute), USGS: *North Manitou* (7.5 minute).

TRIP PLANNING: Only advanced sea kayakers should consider making the 8-mile crossing from the Cannery Beach in Glen Haven to the harbor on the east side of the island. With a southwest wind the Manitou Passage can get very rough. Over fifty ships have found their graves here, so if you have any doubts, it is prudent to take the ferry from Leland. The ferry to South Manitou leaves at 10:00 A.M. daily. The cost is $20 per passenger round-trip with an additional $20 for bringing a kayak. The ferry to North Manitou leaves every day of the week except Tuesdays and Thursdays. For information on the ferry call Manitou Island Transit at (616) 256–9061. If you plan to stay overnight, make reservations for one of the three designated campsites on South Manitou; camping permits are $5.00 per night, backcountry camping outside of the designated sites is not allowed. On North Manitou a designated campsite is available at the island dock, and wilderness backcountry camping is allowed. Camping permits for either are $5.00 per night.

DIRECTIONS

START: Those arriving by ferry will reach the dock at South Manitou at about 11:30 A.M. For those advanced kayakers who paddled across the Manitou Passage from Glen Haven, they will already have logged 8 miles, but we will call the dock the starting point for description purposes. *Caution:* For those who make the crossing, be aware that almost all shipping passes through the Manitou Passage, watch out for freighters. From **South Manitou dock (N 45° 00.72' W 086° 05.68')** head south, then west to circle the island clockwise.

MILE 0.25: As you round the point and leave the harbor, you pass the historic lighthouse, a large brick tower 100 feet high. During the summer tours of the lighthouse are available. The first lighthouse was built here in 1839, with the larger, more elaborate lighthouse that stands today completed in 1871 and under operation until 1958.

MILE 1.0: Paddling along the south shore of the island for about 1 mile, you come to the **Weather Station campsites (N 45° 00.10' W 086° 06.38')**. The camp has group sites ($20.00/night) and individual campsites ($5.00/night), outhouses, and potable water. The sites are not visible

NORTH & SOUTH MANITOU ISLANDS

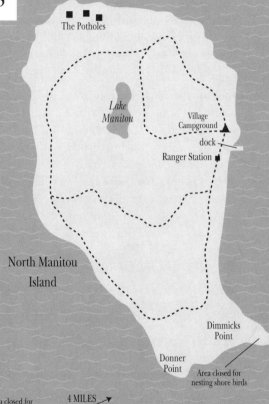

0   1   2   3
miles

Launch site
Lighthouse
Campsite
---- Hiking trail
→ Route

The Potholes

Lake Manitou

Village Campground

dock

Ranger Station

North Manitou Island

Dimmicks Point

Donner Point

Area closed for nesting shore birds

South Manitou Island

Area closed for nesting shore birds

4 MILES →

The Popple Campground

dunes

Gull Point

cemetery

perched sand dunes

Farms

Bay Campground

Florence Lake

Ranger Station and dock

old cedars

Weather Station Campground

risco Morazan *hipwreck*

8 MILES FROM GLEN HAVEN

from the water, and you have to climb a low dune bluff and hike from 300 to 500 feet inland to reach the campsites. Access trails are marked by wooden posts on the beach marked with blue tips.

MILE 2.5: We often think of shipwrecks on the Great Lakes as a thing of the past. Surely with radar, steel-hulled ships, and modern navigation, shipwrecks are avoidable. On November 29, 1960, the 246-foot-long Liberian-registered *Francisco Morazan* ran aground in 15 feet of water on the south end of the island. Three Coast Guard cutters and one helicopter successfully rescued all hands. The wreck—much of it above water—is visible just off shore (**N 44° 59.80' W 086° 08.52'**). Please do not climb on the wreck because it is being used as a gull and cormorant rookery.

MILE 3.0: From 1840 to 1917 most of the island timber was cut for use as fuel for the wood-burning steamships that would refuel at South Manitou. Somehow one area of virgin white cedar remains. Although not visible from shore, if you are willing to climb a dune bluff and hack your way through some brush, you can access the well-worn trails that lead you to the cedars. An arm of the trail that comes closest to the water comes near shore by the wreck of the *Francisco Morazan*. Some of the cedars are over 500 years old, and one tree is about 80 feet tall and over 17 feet in circumference.

MILES 3.5 TO 6.0: After you round the corner and head north along the west side of the island, you pass huge perched sand dunes. The dune bluffs that rise up from the lake are as high as 400 feet in places and are similar to those on the mainland, along the scenic drive.

MILE 7.0: As you leave the dunes and pass along the north side of the island, paddle close to shore and watch for a ladder made of cables and 4 x 4 lumber. This marks the **Popple Campground (N 45° 02.82' W 086° 06.90').** Although you still need to carry your equipment 300–500 feet to get to a campsite from the water, the campsites are quite nice and spaced far apart for privacy. The site has outhouses and potable water.

MILE 9.0: Paddling along the north side of the island, you come to the easternmost point of the island, **Gull Point**. The tip of Gull Point is a sensitive bird-nesting area that is closed to the public to protect endangered gull and shore bird species, such as the piping plover. Keep offshore at a distance so as to not disturb the birds; bring a long lens for your camera or binoculars if you want to do some bird watching.

MILE 11.0: After rounding Gull Point and heading into the east bay, you come to the **Bay Campground (N 45° 00.85' W 086° 05.93')** at Mile 11.0. Wooden posts tipped with blue paint mark the beginning of the trail to the **campsite**. Its a bit of a hike from the water to the campsites, and this area of the bay tends to be a bit crowded with moored sailboats and motorboats. I prefer to camp at either the Popple or Weather Station camps when kayaking. The camp has group sites ($20/night) and individual campsites ($5.00/night), outhouses, and potable water.

MILE 12.0: Paddling southeast along the bay's beach, you return to the dock and ranger station. *Sidetrip:* Paddlers who have a full week to explore the Manitous should consider exploring North Manitou Island. Of the two islands, North Manitou is less heavily visited, so it is your best choice for a wilderness kayak experience. From South Manitou it is about a 4-mile crossing from Gull Point to Donner Point on North Manitou. If you only have time to explore North Manitou, you can take the ferry directly from Leland to the Park Service dock on the east side of the island. At the dock there is a ranger station and designated campground ($5.00/night). Wilderness camping is allowed along the coast of the island with a backcountry permit ($5.00/night). Wilderness camping is not allowed within 300 feet of the Lake Michigan high-water mark, inland lakes, streams, ponds, buildings, or other camps. North Manitou Island has a fascinating history, including abandoned farms, lumber camps, and a lifesaving station. To circumnavigate the 20 miles of shoreline, allow at least two days. The shoreline is quite scenic and varied with low, open sandy dunes on the southeast shore; high sandhills and blowout dunes on the southwest side; and huge steep dune bluffs along the west and northwest side. Please note that the Dimmicks Point area is closed from May to August to protect bird-nesting areas, including those of the endangered piping plover.

Where to Eat & Where to Stay

RESTAURANTS In Empire **Daves, The Village Inn** (616–326–5101), and **The Friendly Tavern** (616–326–5506) are good places to eat. In Glen Arbor there are several options, including the **Beach Break Café**, and the **Good Harbor Grill** (616–334–3555). For a more complete list of dining options call or write the Leelanau County Chamber of Commerce, Box 627, Leland, MI 49654; (616) 256–9895. **LODGING** This area is a very popular tourist destination, and there are many lodging options from motels and bed-and-breakfast inns to rental cabins. For a list of lodging options, call or write the Leelanau County Chamber of Commerce, Box 627, Leland, MI 49654; (616) 256–9895. **CAMPING** Although wilderness backcountry camping is not allowed along the mainland shore of the National Lakeshore, the park does have designated campgrounds at the Platte River, about 8 miles south of Empire, and also the **D. H. Day campground** in Glen Haven. Both are available on a first come, first serve basis. For information on private camp grounds, write or call the Leelanau County Chamber of Commerce, Box 627, Leland, MI 49654; (616) 256–9895.

Route 40:

▬ ▬ ▬ ▬ ▬ ▬ ▬ ▬ ▬ ▬ ▬ ▬ ▬ ▬ ➡

Arcadia to Frankfort

The shoreline from Arcadia to Frankfort consists of beautiful sand beaches and steep dune bluffs that rise up to 300 feet above the lake. From the public beach in Arcadia to just south of Frankfort (Elberta), there is no public land so much of the route must be admired from the water not the shore. Still this paddle is well worth it for the lovely scenery. There is an access point using Lower Herring Lake that allows kayakers access to Lake Michigan between Arcadia and Frankfort. In all, four access locations are available: one in Arcadia, one 5 miles north of Arcadia via Lower Herring Lake, the public beach at the Frankfort harbor, and Point Betsie, 4 miles north of Frankfort. A trip to Point Betsie to visit the historic Point Betsie Lighthouse is worthwhile.

TRIP HIGHLIGHTS: Lake Michigan access, large coastal dune bluffs, historic lighthouses.

TRIP RATING:
Beginner: A 4-mile paddle from the Frankfort public beach to Point Betsie.
Intermediate/Advanced: Extended trips from Lower Herring Lake to Point Betsie (about 10 miles) or Arcadia public beach to Point Betsie (about 14 miles).

TRIP DURATION: Part or full day.

NAVIGATION AIDS: NOAA chart 14907, USGS: *Benzie County* at 1:100,000.

CAUTIONS: Submerged dock pilings, and clapotis off the Frankfort breakwall.

TRIP PLANNING: The shore is almost entirely gently sloping sand beach that would allow a surf landing if weather conditions deteriorated. Westerly winds can build large seas, so a calm day or winds from the east are preferred. From the Arcadia public beach to the Frankfort public beach, there are no public shore access locations (Lower Herring Lake is a possible takeout, but it involves a 1-mile long paddle across an inland lake) so plan on sitting in your kayak for at least three hours without a shore break.

LAUNCH SITES:

Arcadia Beach: Just north of the Arcadia Harbor entrance is a small public beach **(N 44° 29.63' W 086° 14.49')** with parking, easy access to the lake, and porta-john toilets. To get to the beach, simply head south from Frankfort on M 22 to Arcadia. Watch for a LAKE MICHI-

GAN PUBLIC ACCESS sign and head east down the road till it dead-ends at the small park.

Lower Herring Lake Access: From Frankfort head south on M 22 until you see a sign for LOWER HERRING LAKE ACCESS DNR ACCESS. Turn right on Elberta Resort Road and follow it to the boat ramp on Lower Herring Lake. Launch your kayak at the boat ramp and head southwest across the lake until you reach a small channel that leads to Lake Michigan. The end of the stream is often blocked by a sandbar so you may have to carry your kayak over the bar to the water. The beach on either side of the outlet is owned by the Watervale Inn, please don't linger at the beach unless you are a guest at the inn.

Frankfort Beach: There is Frankfort public beach access inside the harbor breakwall and to the north of the breakwall. In addition to

a lovely sand beach, there are porta-johns and ample parking. To get to the beach simply drive into Frankfort on Main Street and continue toward the harbor until you reach the beach.

Point Betsie Beach: Drive north from Frankfort on Highway 22 past Crystal Lake. Turn left (west) on Point Betsie Road and follow it until it dead-ends at Lake Michigan. There are no public toilets at this location and roadside parking only.

D I R E C T I O N S

START: From the **Arcadia public beach** paddle north along the coast.

MILE 1.0 TO 3.0: For the first 1.0 mile, the land is fairly flat with a sand beach shore and low dune bluffs. The low dune bluffs give way to steep dune bluffs that rise about 300 feet above the lake. Some of the bluff faces are wooded, while others are bare sand.

MILES 3.0 TO 4.5: As you approach the outlet to **Lower Herring Lake** at about Mile 4.5, the dunes become much lower, and there is a long, low sand beach. The outlet is often blocked by a **sandbar (N 44° 33.60' W 086° 13.34')**. This is a possible takeout spot: You can paddle into Lower Herring Lake and take your kayak out at the DNR public boat ramp access—about 1.0 mile—**(N 44° 34.24' W 086° 12.52')**.

MILES 4.5 TO 7.5: Continue along about 1.0 mile of lower dune bluffs, then from about Miles 5.5 to 7.5, you pass very steep dune bluffs that rise about 300 feet above the lake.

MILES 7.5 TO 9.5: The dune bluffs continue, ranging from more moderate dune slopes of about 50 to 100 feet to steep bluffs about 150 feet high as you approach **Frankfort Harbor**. The lighthouse at the harbor entrance on the **North Breakwall** is worth checking out. Although there has been a breakwall lighthouse since 1832 here, this newer model was put into service in 1932. You can land at the **beach (N 44° 37.91' W 086° 14.77')** inside or north of the harbor or continue north to Point Betsie.

MILES 10.0 TO 12.0: You pass dune bluffs that rise up to 150 feet from the lake.

MILES 12.0 TO 14.0: The dune bluffs become less steep and the land flattens to smaller rolling coastal dunes as you approach **Point Betsie**. At **Point Betsie Beach (N 44° 41.42' W 086° 15.34')** end your trip. Make

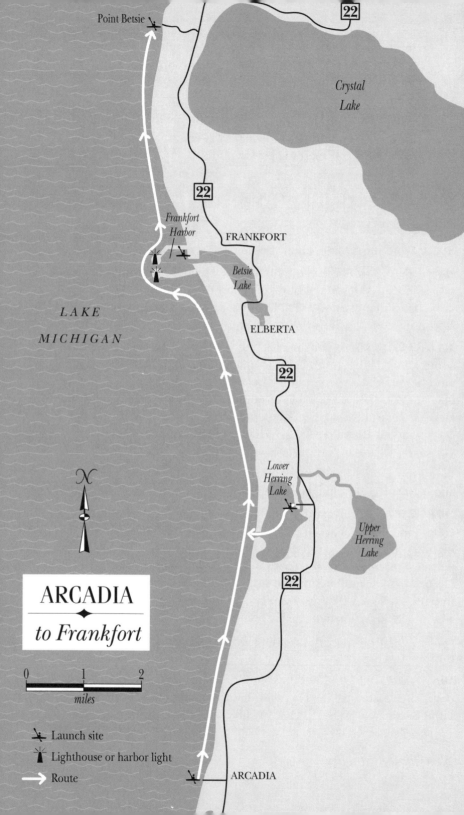

Point Betsie

22

Crystal
Lake

22

*Frankfort
Harbor*

FRANKFORT

*Betsie
Lake*

LAKE

MICHIGAN

ELBERTA

22

N

*Lower
Herring
Lake*

*Upper
Herring
Lake*

22

ARCADIA

to Frankfort

0   1   2
miles

Launch site

Lighthouse or harbor light

Route

ARCADIA

Betsie Bay Kayaks

The Frankfort area is the home to Betsie Bay Kayaks, a company that specializes in handmade Greenland-style kayaks and traditional Greenland-style paddles. For information call (616) 352-7774.

sure you have a good look at the lighthouse. The first lighthouse at Point Betsie was completed in 1858. The original tower remains, but much of the present structure was added in 1894. The lighthouse was not automated until 1983, the last manned lightstation on the eastern shore of Lake Michigan at that time. The many outbuildings associated with the light station are owned by the U.S. Coast Guard and are used to house Coast Guard personnel.

Where to Eat & Where to Stay

RESTAURANTS Main Street in Frankfort provides several dining options. The **Coho Café** (616–352–6053) has good food, and they usually have several vegetarian meals on the menu. For information about other dining options, you can walk across the street to the Frankfort Chamber of Commerce or call (616) 352–7251. **LODGING** There are several motels in the Frankfort area. For those who want to enjoy the beach at the Lower Herring Lake access point guilt free, call the **Watervale Inn** at (616) 352–9083. This resort, located on Lower Herring Lake, is very popular so you will need to make reservations far in advance. For more information on lodging, call the Frankfort Chamber of Commerce at (616) 352–7251. **CAMPING** The **Platte River Campground**, located at the southern edge of the Sleeping Bear National Lakeshore, is north of Frankfort off M–22. Call (616) 326–5134 for information. For private campgrounds the **Betsie River Camp Site** is located in Frankfort; call (616) 352–9535.

Route 41:

━ ━ ━ ━ ━ ━ ━ ━ ━ ━ ━ ━ ━ ━ ━ ━ ➤

Nordhouse Dunes to Ludington State Park

South of the Sleeping Bear National Lakeshore, most of the east shore of Lake Michigan is privately owned. The 12-mile stretch of coast from the north end of the Nordhouse Dunes Wilderness to the south end of the Ludington State Park is a delightful exception to this rule. Although the coastal dune bluffs are not as spectacular as the towering Sleeping Bear Dunes, this beautiful coastal dune wilderness is well worth the visit. The two parks combine to form a total of about 8,000 acres of coastal wilderness, offering miles of dune grass, bare sand bluffs, drifting sand dunes, and old wooded dunes as high as 140 feet. Along the 8-mile section described in this route, there is no road access to the coast, so you will only encounter backpackers or other boaters.

TRIP HIGHLIGHTS: Beautiful sand beaches, coastal dunes, and wilderness.

TRIP RATING:
Beginner/Intermediate: About 8 miles one way.

TRIP DURATION: Part or full day.

NAVIGATION AIDS: NOAA chart 14907, USGS: *Mason County.*

TRIP PLANNING: Westerly winds can produce large seas and surf. Almost all of this 8-mile section of coast is sand beach that would allow for landing if weather conditions deteriorated. Wilderness camping is allowed within the Nordhouse Dunes, but regulations specify that camps must be a minimum of 400 feet from the lake.

For this reason it is more convenient to camp at the national forest campground or state park (see Camping).

LAUNCH SITES:

Lake Michigan Recreation Area Beach: From Ludington head east on Highway 10 for about 5 miles, then turn north on Stiles Road. Head north on Stiles for about 8.5 miles, then right on Townline Road for about 0.5 mile, until turning north again (left) onto Quarterline Road. Stay north on Quarterline Road for about 3.5 miles, then go left (west) on Forest Trail Road. About 5.7 miles down Forest Trail Road, you come to the beach parking lot. The parking lot is about 1,000 feet from the water, and you have to hike down stairs and a dune bluff about 50 feet in elevation to get to the lake. The parking lot area has outhouse bathroom facilities. Potable water is available at the nearby campground.

Ludington State Park Beach: From Ludington simply follow the signs to the state park. You follow Highway 116 north along the coast until it dead-ends within the park. Follow the signs for the "Park Café" and Lake Michigan Beach. Changing rooms and bathroom facilities are available at the beach. It is about 300 feet from parking lot to the water over level ground.

DIRECTIONS

START: From the **Lake Michigan Recreation Area Beach (N 44° 07.29' W 086° 25.67')** head south into the **Nordhouse Dunes Wilderness Area**.

MILE 3.0: For the first 3.0 miles, you pass along a beautiful sand beach with a narrow band of low coastal dunes about 50 feet high or less covered with dune grass. There are wooded sand dune bluffs a short distance inland.

MILE 4.0: Between Miles 3.0 and 4.0, you cross from the Nordhouse Dunes Wilderness Area to the **Ludington State Park**.

MILES 4.0 TO 6.0: At about Mile 4.0 the width of coastal dunes expands until the coastal dunes stretch off into the distance. The dunes are still less than 100 feet high in most cases. Make sure you save some time to hike inland to explore the lovely dune landscape. Take care not to walk on the fragile dune vegetation.

Nordhouse Dunes to Ludington State Park

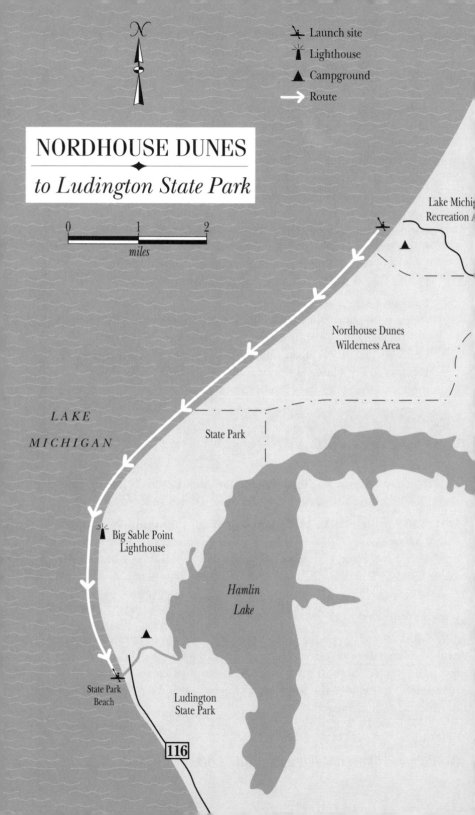

N

Launch site
Lighthouse
▲ Campground
→ Route

NORDHOUSE DUNES
to Ludington State Park

0   1   2
miles

Lake Michigan
Recreation Area

Nordhouse Dunes
Wilderness Area

LAKE

MICHIGAN

State Park

Big Sable Point
Lighthouse

*Hamlin
Lake*

State Park
Beach

Ludington
State Park

116

MILE 6.0: At Mile 6.0 you come to the **Big Sable Point Lighthouse**. The first lighthouse was established here in 1867, a conical brick tower about 112 feet high. In the early 1900s additional work was done on the lighthouse, and both the watch building and tower were encased in steel plates.

MILES 6.0 TO 8.0: The sand beach and wide band of coastal dunes continues until you reach the **Ludington State Park Beach (N 44° 01.93' W 086° 30.52')** and complete the trip.

Where to Eat & Where to Stay

RESTAURANTS   For convenience it is tough to beat eating at the **Park Café** at the end of the trip. The park has both a Big Boy and a Pizza Hut concession at the swimming beach. Not haute cuisine, but convenient. Ludington has a number of restaurants, call the Ludington Chamber of Commerce for a complete list (616–845–0324).   **LODGING**   Ludington is a resort town, and there is no shortage of motels to chose from. For a list of motel options, call the Ludington Chamber of Commerce (616–845–0324).   **CAMPING**   At the beginning of the trip, the most convenient camping is at the **Lake Michigan Recreation Area National Forest Service Campground**. For information call (616) 723–2211. At trip's end there's **Ludington State Park**. For information call (616) 843–8671.

Route 42:

■ ■ ■ ■ ■ ■ ■ ■ ■ ■ ■ ■ ■ ■ ■ ■ ■ ■ ➤

Van Buren State Park to South Haven

The Van Buren State Park has a beautiful 1-mile long beach with sand dunes and dune bluffs that rise 50 to 100 feet up from the lake. With the exception of the state park and the South Haven Public Beach, most of the land along this route is private so you will need to enjoy the view of the dune bluffs and sand beaches from the water. South Haven has a great public beach and a long harbor breakwall with lighthouse and raised catwalk.

TRIP HIGHLIGHTS: Dune bluffs, beautiful sand beaches, lovely harbor and lighthouse.

TRIP RATING:
Beginner: 5 miles one way.

TRIP DURATION: Part day.

NAVIGATION AIDS: NOAA chart 14905, USGS: *Van Buren County* at 1:100,000.

CAUTIONS: Clapotis off harbor breakwall, boat traffic in harbor.

TRIP PLANNING: Avoid paddling on a day with strong westerly winds because large seas are likely. The sand beaches allow for an emergency surf landing almost anywhere along the coast if weather conditions deteriorate. On the 5-mile trip there is only public shore access during the first and last miles so plan on staying your boat for the middle three.

LAUNCH SITES:
Van Buren State Park: From South Haven head south on Highway I–196 and after about 5 miles take exit 13 (Covert) which is 32nd Avenue. Go about 0.25 mile on 32nd, then right on the Blue Star

Highway. Follow the Blue Star for 3.4 miles to County Road 380, go left for about 0.1 mile to Ruggles Road, then turn left again. This road dead-ends into the state park after about 0.5 mile. The directions sound complicated, but the turns are well marked with signs to the state park. Follow the park road to the Harry Labar Drake Picnic Area. The swimming area nearby has changing rooms and bathroom facilities. There is a concrete sidewalk that leads to the beach. It is about a 1,000 foot carry, so if you have a wheeled portage cart, bring it on this trip. State park day-use fees are $4.00 and an annual permit is $20.

South Haven–Black River Boat Ramp: Follow Business I–196 into town from the south (Broadway Street), then turn left on Dyckman. Just before Dyckman crosses the river, turn right on Dunkley Avenue and follow it to the DNR public boat ramp access **(N 42° 24.63' W 086° 16.36')**. There is an automated gate to the parking lot that will accept either $5.00 or $1.00 bills to pay the required $5.00 parking and launch fee. Bathroom facilities are available at the boat ramp.

DIRECTIONS

START: From the **Van Buren State Park beach (N 42° 19.98' W 086° 18.64')**, head north along the shore. Just to the south is the **Palisade Nuclear Plant** so keep your eyes pointed north for beautiful scenery.

MILE 1.0: The Van Buren State Park has about 1 mile of gorgeous sand beach with lovely sand dunes and dune bluffs that rise up to 100 feet above the lake. At about Mile 1.0 you will see the remains of an old pier or dock, roughly marking the end of public land. For the next 3.0 miles you will be paddling along private beaches.

MILES 1.0 TO 4.0: More lovely beach and low dunes, but this is private land so do not land unless it is an emergency. At Mile 4.0 you approach the **South Haven Harbor entrance (N 42° 24.09' W 086° 17.28')**, and pass along the **South Haven Public Beach**. At the end of the breakwall is a lighthouse that was built in 1903. Rounding the breakwall enter the

Michigan Maritime Museum

The Michigan Maritime Museum in South Haven is open to the public Wednesday to Sunday year-round, 10:00 A.M. to 5:00 P.M. The museum is located on the Black River on Van Dyckman Road. Simply follow the directions listed earlier for the Black River boat ramp, but cross the river on Dyckman Road: The museum is just across the bridge on the left.

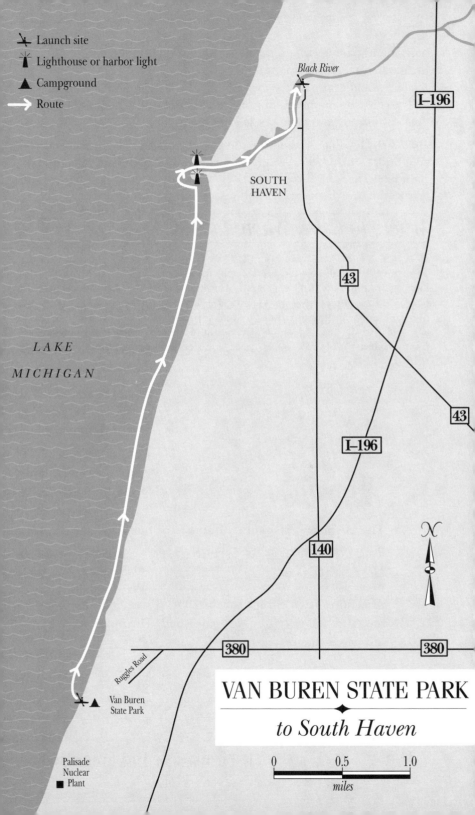

Launch site
Lighthouse or harbor light
Campground
Route

Black River

I–196

SOUTH
HAVEN

LAKE

MICHIGAN

43

43

I–196

N

140

380   380

Ruggles Road

Van Buren
State Park

VAN BUREN STATE PARK
◆
to South Haven

Palisade
Nuclear
Plant

0   0.5   1.0
miles

harbor and paddle east up the Black River. *Caution:* The end of the breakwall can create clapotis if there is significant wave action. Although the city would prefer to keep kayaks out of the swimming area, it may be safer to land on the beach in rough conditions, there may also be a great deal of boat traffic entering or leaving the harbor.

MILE 5.0: Heading up the river you pass the marinas. Go under the bascule bridge at Dyckman Avenue and land at the DNR boat ramp on the right bank.

Where to Eat & Where to Stay

RESTAURANTS & LODGING South Haven has been a popular resort town since the late 1800s so there is no lack of choices for dining or lodging in the area. Call the South Haven Chamber of Commerce at (616) 637–5171 for complete listings. **CAMPING** Van Buren State Park has well over 200 modern campsites available. Call (616) 637–2788 for information. There are two private campgrounds in South Haven: **Cousins Restaurant and Campground** (616–637–1499) and **Jensen's Campground and Motel** (616–637–3544).

Lake Michigan
Illinois

Route 43:

Chicago Lakefront

Kayaking along the Lake Michigan waterfront provides a unique view of the city skyline. You get all of the beauty of the tall buildings, while sitting far enough from shore to avoid the noise and the hassles of city traffic. I was fortunate enough to paddle this route during the evening rush hour. There is something eminently satisfying about gliding along in your kayak while the rest of the city is bumper to bumper in a traffic jam. The skyline is even more impressive at night with the buildings lit up and the Ferris Wheel on Navy Pier ablaze with lights. I personally have always preferred wilderness paddling to urban paddles. In spite of my prejudice against urban paddling, I was pleasantly surprised by this and the following Chicago routes.

TRIP HIGHLIGHTS: World-class city skyline scenery, people watching, and sand beaches.

TRIP RATING:
Beginner/Intermediate: 10 miles from Diversey Harbor to 12th Street and back.

TRIP DURATION: Part day (less than four hours unless you have someone feed the parking meter at Diversey Harbor).

NAVIGATION AIDS: NOAA charts 14937 for general coast and 14928: *Chicago Harbor.*

CAUTIONS: Small craft and tour boat traffic; clapotis from breakwalls or sheet piling walls.

TRIP PLANNING: The second half of the trip is sheltered within the Chicago Harbor so weather is less of a factor. An east or northeast wind could bring in larger seas, but there are enough sand beaches for an emergency landing to make the route fairly safe (car access to some of the beaches would be difficult). Plan for city traffic: Drive before or after rush hour traffic and paddle while everyone else is stuck in traffic.

LAUNCH SITES:

12th Street Beach: From Lake Shore Drive take the exit for Adler Planetarium, Shedd Aquarium, and the Field Museum of Natural History. The 12th Street Beach is located between the planetarium and Meiggs Field. There are pay lots and metered parking that will allow you to park for up to ten hours. Parking is 500 to 1,000 feet from the beach, but you can usually ask permission to drop off your kayak and gear from the police officer at the barricades that keep cars from driving up to the beach. If no one is on duty, drive past the barricades and drop off your boat, but do not park unless you want to pay $150 to get your car out of a very unpleasant impound lot. Launch your boat from the south end of the beach, avoiding the buoyed swimming area.

Diversey Harbor: From 12th Street get on Lake Shore Drive and head north. Exit to go west on Fullerton Avenue and circle around Diversey Harbor to the north end (north on Canon Drive, right on Lake Shore Drive—not the same Lake Shore Drive that you started on—to Diversey Parkway, a dead end that brings you to the north end of the harbor). There is metered parking close to the water, but parking is limited to four hours, so get your trip completed in under four hours or have someone feed the parking meter for you. There is a low rock and concrete shelf next to the parking spaces that makes a good kayak launch site.

DIRECTIONS

START: Head east out of Diversey Harbor through a tunnel that goes under Lake Shore Drive. Now turn right out of the harbor and head south toward **Diversey Harbor (N 41° 55.97' W 087° 38.04').**

MILES 1.0 TO 2.0: Head for Chicago Harbor. The harbor entrance is roughly in line with the two towers on the end of Navy Pier. You will pass along some lake shore parks and beaches as you paddle about 0.5 mile offshore.

Chicago Lakefront

CHICAGO LAKEFRONT

Belmont
Harbor

Diversey
Harbor

0 _____ 1
miles

✕ Launch site
✵ Harbor Light
→ Route

Chicago River North Branch

Water
Filtration
Plant

Navy Pier

Chicago River

Chicago River
locks

Grant Park Fountain ▪

Chicago
Harbor

Chicago River South Branch

Shedd Aquarium ▪

Adler Planetarium ▪

12th Street
Beach

Merrill C. Meigs
Airfield

MILES 2.0 TO 3.5: Heading into the harbor through the opening in the breakwall, you first pass the **Water Filtration Plant** at about Mile 2.75. At about Mile 3.5 you reach the end of **Navy Pier**. Formerly a Navy facility, the pier now serves the public with an amusement park, sculpture garden, concerts, etc. There is almost always something interesting going on here. Unfortunately the steep sheet piling sides don't allow for an easy landing by kayak, so you will have to visit Navy Pier by land.

MILES 3.5 TO 4.5: Heading south from Navy Pier, you pass the mouth of the Chicago River and the **Chicago River locks**. *Caution:* Watch for tour boat and small craft traffic coming from the docks along Navy Pier and from the river. You now are in front of spectacular city skyline. Continue south where at about Mile 4.5, you pass in front of Buckingham Foun-tain at **Grant Park**, which you may be able to see even though it is nearly a mile away.

MILE 4.5 TO 5.5: Continue south toward **Meigs Field** and the **12th Street Beach (N 41° 51.88' W 087° 36.46')**. As you approach the end of the trip, you pass the **Shedd Aquarium** and **Adler Planetarium** before landing at the south end of the 12th Street Beach, between the planetarium and Meigs Field.

Where to Eat & Where to Stay

For information on restaurants and lodging, see Route 44: Chicago River.

Route 44:

Chicago River

This may be the best downtown urban paddle in the country! By heading up the Chicago River in a kayak, you pass some of the largest and most interesting buildings that Chicago has to offer. As you paddle you also pass under fourteen historic bascule bridges before you complete your journey. The river is also one of the few large open spaces that allows you enough room to get a good view of the many tall buildings. Gliding along peacefully in your kayak as the rest of the city roars with activity is a wonderful contrast.

TRIP HIGHLIGHTS: Spectacular downtown scenery: locks, historic architecture, mechanized bridges.

TRIP RATING:
Beginner/Intermediate: About 8 miles round-trip.

TRIP DURATION: Part day.

NAVIGATION AIDS: NOAA chart 14928: *Chicago Harbor.*

CAUTIONS: No easy landings, sheet piling walls with few ladders, small craft and tour boat traffic.

TRIP PLANNING: The route is sheltered within the harbor so wind and waves are less of a concern. Landings are few, and much of the shore is sheet piling with few if any ladders. Paddle this route only if you have good self-rescue skills and are comfortable sitting in a kayak for hours without access to shore. The best time to head downtown on the Chicago River is at the peak of rush hour when the city's energy and level of activity reaches a crescendo!

LAUNCH SITE: See directions to 12th Street Beach in Route 43.

DIRECTIONS

START: Launch your kayak from the south end of the 12th Street Beach. Head north past the **Adler Planetarium** and the **Shedd Aquarium**, heading roughly toward the end of Navy Pier.

MILE 1.0: At about Mile 1.0 you pass the entrance to inner harbor and the Chicago Yacht Club. You are now in front of Grant Park, and you may be able to catch a glimpse of Buckingham Fountain even though you are far from shore.

MILE 2.0: At about Mile 1.5, as you are nearing **Navy Pier,** you turn the corner and head west into the **Chicago River locks**. There is a simple system for entering the locks. Just wait for the green light as at a traffic intersection and paddle into the lock. You are then lowered several feet below the Lake Michigan level to match the Chicago River elevation. At Mile 2.0 exit the locks and continue west past the **police dock** and into downtown.

MILE 3.0: Heading west up the Chicago River you enter the heart of downtown. Nearing Mile 3.0 you pass the **Tribune Tower**, the **Wrigley Building**, and the **Equity Building**. Check out the funky architecture of

Chicago River

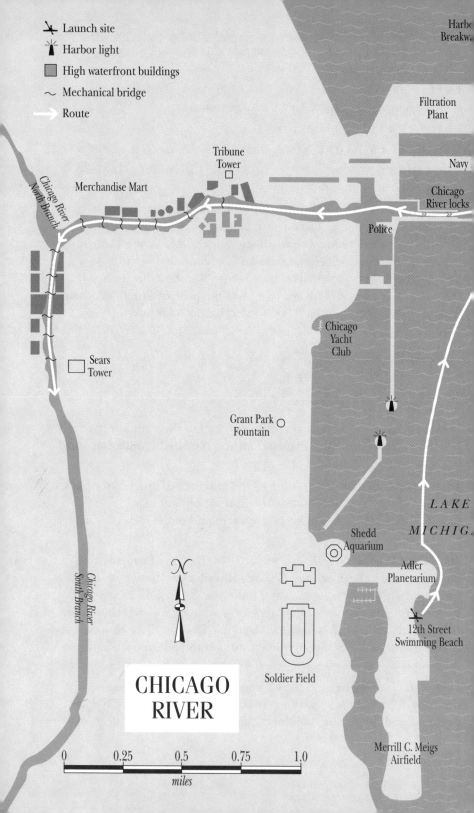

Legend

- ✈ Launch site
- ☀ Harbor light
- ▦ High waterfront buildings
- ~ Mechanical bridge
- → Route

Harbor Breakw...

Filtration Plant

Navy

Chicago River locks

Tribune Tower

Merchandise Mart

Chicago River North Branch

Police

Chicago Yacht Club

Sears Tower

Grant Park Fountain

Shedd Aquarium

LAKE MICHIG...

Adler Planetarium

Chicago River South Branch

N

12th Street Swimming Beach

Soldier Field

CHICAGO RIVER

| 0 | 0.25 | 0.5 | 0.75 | 1.0 |

miles

Merrill C. Meigs Airfield

Marina Towers (I am pretty sure George Jetson lives here).

MILES 3.0 TO 4.0: Heading farther up river, you pass a total of seven bascule bridges and come to the **Mechandise Mart**. Here the river splits into its north and south branches. Turn left to take the South Branch and continue past many high buildings (**Civic Opera House, Northwestern Atrium Center, Chicago Mercantile Exchange,** and the **Sears Tower)** that are near the riverfront and pass under another seven bascule bridges. On reaching the Sears Tower, you are at the end of the route and can retrace your route back to the 12th Street Beach. The South Branch of the Chicago River beyond this point gets more industrial, more polluted, and less interesting, but if you are looking for extra miles you can continue on as far as New Orleans!

Where to Eat & Where to Stay

Chicago has such an overwhelming number of restaurants and lodgings that it is hard to make a recommendation. Ask a local friend or contact the Chicago Convention and Tourism Bureau (312–567–8500) or the Convention and Visitors Hotel Information (800–445–8849).

Lake Michigan
Wisconsin

Route 45:

━━ ━━ ━━ ━━ ━━ ━━ ━━ ━━ ━━ ━━ ━━ ➤

Milwaukee: Bradford Beach

This quiet and surprisingly scenic paddle is a good get-away from the noise and bustle of the city, particularly on weeknights. The tall bluffs north of Bradford Beach are still wooded for the most part, making this a pleasant stretch of shoreline. There is no real destination here, though the prettier shoreline doesn't start until you're about a half-mile north of the launch site. Paddle as long as you like and return. Local paddlers have had to negotiate with the county parks to get permission to use this beach, and Bradford is one of the few where they have agreed to let kayakers launch.

TRIP HIGHLIGHTS: Wooded shoreline, fairly quiet paddle.

TRIP RATING:
Beginner/Intermediate: 2–4-mile paddle north of the beach and back.

TRIP DURATION: Part day.

NAVIGATION AIDS: USGS: *Milwaukee* and *Thiensville* (7.5 minute).

CAUTIONS: Some boat and Jet Ski traffic, shoals, reflection waves.

TRIP PLANNING: If you pick a hot weekend day during the summer, you may have to fight a crowd to get to the beach. Try week-days, evenings, or early mornings for a quieter launch.

LAUNCH SITE: From downtown Milwaukee (e.g., from I–794) take Lincoln Memorial Drive north along the shore. Look for the main parking lot for Bradford Beach just beyond North Avenue, which is your first option (it's busy, though) or continue driving and look for parking along the road. If you use this last option, be careful as you unload the kayak from your car.

DIRECTIONS

START: Whatever point on **Bradford Beach** beach you start from, paddle north along the shore. At the north end of the beach, the sand ends and the shore is lined with large boulders. Ahead is a part of the University of Wisconsin-Milwaukee campus.

MILE 0.5: *Caution:* There is a section of vertical wall next to shallow water that can produce some surprisingly large reflection waves. Paddle well out from shore to avoid the chop.

MILE 1.0: After the wall ends, the land rises up to form bluffs with narrow or boulder-strewn beaches, most of which are privately owned. *Caution:* If you paddle close to shore, beware of submerged pilings, rubble, etc., which may be hard to see if the waves have stirred up sediment.

MILES 2.0 TO 4.0: Paddle as long as you like and return to Bradford Beach.

Where to Eat & Where to Stay

RESTAURANTS & LODGING Many options here, especially so close to downtown. Call (800) 554–1448 for a visitor's guide and more information.

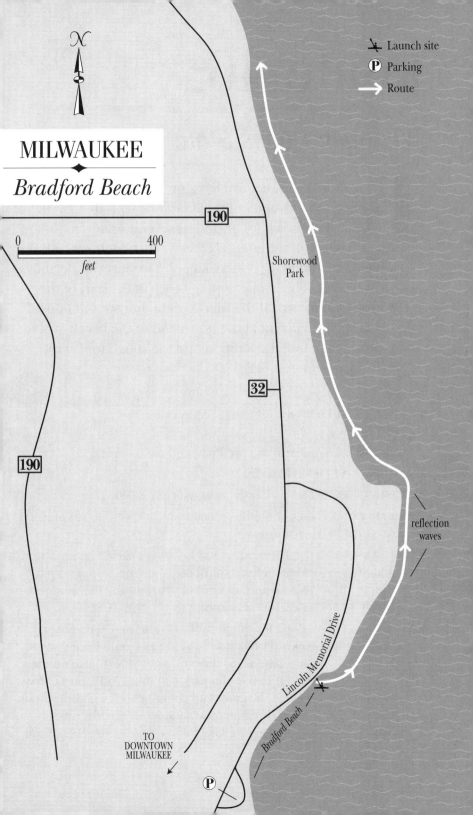

N

MILWAUKEE
Bradford Beach

190

0   400
feet

190

32

Shorewood
Park

⚓ Launch site
Ⓟ Parking
→ Route

reflection
waves

Lincoln Memorial Drive

Bradford Beach

TO
DOWNTOWN
MILWAUKEE

Ⓟ

Route 46:

▬▬ ▬▬ ▬▬ ▬▬ ▬▬ ▬▬ ▬▬ ▬▬ ▬▬ ▬▬ ▬▬ ▬ ▬ ➤

Whitefish Dunes State Park

This short and sweet trip has a great sand beach and some very good examples of the limestone cliffs that Door County is known for, including several stone grottos and caves. The clear but intensely green water contrasts with the white sand and gray rock, making the scenery wonderfully rich in color. The gently sloping beach at the start of the trip is good for surf if the wind is right, but see Cautions about the rip current at the north end of the beach. There is a shoreline trail if conditions are too rough to visit the cliffs by water.

TRIP HIGHLIGHTS: Limestone cliffs, caves.

TRIP RATING:
Beginner: 1.5-mile trip to Cave Point and back.

TRIP DURATION: Part day.

NAVIGATION AIDS: USGS: *Jacksonport* at 1:24,000.

CAUTIONS: Exposed shoreline, sections of cliffs with no landing and potential for refection waves.

TRIP PLANNING: The weather will be calmer earlier in the season and in the mornings before afternoon winds come up. This park, like much of Door County, can be very busy during the summer, which is another reason to start early in the day.

LAUNCH SITE: Look for the turnoff to Whitefish Dunes about 1 mile north of Valmy on Highway 57. Turn east onto County Road WP, then continue east for 3.8 miles to the park entrance on the south side. Turn south on to the park entrance road (you will have to pay a day-use fee at the gate) and continue to the nature center. If the park is busy, as it will be most summer weekends, you will have to go on to the main parking lot and unload your boat from

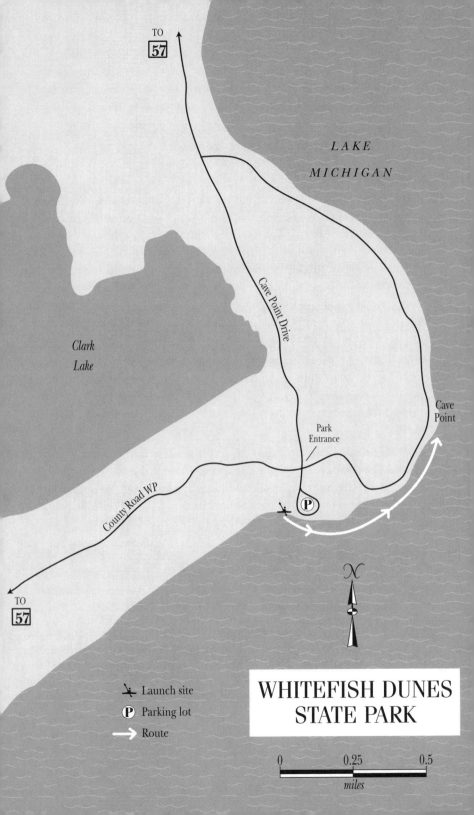

TO
57

LAKE

MICHIGAN

*Clark
Lake*

Cave Point Drive

County Road WP

Park
Entrance

Cave
Point

P

TO
57

N

Launch site

P Parking lot

Route

WHITEFISH DUNES
STATE PARK

0   0.25   0.5

miles

there. If you're lucky and it's not crowded, you may be able to (quickly) unload your boat from the five-minute parking lot next to the nature center, which makes for a much shorter carry, before moving your car to the main lot. If you're not sure, ask.

DIRECTIONS

START: Launch from the beach and paddle east, then turn north, then east along the shore. *Caution:* Strong southerly winds will create several lines of breakers on the beach; they often cause a rip current at the north end where the shore turns east. Rip currents flow away from shore toward the lake and may take you farther out from shore than you want to be, but they may also provide a good place to paddle through the surf because rip currents generally flow out through deeper channels. If you do encounter one but don't want to be there, paddle parallel to the shore to escape because they are usually localized to one section of beach.

MILE 0.25: The shoreline changes from sand to a low rock shelf and finally to the taller cliffs around Cave Point. *Caution:* There is potential for reflection waves along the cliffs, and the shoals extending out from shore can cause waves to increase in height and even break in rough weather.

MILE 0.75: Take your time and explore the caves and grottos. The land around **Cave Point** is a county park, and some of the caves can be viewed from the picnic area if conditions are too rough to approach the caves by water. The best of the caves are around Cave Point, but continue north if you like along the shore before heading back.

Where to Eat & Where to Stay

RESTAURANTS & LODGING No shortage of places to eat or stay in Door County. Call the Door County Chamber of Commerce at (800) 527–3529 for more information. **CAMPING** Whitefish Dunes State Park is a day-use only park with no camping. The two closest state parks with camping are **Potawatomi** (920–746–2890) west of Sturgeon Bay and **Peninsula State Park** near Fish Creek (920–868–3258). All are busy during the summer season, and reservations are recommended. There are also a number of private RV/tent campgrounds in Door County, call the Door County Chamber of Commerce for a list.

Route 47:

■■ ■■ ■ ■■ ■■ ■ ■■ ■■ ■■ ■■ ■■ ■■ ■■ ➤

Newport State Park

A lthough this park doesn't have some of the more dramatic scenery of other areas in Door County, it is a good place to escape the crowds. Campsites must be accessed by foot, bike, or boat, which makes this park a little quieter than others. The southern end of the park has some low rock shelves, while the northern section has more sand. Some paddlers use the northern end as a starting point for a trip farther north along the shore to Northport and then to Plum, Washington, and Rock Island. If you manage to get one of the good kayak sites, this is a great place to spend a weekend relaxing, and if not, a good place for a quiet day's paddle.

TRIP HIGHLIGHTS: Good scenery, undeveloped and relatively quiet shoreline.

TRIP RATING:
> *Beginner:* 4 miles: Newport Beach to Duck Bay, round-trip.
> *Intermediate:* 8-mile trip from Europe Bay to Varney Point and back.
> *Advanced:* Continue on to Washington, Rock Islands (see Rte. 48).

TRIP DURATION: Part day to multiday.

NAVIGATION AIDS: USGS: *Spider Island* and *Washington Island SW* at 1:24,000

CAUTIONS: Exposed shoreline, some sections of rocky cliffs with no landing and possible reflection waves, poison ivy in the woods.

TRIP PLANNING: If you are planning on doing a day trip, you only need to pick a nice day to paddle. If you want to camp at the park, make sure to reserve a site as soon as possible. The park is booked through Labor Day and on fall weekends, too. Ask the park staff for a copy of the list of campsites, which has a brief description of the type of shoreline at each site (cobble, sand, rock) to help you choose. Most of the sites at the southern end of the park (5–13) are located on shoreline consisting of a 2–4-foot-high rock shelf and are not easily accessible to kayakers. Sites 1–4 and 16 have sand or gravel beaches at or near the campsites, and sites 14 and 15 are located on the inland Europe Lake.

LAUNCH SITE: There are three parking lots in the park, and parking for each campsite is assigned to a certain lot. Ask the park staff which lot you should park in. Unfortunately, the two lots on Newport Bay are some distance (300-400 yards) from the water. Europe Bay offers the easiest launch site for paddlers, and it should be used by those doing a day trip. To get to Newport State Park, take County Road NP from Highway 42 (the turnoff is located just north of Ellison Bay). To go to the main park entrance (you will need to do this to purchase a day-use permit if you don't have one), continue on NP, which ends at the park gate 2.5 miles from Highway 42. To get to the Europe Bay Beach, take NP from the park gate 0.3 miles west, then turn north onto Timberline Road. Continue 1.1 miles north, then turn east onto Europe Bay Road. Stay on the road for another 1.1 miles to the beach parking lot (the park map, available at the gate or park office, will show these roads and parking lots, so pick one up when you get your permit).

DIRECTIONS

START: Launch from **Europe Bay** and paddle south. Europe Bay is a long beach, and in southerly winds it may have a slight current moving north along the shore.

MILE 1.0: The shoreline becomes rocky; shoals extend out from the shore. **Lynd Point** has two forks, and between the forks is a very small gravel beach that is probably the best access to the two campsites on the point. *Caution:* In a southerly wind, there may be some reflection waves around the point.

MILE 1.5: As the shoreline turns briefly west, the shore once again becomes sandy, and you are now in Newport Bay.

MILE 2.5: Pass small rocky point and find **Sand Cove** just beyond.

MILE 3.0: Between Sand Cove and **Duck Bay**, the shoreline is rocky, the

GILL'S ROCK

42

NORTHPORT

NEWPORT STATE PARK

N
S

Launch site

Ⓟ Parking lot

→ Route

0   0.5   1.0
miles

42

Europe Lake

PARK BOUNDARY

PARK BOUNDARY

LAKE MICHIGAN

42   Europe Bay Rd.

Ⓟ   *Europe Bay*

Timberline Rd.

PARK BOUNDARY

Gravel Island

NEWPORT STATE PARK

Lynd Point

PARK BOUNDARY

Office

Ⓟ

Newport Bay

Park Gate

Ⓟ

Sand Cove

Rowley Bay

Duck Bay

Varney Point

Spider Island

water shallow, and shoals extend a long way out from shore. If conditions are not calm you may have to go some distance out to get around waves breaking on the shoals. Duck Bay is the last sandy bay in the southern part of the park, so if you are looking for a soft landing, take a rest here.

MILE 3.5: The shoreline becomes rocky with a few scattered cobble beaches near the point, followed by a very shallow and swampy bay.

MILE 4.0: Continue west beyond **Varney Point** if you like, but the scenery is fairly uninteresting west of here.

MILES 5.5 TO 8.0: Return to Europe Bay.

Where to Eat & Where to Stay

RESTAURANTS & LODGING Ellison Bay and Sister Bay have plenty of dining and lodging. Call the Door County Chamber of Commerce at (800) 527–3529 for more information. **CAMPING** If no campsites are available in the park, try one of the private RV/tent campgrounds in Door County. Call the Door County Chamber of Commerce for a list.

Route 48:

▬ ▬ ▬ ▬ ▬ ▬ ▬ ▬ ▬ ▬ ▬ ▬ ▬ ▬ ➤

Rock Island State Park

Off the tip of the Door County Peninsula is a chain of islands that stretch north across the entrance to Green Bay all the way to Michigan. These limestone islands are known for their scenery and beaches, and Washington Island in particular is an extremely popular vacation spot. North of Washington lies Rock Island, a state park that is a well-known destination for kayakers and backpackers (there are no cars or bicycles on the island). The island can be reached by paddling or taking a small ferry from Jackson Harbor at the north end of Washington Island. The island has brilliant white cliffs and cobblestone beaches, and as in the Whitefish Dunes paddle, the combination of colors— green water, white rock, and blue sky—can be quite stunning on a fair day. The island also has a system of hiking trails that circle the island, giving you a change of pace or an alternate activity when the weather's rough.

TRIP HIGHLIGHTS: Excellent scenery, good camping in an undeveloped setting, Potawatomi Lighthouse, and the Viking Hall of the Thordarson estate.

TRIP RATING:

Beginner/Intermediate: Paddle or take the *Karfi* ferry from Jackson Harbor and do day trips from the campground on Rock Island (3–8 miles round-trip), or paddle to Rock Island from Jackson Harbor and circumnavigate the island as an 8-mile day trip.

Advanced: Start from Northport or Newport State Park and paddle by Plum, Detroit, Washington Islands on the way to Rock Island, about a 40-mile round-trip.

TRIP DURATION: Day trip to multinight

NAVIGATION AIDS: USGS: *Washington Island NE* at 1:24,000 covers all of Rock Island and Jackson Harbor. For complete coverage of Washington Island and Northport see *Washington Island SW*, *Washington Island NE*, and *Washington Island NW* maps. NOAA chart 14909 covers the northern half of Door County and surrounding waters, but it does have useful information about water depths and channel locations that can be useful for paddling.

CAUTIONS: Currents; exposed crossings and shoreline; rocky shoreline with limited landings, particularly in rough weather; reflection waves; and boat traffic.

TRIP PLANNING: Unless you are looking for a challenge, plan your trip early in the summer before the winds pick up. Plan to paddle early in the day, and check the marine forecast before setting out. Strong winds and changes in atmospheric pressure over Lake Michigan cause water to flow in or out of Green Bay through the restricted channels between islands. Although currents are at most 2 knots, this has been enough to push some paddlers out into the lake, where they were picked up by the Coast Guard. Although 2 knots may not seem like a lot, many kayakers paddle at a speed of around 2–3 knots, and paddling speed drops farther in a head wind. Death's Door Passage between Northport and Washington Island has the worst reputation, but paddlers have had trouble around Rock Island, too. Don't let it happen to you: Allow extra days in your plans to sit out bad weather, or consider taking one or both of the ferries available. For information about the Washington Island ferries from Northport, call (800) 223–2094 for schedules and fares. For the ferry to Rock Island, call (414) 847–2252.

LAUNCH SITE: After reaching Washington Island, stop at the tourist information center near the ferry dock on Lobdells Point Road and pick up a free map of the island. Continue north to its intersection with Main Road, then turn north. Continue on Main Road to Jackson Harbor Road and turn east. Continue east for 3.6 miles, following Jackson Harbor Road. It makes a right-angle turn and continues north for another 0.4 miles (becoming Indian Point Road) to the Rock Island State Park lot on the east side of the road. The ferry leaves from the dock, or you can launch your boat from the ramp or the narrow gravel beach next to the ramp. There is no launch fee or charge to park. If leaving from the mainland, you can launch from Newport State Park (see Rte. 47) or launch from the cobble beach at Northport. During peak season when Northport is quite busy, and it may be hard to get close to the beach to unload your kayak, Newport may be the better choice. Parking at the ferry lot at Northport is free, while there is a vehicle permit fee at the park (annual stickers are also available).

DIRECTIONS

Note: If you leave from the mainland, you will have to complete your trip to Rock Island in one day, as there are no places to camp on the shores of Washington Island. Landing is permitted at the following public areas only: Plum Island, Sand Dunes Beach, Percy Johnson Park, and, on the north side of the island, Jackson Harbor Ridges (a Nature Conservancy property located on the eastern point of Jackson Harbor) and School-house Beach in Washington Harbor. Paddling up the east side of the island is recommended because there are no public landing areas on the west side, and the shoreline is mainly composed of bluffs exposed to prevailing northwest winds. *Caution:* Porte des Mortes (Death's Door) is known for its currents, and, furthermore, the channel is deep enough to allow large ships out of Escanaba, Michigan, to pass through there, so be aware of any approaching boat traffic, not to mention the frequent Washington Island ferries. It can be a hazardous crossing, so don't attempt it unless you are confident of good weather.

START: Launch from the beach at the **Rock Island Ferry** parking lot and paddle northeast to the **Jackson Harbor** entrance. On your left are the docks for the fishing boats still running here, though they are gone from most places on the Great Lakes. There is also a maritime museum with displays of old fishing rigs and model boats. Paddle toward the harbor entrance. To the left is a light set at the end of a line of shoals, and just beyond are the red and green channel marker buoys. *Caution:* The channel is the only route in and out for boats with any significant draft, such as the ferry and fishing boats. They have little room to maneuver so please stay well out of their way.

MILE 0.5: Leave the harbor entrance and head to **Rock Island**. *Caution:* Most of the channel between the islands is extremely shallow. Strong north or northwest winds will make this passage extremely rough, with

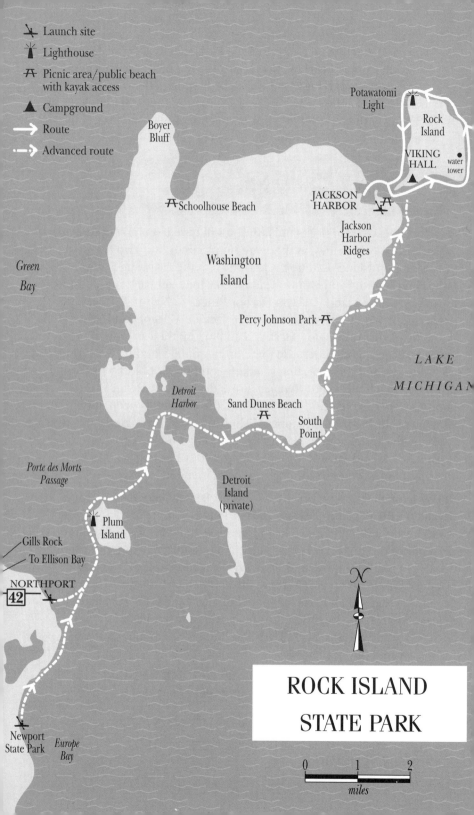

Launch site
Lighthouse
Picnic area/public beach
with kayak access
Campground
Route
Advanced route

Potawatomi
Light

Rock
Island

VIKING
HALL

water
tower

Boyer
Bluff

Schoolhouse Beach

JACKSON
HARBOR

Jackson
Harbor
Ridges

Green
Bay

Washington
Island

Percy Johnson Park

LAKE
MICHIGAN

Detroit
Harbor

Sand Dunes Beach

South
Point

Porte des Morts
Passage

Detroit
Island
(private)

Plum
Island

Gills Rock
To Ellison Bay

NORTHPORT
42

Newport
State Park

Europe
Bay

ROCK ISLAND
STATE PARK

0   1   2
miles

The Story of Viking Hall

The buildings on the south side of Rock Island are the remains of the deluxe country estate built by Chester Thordarson, a wealthy Icelandic immigrant who settled in Chicago. (Washington Island was home to a community of Icelanders.) The small buildings house a ranger, a generator, and rest rooms. The largest building is Viking Hall, an unusual combination dining hall (above) and boathouse (below). Inside are several displays, including some photographs from Thordarson's time, some old fur trade relics, and some of the original furniture, including carved chairs, each with a different scene on its back. The pagoda shelter is all that remains of a Japanese garden, bulldozed by Thordarson after the Pearl Harbor bombings. The estate eventually became the property of the State of Wisconsin when Thordarson's heirs failed to pay property taxes, and the main building was demolished when the state decided not to maintain it.

breaking waves more common with increasing wind. If it is calm, head directly for the end of the gravel spit at the south end of the island; if it is rougher, stay in deeper water to the northwest of the harbor entrance.

MILE 1.5: The long spit extending southwest from Rock Island has a cobblestone beach all along the west side, but a good sand beach can be found on the east, the best landing spot for kayaks, although a bit of a walk to the farther campsites. When weather permits, do a trip around the island, going counterclockwise. *Caution:* Most of the island's shore is cobble beaches with a sheer bluff of varying height at the back. Landing on these beaches in surf can be very difficult and risky. Also shoals extend out from the shore, causing waves to increase in height when they reach the shallows. In other words, pick a calm day for this trip.

MILE 2.5: After the shoreline turns north, you find the remains of an **old fishing operation,** and the **water tower** built to serve the estate. These landmarks may be best accessed by the trail on land. The shoreline is characterized by cobblestone beaches and short stretches of small cliffs all the way to the northwest point of the island.

MILE 4.5: Just as the land starts to curve south, look for a staircase that leads up to the top of the bluffs, the start of the short trail to **Potawatomi Light.** The lighthouse itself is no longer in service, and the light is now on a tall metal tower nearby. Built in 1836, Potawatomi Light is the oldest light in Wisconsin. (The Potawatomi were one of the tribes that originally lived on the islands.) Around the bend are the striking white limestone cliffs of the west side. At sunset these turn pink and orange, reflecting the colors in the sky.

MILE 6.0: The **Viking Hall** boathouse is right on the water, but the boulder/cobblestone beach next to it makes an uncomfortable landing place in any waves. It may be easier to visit it by paddling to the other side of the point and walking from the sand beach.

MILES 6.5 TO 7.0: Cross back to Jackson Harbor from Rock Island following the same route (see Caution in Mile 0.5).

Where to Eat & Where to Stay

RESTAURANTS There are no restaurants on Rock Island, so bring your own food! There are several restaurants on Washington Island. Call the Chamber of Commerce at (920) 847–2179 for a map and listing. There is also a restaurant at the Northport ferry dock. **LODGING** Call the Washington Island Chamber of Commerce for information on lodgings. Most convenient to Rock Island is the **Jackson Harbor Inn**, located a short walk away from the *Karfi* ferry dock. Call (920) 847–2454 for more information. **CAMPING** There are about thirty campsites on Rock Island itself, most are located at the point at the southwest tip of the island. There are also a few backpacking sites located some distance away from the main campground. Reservations are recommended from June to Labor Day. Call (920) 847–2235 for more information. There is also a private campground located inland on Washington Island. Call (920) 847–2640 for information.

Route 49:

---- ---- ---- ---- ---- ---- ---- ---- ---- ---- ---- ----→

Peninsula State Park

Peninsula State Park has a little of everything: bike and hiking trails, beaches, bluffs, a lighthouse, and an easily accessible offshore island for paddlers.

TRIP HIGHLIGHTS: Hiking and bicycling trails, lighthouse.

TRIP RATING:

Beginner: 2.5 mile round trip from Nicolet Beach to Horseshoe Island.

TRIP DURATION: Part day.

NAVIGATION AIDS: USGS: *Ephraim* at 1:24,000.

CAUTIONS: Some exposure to north or northwest winds, powerboat traffic, and poison ivy in woods.

TRIP PLANNING: As long as you don't try this trip on a windy day, it won't be too exposed to wind and waves from the open lake. Nonetheless, a morning paddle is usually quieter.

LAUNCH SITE: Nicolet Beach is the most convenient to Horseshoe Island and has real sand. The entrance to Peninsula State Park is located on Highway 42, just north of Fish Harbor. Turn west onto the park road and stop at the park gate to pick up a park map and vehicle permit. If you would like to camp in the park, reservations are strongly recommended, even after fall. Continue west along the road that follows the shoreline as it curves around back east. Take the turnoff for the Nicolet Beach picnic area.

START: Launch from **Nicolet Beach** and head east to **Horseshoe Island**.

MILE 0.5: *Caution:* Powerboats round **Eagle Bluff** on their way to **Eagle Harbor**, and as this is sort of a blind corner, keep your ears open for the sound of a boat approaching.

MILE 1.0: There is a cobblestone beach and dock in the U-shaped harbor on the south side of Horseshoe Island. This harbor is a good place to stop for a break or stretch your legs on the trail that circles the small island. If weather permits, go around to the outside of the island to see the small bluffs on the north side. *Sidetrip:* If you feel like paddling a little more, paddle back to the peninsula and continue paddling around the tip of the peninsula as it curves toward Fish Creek. At the point before Tennison Bay, there is a good view of Eagle Bluff Lighthouse from the water. The lighthouse is best visited from the road, however.

MILES 2.5 TO 3.0: Return to Nicolet Beach.

Where to Eat & Where to Stay

RESTAURANTS & LODGING There are many choices in Fish Creek. Call the Fish Creek Information Center at (800) 577–1880 for a list and town map. **CAMPING** Peninsula State Park has literally hundreds of campsites. Nonetheless it is often full through summer and fall, so call (920) 868–3258 to make reservations if you plan to stay at the park.

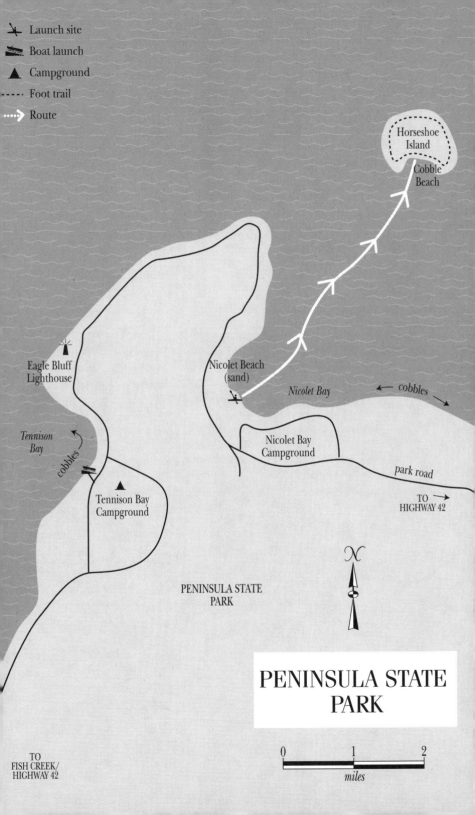

Launch site

Boat launch

▲ Campground

- - - - Foot trail

···▷ Route

Horseshoe Island

Cobble Beach

Eagle Bluff Lighthouse

Nicolet Beach (sand)

Nicolet Bay

← cobbles →

Nicolet Bay Campground

Tennison Bay

cobbles

Tennison Bay Campground

park road

TO → HIGHWAY 42

PENINSULA STATE PARK

N

PENINSULA STATE PARK

TO FISH CREEK/ HIGHWAY 42

0   1   2

miles

Appendix A
Further Reading

Chisholm, Barbara, Andrea Gutsche, and Russel Floren. *Superior: Under the Shadow of the Gods: A Guide to the History of the Canadian Shore of Lake Superior.* Toronto: Lynx Images, 1998.

Dahl, Bonnie. *The Superior Way: A Cruising Guide to Lake Superior* (2nd ed.). Duluth: Lake Superior Port Cities, 1992.

Dufresne, Jim. *Isle Royale Park: Foot Trails and Water Routes.* Seattle: Mountaineers Books, 1991.

Marshall, James R. (Ed.) *Shipwrecks of Lake Superior.* Duluth: Lake Superior Port Cities, 1987.

Pye, E. G. *Roadside Geology of Lake Superior: North Shore of Lake Superior.* Sudbury: Ontario GEOservices Centre, 1997.

Zimmerman, Craig. *Teasing the Spirit: A Comprehensive Guide to Paddling Pukaskwa National Park's Coastal Waters, Pic River to Michipicoten Harbor.* Marathon, Ontario: Words for Wildlands, 1996.

Appendix B
Kayak Clubs in the Great Lakes Region

Chicago Area Sea Kayakers
4019 North Narragansett
Chicago, IL 60634

Great Lakes Sea Kayaking Club
3712 Shallow Brook
Bloomfield Hills, MI 48013
Web site: www.threecat.netgate.net/glskc/glskcl.htm

Great Lake Sea Kayaking Association (GLSKA)
P.O. 22082
45 Overlea Boulevard
Toronto, ONT, M4H 1N9 Canada

International Klepper Society
P.O. Box 973
Good Hart, MI 49737

Lansing Oar and Paddle Club
P.O. Box 26254
Lansing, MI 48909

Mad City Paddlers
1710 Yahara Place
Madison, WI 53703

Negwegon Kayak Club
218 West Bay Bay Street
East Tawas, MI 48703

Peninsula Paddlers
822 North Fourth Avenue
Sturgeon Bay, WI 54235
E-mail: rcross@sturbay.k12.wi.us

RASKA
4805 South Lakeshore Drive
Racine, WI 53403-4127

Twin Cities Sea Kayak Association
P.O. Box 581792
Minneapolis, MN 55458–1792

University of Minnesota Kayak Club
108 Kirby Student Center, UMD
10 University Drive
Duluth, MN 55812–2496

Upper Midwest Kayak Touring News
P.O. Box 17115
Minneapolis, MN 55417–0115

West Michigan Coastal Kayakers Association
c/o Karl Giesel
1025 Griswold SE
Grand Rapids, MI 49507

Appendix C

Guided Tours, Rentals, and Outfitters

Lake Superior

Michigan

Cascade Kayaks has details about outfitting and guided trips. For information contact them at 20 East First Street, P.O. Box 215, Grand Marais, MN 55604; (800) 720–2809; Web site: www.boreal.org/ckayaks.

Down Wind Sports in Marquette sells kayaks and kayak equipment, but does not have rentals. It can also provide information on local kayaking routes. Contact Jeff Stasser at (906) 226–7112.

Keewenaw Adventure Company offers guided day trips, lessons, and rentals. For information call (906) 289–4303 or write to P.O. Box 70, Copper Harbor, MI 49918.

Northern Waters in Munising is the largest and most active kayak guide and boat rental company in the area. For information about rentals or guided trips, call them at (906) 387–2323.

Quick Stop Bike and Kayak in Marquette sells kayaks and equipment, but no rentals. It can offer information on local kayaking routes. Contact David Wert at (906) 225–1583.

Superior Access is a nonprofit organizatoin that offers guided trips in the Marquette area. For information call (888) 999–5919.

Wisconsin

Adventures in Perspective offers trips to/in the Apostle Islands. For information call (715) 779–9503; or visit their Web site: www.livingadventure.com.

Superior Vision offers trips to the Apostle Islands as well as kayak instruction. For information call REI at (612) 884–4315 or Superior Vision at (612) 331–2558; or visit their Web site: www.superiorvision.com.

Trek and Trail is the oldest and largest outfitter in the Bayfield area. It offers both guided tours (including to/in the Apostle Islands) and kayak rentals. For information call (800) 354–8735.

Minnesota

Cascade Kayaks has details about outfitting and guided trips along the Lake Superior water trail. (See page 269 for contact information.)

KCI offers guided harbor tours and wildlife viewing tours in St. Louis Bay during the summer months. Rentals and safety lessons are also available. For information contact Randy Carlson at (218) 726–6177.

Ski Hut in Duluth, Minnesota, offers sea kayak rentals. However, before renting kayakers must have previously taken a safety course that included self-rescue skills to qualify. Call (218) 724–8525 for information.

Superior Vision offers trips to the North Shore as well as instruction. (See page 269 for contact information.)

Ontario

Caribou Expeditions offers guided trips, including tours in the Pukaskwa region and Lake Superior Provincial Park. For information contact them at RR 2, 76 Island Road, Goulais River, Ontario, POS 1EO, Canada; (800) 970–6662; Web site: www3.sympatico.ca.caribouexp.

Cascade Kayaks offers guided trips in the Pukaskwa region. See above for contact information.

Naturally Superior Adventures offers guided trips, rentals, and outfitting. For information contact them at RR 1, Lake Superior, Wawa, Ontario POS 1KO, Canada; (800) 203–9092; Web site: www.naturallysuperior.com.

Superior Ecoventures offers guided trips. For information contact them at Site 3, Comp 23, RR 16, Thunder Bay, Ontario, P7B 6B3, Canada; (807) 683–7499 or (888) 290–1337. For guided trips in the Rossport area, contact their Thunder Bay office at (807) 683–7499 or (888) 290–1337. Rentals and outfitting are available from their office in Rossport. Call (807) 824–3314 for details.

Superior Vision offers trips to Pie Island and the Ontario coastline. (See page 269 for contact information.)

Lake Michigan

Michigan

Back Country Outfitters in Traverse City sells kayaks and kayak equipment but does not rent boats. Contact John Lewis at (616) 946–1339 for information.

Northwest Outfitters in Traverse City offers guided tours and sea kayak rentals. For information call (616) 946–4841.

INDEX

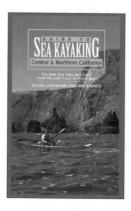
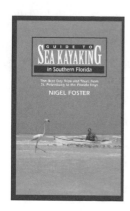